A PRACTICAL GUIDE
TO
ECUMENISM

A Practical Guide to Ecumenism

(Revised Edition)

by

John B. Sheerin, C.S.P.

PAULIST PRESS DEUS BOOKS

NEW YORK   GLEN ROCK   WESTMINSTER

TORONTO   AMSTERDAM

This book was originally published under the title *Christian Reunion: The Ecumenical Movement and American Catholics,* copyright © 1966 by Hawthorn Books, Inc., New York.

Nihil Obstat:
Gail Higgins, O.F.M. Cap.
Censor Librorum

Imprimatur:
✠ Terence J. Cooke, D.D., V.G.

April 27, 1966

The Nihil Obstat and Imprimatur are official declarations that a book or pamphlet is free of doctrinal or moral error. No implication is contained therein that those who have granted the Nihil Obstat and Imprimatur agree with the contents, opinions or statements expressed.

Copyright © 1967 by
The Missionary Society
of St. Paul the Apostle
in the State of New York

Library of Congress
Catalog Card Number: 66-13619

Published by Paulist Press
Editorial Office: 304 W. 58th St., N. Y., N. Y. 10019
Business Office: Glen Rock, New Jersey 07452

Printed in the
United States of America
by Our Sunday Visitor Press

Contents

INTRODUCTION		1
I	The Means and Meaning of Unity	4
II	The East and West at Odds	15
III	The Reformation	23
IV	The Catholic Church Against the World	34
V	The Catholic Church and Ecumenism in the Past	41
VI	Ecumenism in the Constitution on the Church	56
VII	The Decree on Ecumenism: General Principles	66
VIII	The Decree's Practical Recommendations	76
IX	The Decree and the Orthodox	96
X	The Decree and the Protestants	105
XI	American Protestantism	118
XII	Obstacles to Unity	130
XIII	The Future	170
XIV	Secular Ecumenism	173
APPENDIX ONE: DECREE ON ECUMENISM		190
APPENDIX TWO: INTERIM GUIDELINES FOR PRAYER IN COMMON AND COMMUNICATIO IN SACRIS		220
APPENDIX THREE: DIRECTORY FOR THE APPLICATION OF THE DECREES OF THE SECOND ECUMENICAL COUNCIL OF THE VATICAN CONCERNING ECUMENICAL MATTERS, PART ONE		229
INDEX		250

Introduction

This book is designed to give basic information about the ecumenical movement as seen from a Roman Catholic viewpoint. I have tried to present this information as clearly as possible in order to prevent misunderstandings but I am under no illusion that the materials presented represent the final truth about ecumenism. We are in the experimental stage of the movement and time and experience are needed to test its central themes and policies. Yet the goal is clear and only the spiritually insensitive will deny that the search for unity is God's will for our time.

Unfortunately some Roman Catholics are puzzled and bewildered by the fast pace of ecumenical developments. Through the Second Vatican Council the Church has called them to action but they are uncertain as to what they should do. For this reason I have tried to give a clear, balanced, and accurate report on the ecumenical movement.

I have tried especially to dissipate the notion that ecumenism is a radical revolution in the Church. To do so is to deny the divine guidance of the Second Vatican Council. The Holy Spirit's message to our times is necessarily different in form from that addressed to the medieval or Renaissance world but it is not turning the Church upside down or perverting the Gospel message. In essence the message is still the same good news of Christ, the light of the world.

This volume is a primer on ecumenism. Although striving for accuracy, I have not attempted a work of scholarship. This would be a task beyond my competence and beyond the purpose of the book. Not all readers will agree with the emphases I have given to certain topics or with my omission of others. Why not more space for Orthodox Churches? Why not greater attention to the obstacles that bar the way to unity? I have tried to present the topics that have a special relevance to the American scene and to give special emphasis to the practical rather than to the speculative features of these topics. Professional theologians may consider it simplistic to discuss ecumenism without plunging deeply into all aspects of the question but my conviction is that ecumenism in America, discussed as it is on television, radio, and in the press, cannot be restricted to scholars.

There is nothing here about the Jews. Some may regard this as a glaring omission. I take my cue, however, from the Council Decree on Ecumenism which is limited to the pursuit of unity among Christians. The Council's declaration on the Jews (the summons to a long-awaited campaign against anti-Semitism) will inaugurate a new era of Catholic-Jewish dialogue but that dialogue will present a very different set of problems. In this volume, space limitations do not permit the extended treatment of Catholic-Jewish dialogue that its importance deserves.

Activism may be a bad word in some quarters but not in America; and I confess that this volume is geared to action. The Second Vatican Council did not study and debate and agonize over ecumenism in order to publish an abstract dissertation on interfaith relations. The bishops viewed ecumenism as a dynamic force that has extraordinary implications for the practical order.

Ecumenism is spurious if it amounts to nothing more than exchange of theological monologues or if it means polite coexistence until the Second Coming of Christ. Christian unity demands hard work, the same kind of effort that activated a Paul, a Patrick, or a Francis Xavier. Indeed, the ultimate aim of Christian ecumenism is unity for the sake of a more effective preaching of the Gospel. Theologians have a large role to play in the attainment of Christian unity but to leave ecumenism entirely to theologians would be a new form of clericalism. As Pope Pius XII said, "Laymen and laywomen must become increasingly aware of the fact that they do not simply belong to the Church. They are the Church."

Introduction

It is, of course, my humble hope that this book will make a practical contribution to the Catholic-Protestant dialogue so urgently requested by the Second Vatican Council. Ecumenism is moving forward rapidly but in places it is still somewhat romantic or sentimental. My aim is to urge Catholics to put to practical use in their everyday relations with Protestants the fundamental Christianity that is our common heritage. The final result is in the hands of God.

J.B.S.

I
The Means and Meaning of Unity

The central theme of this book is ecumenism. After centuries of isolation from other Christian churches, the Roman Catholic Church has now joined the world-wide ecumenical movement. The Second Vatican Council has officially praised the movement and urged the bishops to promote and encourage it. There are Catholics who welcome the new policy, wax almost ecstatic over it, and laud it to the skies. Others accept it in good spirit and try to adjust themselves to a more genial attitude toward Protestants and members of Orthodox Churches. But there is a third group that regards ecumenism as a dangerous innovation. Profoundly disturbed by the pace and scope of the whole Council program of renewal, this last group feels particularly distressed by any form of Catholic participation in interfaith dialogue. They see it as a movement that might easily get out of control and shake the Church to its foundations.

That such a reaction should be found among certain American Catholics is not at all surprising. At the beginning of the Second Vatican Council, October 11, 1962, there were bishops who had serious misgivings about Pope John's whole program of *aggiornamento*. They listened to talk about Church reform with about as much relish as their sixteenth-century predecessors listened to Luther. During the Council's first session, one venerable prelate remarked, "The old miasma comes again over the Alps."

It is perfectly natural, then, to expect that certain

The Means and Meaning of Unity

American Catholics will look upon ecumenism as a concession to the spurious togetherness of our times even though they know it has been endorsed by the highest assembly in Christendom. They view it as a disturbance of the status quo that will turn the Church upside down and leave in its wake a diluted theology. For many reasons, then, an appraisal of ecumenism, with all its risks and dangers, is very much in order.

Ecumenism is promotion of Christian unity but the adjective "ecumenical" has been used in various meanings, sometimes bewilderingly disparate. In "the Ecumenical Council" it means universal; and some lecturers and journalists have taken the word "ecumenical" to mean civil, tolerant, undenominational. At times it has been taken to indicate relations between Christian and non-Christian faiths but in the term "ecumenical movement," it generally refers to relations among Christians and I use it here in that sense.

The ecumenist is simply trying to persuade Christians to pool their religious resources, if they can do so without violating conscience, in order to make the best possible use of whatever Christianity is present in our world. They look forward hopefully to the eventual unity of all Christian Churches. But we cannot wait for that before we begin to work together, think together, pray together, and stay together.

The success of the ecumenical movement, then, does not depend entirely on the achievement of corporate unity. It will be successful day by day if we make the maximum use of the wonderful gifts that have come to this world from Jesus Christ through His Holy Spirit, some of which exist outside the visible borders of the Catholic Church. I don't want to give the impression that we will never achieve corporate unity. As a matter of fact, I agree with Bishop Oliver Tomkins of Bristol, England, who has said that we can begin thinking of attaining corporate unity in our own lifetime. It is important, however, to realize that we can gather the fruits of unity daily as we work toward a golden harvest of unity in the dim future.

The desire for Christian unity is a free and voluntary choice of the Roman Catholic Church, not something imposed from above by the hierarchy of the Church. When we speak of ecumenism as a new policy of the Catholic Church, there is a danger of thinking of it as the dictate of Church officials forced upon reluctant laymen and laywomen. Ecumenism is not our policy simply because the bishops in Council have approved it; the bishops have approved it because it comes from the believing Church in free obedience to the command of Christ. His command is crystal clear in His prayer to His heavenly Father at the Last Supper: "that all may be one, even as Thou, Father, in Me and I in Thee; that they also may be one in Us, that the world may believe that Thou hast sent Me" (John 17:21).

The desire for unity, then, is bound up with our faith in Christ; it is our free and voluntary response to the divine call. If our faith in Christ were not free, it would not be faith at all and if our desire for unity were not a voluntary desire, then it would be spurious. Yes, there is pressure on Catholics to take part in the ecumenical movement but it is pressure from God speaking to us in conscience.

God is calling us to unity not only through the voice of the bishops at the Council but also through the events and circumstances of our times. The philosopher Hegel said that "the only thing we learn from history is that we never learn from history." The fact is that we learn much from history. As Pope John said in his address at the opening of the Council, the prophets of doom he met in his daily ministry failed to learn from history. "They say that our era, in comparison with past eras, is getting worse and they behave as though they had learned nothing from history, which is nevertheless the teacher of life." Pope John, on the other hand, read history as though it were a daily news story of God working through His providence for the greater good of the Church and humanity.

God has been speaking to us about Christian unity through the mysterious factors and forces that have prepared the minds of Christians to realize the need of unity and warmed their hearts to yearn for it. These factors and forces have appeared with startling persuasiveness in the twentieth century.

The Means and Meaning of Unity

To be faithful to history, there have been men in the last four centuries, like Erasmus, Bossuet, and Leibnitz, who were painfully saddened by the schisms in Christianity and who engaged in ecumenical work, but their efforts seemed to result in no lasting ecumenical enterprises.

The tragic fact is that the Christian Churches were largely unconcerned about Christian unity until this century. There was such a mass of perverse thinking, muddled loyalties, misconceptions, and misunderstandings among the various Christian groups that the tender bud of brotherly love was unable to break through the hard ground of sectarianism. The pathos of it all was that in so many cases the most virulent sectarian hatreds were nurtured by men of deep sincerity and fidelity to Christ. Catholic churchmen, we must confess, played their role in the unhappy cold war of the last four centuries. Without undue breast-beating and with humility, we have to admit Catholic blame. As The Decree on Ecumenism (Appendix One of this book) says: "But in subsequent centuries much more serious dissensions appeared and quite large Communities became separated from full communion with the Catholic Church—for which, often enough, men of both sides were to blame" (Article 3).

The first and primary factor that fostered the rise of ecumenism in the Catholic Church in this century was the realization of a need for a thorough renewal of spiritual life in order to revitalize the Church. This renewal was bursting out in many forms before the Second Vatican Council. There were the biblical revival, the liturgical revival, the resurgence of interest in catechetics. These movements had vitality but they needed the blessing of an Ecumenical Council as there were some Catholics who assumed a flippant and condescending attitude toward them.

Along with these movements there has been an increasing awareness among Catholics in recent days that the Church was not making a strong impact on the modern world, hemmed in as it was by impersonal and anachronistic forms of Church administration, by legalism at the top levels, and by archaic language and ceremonies that were entirely out of line with evangelical simplicity.

In Europe a wide-ranging apostasy during this century

has led to demands for a shakeup of the Church at all levels. During the period just before the Second Vatican Council, in the Church in the United States, alert observers saw a fervent devotional life, no anticlericalism, and an unhesitating loyalty among the faithful but there were alarming indications, nevertheless, that secularism and religious indifference were making their way into Catholic life. The close ties that existed between priest and people in the days of the immigrant Church in America were disappearing, and educated Catholics were beginning to protest that the Church was becoming irrelevant and its priests inaccessible. They wanted the Church to move out into the modern world and to abandon the cold war that kept Catholics and Protestants apart.

Pope John's genius was not in diplomacy or intellectualism but in reading the "signs of the times" and in sensing the mood of the age. He looked at the spiritual needs and yearnings of modern men, and decided that the Church must be taken "out of moth balls" and used for the benefit of humanity. He flung open the windows of the Church, then opened his arms to the whole world, and his warmest welcome went out to separated Christians divided from the Catholic Church, not by divine law, but by human ignorance and misunderstanding.

Another factor that has aided the growth of the ecumenical spirit among Catholics has been our awareness of the scandal of Christian disunity in the mission field. This was the motivating cause of the first great ecumenical meeting of this century, at Edinburgh, Scotland, in 1910. Protestant missionaries realized not only the duplication of resources and the confusion resulting from creeds in competition for the souls of the natives, but also the scandal of competition. This race to win converts was no more inspiring than today's armaments race, so men like the Anglican Bishop Brent organized this meeting ostensibly to bring about greater cooperation among Protestant missionaries but in the back of their minds they undoubtedly hoped the meeting might lead the way to some greater degree of theological unity.

Thoughtful Catholics have lamented the profusion of Christian missionaries abroad working at cross-purposes

The Means and Meaning of Unity

but they have also regretted the lack of unity among the Christian Churches at home. The First Amendment to our Constitution states that Congress shall make no law respecting an establishment of religion and its framers undoubtedly designed it to forbid support of a particular religion by the Federal Government. Such support would give that religion a privileged position in America and thereby lead to endless bickering and wrangling. Yet American history reveals disheartening facts about Christian Churches fighting to advance their own vested interests, thereby entangling themselves in litigation and causing dissension in the community. At times they acted justly, as when certain proposals threatened to infringe the religious freedom of their members, but there have been times when Christian Churches have stirred up a witches' brew in the local community out of sheer selfishness.

The non-Christian and the unbeliever have not been impressed by the wrangling. The quarrels have confirmed their conviction that Christianity is and always has been a source of rancor, discord, and even bloodshed. The prestige of Christianity has suffered immeasurably in the United States precisely because of the spectacle of Christian Churches jockeying for position in politics or public life. Some day, God willing, the Christian Churches will become a unifying rather than divisive force in American life.

Another reason for the surge of interest in ecumenism in recent times, after centuries of neglect, has been the sufferings of European Catholics who endured the agonies of concentration camps together with European Protestants. In these camps, the ecclesiastical externals that often divide Christians were absent, with the result that both Catholic and Protestant had to stay close to fundamentals such as faith in Christ; and they came to realize how very close they were in these fundamentals. Catholics who had to dispense with sacramentals began to realize the common heritage of belief they shared with their Protestant fellow prisoners.

The ecumenical movement has undoubtedly also been spurred by the dwindling proportion of Christians in the world. The Western world (and most Christians are in the Western world) has a low birth rate, but the teeming millions of Asia and Africa have a very high birth rate. While this could never become a genuine motive for unity, it is nevertheless a consideration that induces us to take a little more interest in it. We have no intention of organizing a Christian bloc against the non-Christian world but we do want to make the most of whatever Christian values we have since time seems to be running against us.

We used to think of Protestants as rugged individualists who tended to scorn organization, but that is a thing of the past. The trend toward mergers, for instance, is considered by Protestants not only an abandonment of disunity but also a commitment to the more effective accomplishment of the Church's missionary task. Of course there are many Protestants who are still reluctant to cooperate with this trend. Conservative Evangelicals look dubiously on any merger that might rob individual churches of independence. Merger smacks to them of worldliness and techniques; and they feel that it is the preaching of the Word of God, not the well-oiled and beautifully synchronized machinery of Church government, that will advance the cause of the Church. They look askance at ecclesiastical wheelhorses and desk-bound bureaucrats. However, the fact is that the general direction of Protestant Church life today is toward communal rather than individual activity.

Probably the reason for this is that modern Protestantism has gone beyond the thinking of the seventeenth, eighteenth, and nineteenth centuries and has returned to the thinking of the Reformers. The Protestant theologian Robert Nelson points out that Luther was profoundly interested in the communal life of the Church; in fact, Nelson claims that traditional Protestantism has been more community-minded than Catholicism.[1]

An increasing desire to associate with Protestants has also tended to foster ecumenism among Catholics. In the early days in this country, Catholic clergy often shielded their flocks from the other Christian groups around them. They asserted that love for the faith should deter us from entering into any alliances that might endanger faith, but

---

[1] J. Robert Nelson, *The Realm of Redemption* (London: The Epworth Press, 1962), p. 63.

The Means and Meaning of Unity

this was probably mixed with a fear that Catholics might be enticed away from their faith by social and educational features of the Protestant life around them.

There were, however, certain factors that tended to break down the ghetto aloofness of Catholics. First, the realization that the commandment of brotherly love was scarcely consonant with isolation from their neighbors. Second, most Catholics did have a reverence for religious liberty. Because his ancestors had been persecuted for the faith, the American Catholic had a sincere respect for the freedom of conscience of every man.

A counterforce, however, to this respect for the freedom of every man's conscience was the habit of thinking of the Protestant's religious faith as heresy. The early American Catholic, German or Irish, considered the Protestant a "heretic," and vaguely remembered a scriptural injunction to avoid heretics. But Cardinal Bea has helped immeasurably to clarify for our times this whole question of "heresy." He has shown that the term can be applied only to one who deliberately rejects what he knows to be the truth.

Contemporary Protestants cannot be placed in this category. They have not deliberately rejected a faith they had previously accepted. They have been born into Protestantism and are no more responsible for being born out of the Catholic faith than Catholics are responsible for being born in the faith. Both Catholic and Protestant will be judged on fidelity to conscience but we have no good reason to judge that a Protestant is in bad faith.

A writer in the Italian Jesuit periodical *La Civiltà Cattolica* recently stated: "Some Catholics talk as if nothing had happened in the Church during the last few years, and their mentality still retains the anti-Protestant attitude of the past. But the real thinking of the Church about the problem of unity is expressed in the Vatican Council's Decree on Ecumenism. This document does not speak about the 'return' of 'heretics' and 'schismatics' but of a movement, not only in the direction of separated Christians toward the Church, but also of the Catholic Church toward the other Christians. Unity will thus be a meeting in which the Catholic Church will give the separated Christians what they lost when they left it. But it will also receive the really Christian heritage which has been produced by the separated Christians during the centuries of separation, under the impulse of the Holy Spirit."[2]

These are great days to be alive. Was the presence of the Holy Spirit in world events ever so obvious as it is today! It was no mere coincidence that at a critical time in Catholic history the right man appeared with the right idea at the right time: Pope John. We must make the most of this opportunity God has given us. As Father Yves Congar says in his *Report from Rome* on the Second Session of the Council: "We are living at an extraordinary moment of grace. How careful we must be not to frighten away the gentle dove of peace and the Holy Spirit. What patience must be ours, what understanding of the delays, what deference for the circuitous ways and the slowness of a Providence for whom a thousand years are like a day . . ."[3]

At long last, Christians are finally taking the words of our Lord at the Last Supper seriously. For centuries they seemed to feel His prayer for unity was a vague aspiration or else a pretext for condemning other Christians for the divisions in Christianity. Pope John has recommended that we leave the question of personal blame to the judgment of God. "We do not intend to conduct a trial of the past, we do not want to prove who was right and who was wrong. All we want to say is 'Let us come together. Let us make an end of our divisions.' "

Some of the faithful who are disturbed by ecumenism seem to think their Church is losing its grip, losing confidence in its infallibility and in its centuries-old claim to its uniqueness, losing faith in its assurance that Christ as a matter of historical fact established one and only one Church. Ecumenism however implies no change in essential Catholic teaching. The Second Vatican Council studied the nature of the Church and penetrated deeply into its mystery, cutting away some of the nonessential

---

[2] Yves Congar, O.P., quoted in *Herder Correspondence*, Vol. 2, No. 4 (April 1965), p. 111.

[3] Yves Congar, O.P., *Report from Rome II* (London: Geoffrey Chapman, Ltd., 1964), p. 35.

The Means and Meaning of Unity

customs and practices that had developed, but it did not dare tamper with the fundamental teaching on the Church as recorded in the Scriptures.

This elimination of nonessentials has not enfeebled the old Church but has given her new life. To those Catholics who say that they are too old to adjust to the Council reforms, Bishop G. Emmett Carter of London, Ontario, says: "Let no one say 'I am too old to change.' The Church is older than any of us and behold she comes to us once more arrayed as a young bride and she is more beautiful than ever."

Theological age, of course, is not a matter of years but of temperament. There are some young parishioners who are more distressed by Council reforms than are the eldest of our senior citizens. The laity (and priests as well) are either alarmed or elated over the vigor with which young-at-heart but old-in-years Pope John threw open the windows to let fresh air into the Church. The alarm or elation, however, bears no relation to age. We find young conservatives and old progressives.

It seems to me, therefore, that we need an ecumenical movement within Catholicism wherein ecumenically minded Catholics will engage in dialogue with those of their Catholic brethren who do not share this enthusiasm for ecumenism. Should not the Catholic ecumenist listen patiently to discover if perhaps the traditionalist has some insights that will be helpful to the Church in these days of *aggiornamento* that may be moving too fast in places? The discussion, however, must be carried on in an ecumenical spirit. If polemics are out of place in Catholic-Protestant dialogue, they are also out of order in discussions among Catholics who differ on ecumenism.

The traditionalist, on the other hand, should not play down the Council. He can talk all he wants about clerical politics but as a Catholic he cannot in conscience deny that the Holy Spirit presided over the Council. Moreover, he realizes that the Church must make an agonizing reappraisal of itself from time to time and it has been a century since the last Ecumenical Council. The Church is not precipitate in calling councils.

Léon-Joseph Cardinal Suenens says that much of the

"healthy tension" in the Church today is rooted in the sensitivity of some to the need of preserving the deposit of faith and in the contrary tendency of others to develop "the talents" God has given the Church. Both the conservers and developers, says the cardinal, have their proper roles. But he also adds that what is needed by both groups is a fine sense of distinguishing between the essential and nonessential.

I feel certain that many Catholics are needlessly disturbed by ecumenism. They are alarmed over the new respect shown to Protestant churches. But if they take the trouble to read up on ecumenism, they will find theirs is a false alarm. The Council's ecumenism decree is not changing essentials. Genuine reform is not necessarily revolution. "The reform at which the Council aims," said Pope Paul in his opening address at the Second Session, "is not therefore a turning upside down of the Church's present way of life or a breaking with what is essential and worthy in her tradition but it is rather an honoring of tradition by stripping it of what is unworthy or defective so that it may be rendered firm and fruitful."

II
The East and West at Odds

Christianity made its first appearance on the eastern shores of the Mediterranean. Flourishing colonies of Christians in the first century—at Alexandria in Egypt, at Antioch in Syria, at Jerusalem in Palestine—all shared the same essential faith. Apostles carried the faith from the East to Europe and Peter set up the Church in Rome. In a few centuries, however, the Christians in the East and those in Europe, which we call the West, came to a parting of the ways and are still divided into the Eastern Orthodox Church and the Roman Catholic Church. The history of the events that led up to separation is a long, tragic story.

The year 1054 is often cited by historians as the date of the separation. This is a convenient date for purposes of historical research but it would be a grave mistake to think that the break came suddenly and without warning in that year. For seven centuries the Christians of East and West had become progressively estranged from each other. In A.D. 330 Emperor Constantine changed the seat of government of the Roman Empire from Rome to a Greek city named Byzantium, later called Constantinople in his honor. The bishop of Byzantium enjoyed the special friendship of his neighbor the Emperor, and this close relationship made the bishop a very important prelate in the eyes of the Christian public. In fact, an ecumenical council was later held at Chalcedon near Constantinople in A.D. 451, and in the absence of the Pope, the bishops decided that Constantinople should be given the same ecclesiastical privileges as Rome.

However, the Pope refused to recognize this decision because it asserted that since Constantinople, the new Rome, had supplanted the old Rome, so, too, the spiritual ruler of the new Rome should have at least as great spiritual power as the Pope, the spiritual ruler of old Rome. The Pope insisted that the supremacy of the Bishop of Rome was of divine origin.

Meanwhile, time was wreaking havoc with the city of Rome, which was battered by invasions of barbarians while Constantinople prospered politically, financially, and culturally. Things came to a climax in A.D. 800 when the Pope crowned Charlemagne as emperor of the West. This infuriated the East which still held strongly to the concept of one Christian emperor for both East and West, and the cultured East was particularly annoyed because Charlemagne was an illiterate barbarian.

To the political quarrels were added other factors that widened the breach and increased the disaffection. Certain Christians of the East differed from the Christian West on points such as the two natures in Christ and the veneration of images; and political rivalries prevented East and West from remaining in close contact. One particularly unhappy episode occurred in the ninth century, involving Patriarch Photius of Constantinople whose election was challenged by some Eastern bishops. An appeal was made to Rome and Pope Nicholas sent legates to adjudge the quarrel over the election but they ruled in favor of Photius instead of merely reporting the facts to Rome. Pope Nicholas annulled the decision of the legates. Other papal actions, however, displeased the Patriarch and at the Council of Constantinople in A.D. 867 he excommunicated the Pope. One of the Patriarch's grievances against the Pope was his claim that the West was in heresy and therefore Photius wanted to withdraw from unity with it, especially because the West held that the Holy Spirit proceeds from Father and Son, while Photius held that the Spirit proceeds only from the Father.

Another incident occurred in A.D. 1054. Patriarch Michael Cerularius closed some Latin churches in Constantinople, criticized a number of Latin customs, and assailed Pope Leo IX. The Pope sent Cardinal Humbert as

The East and West at Odds

his legate to handle the matter but the Patriarch claimed the legate did not have proper authorization. Whereupon, Humbert, in high dudgeon, brusquely laid a bull of excommunication on the altar of Santa Sophia during a ceremony on July 16, 1054, and, shaking off the dust from his feet, left the basilica.

The document excommunicated the Patriarch. It accused him of all manner of heresies and the city of Constantinople was enraged. The Patriarch then proceeded to excommunicate Cardinal Humbert and his confreres and burned a copy of the bull which excommunicated himself. It was an explosive incident but not of colossal proportions due to the very isolation of the two groups from each other. Often the Orthodox did not even know the names of the popes at this time.

One Orthodox calendar lists A.D. 1054 as the date of the beginning of the Roman Catholic Church, following upon the "Great Separation" by which the Roman Church "broke away" from the Mother Church—the Eastern Orthodox Church. Yet total alienation was not really felt until 1204, the date of the Fourth Crusade. Eastern Christians had been scandalized and hurt by crusaders on the first three crusades, a tragic period of Christian history. For the crusades, as far as they related to the Christian East, were barbarian invasions by brutal, greedy brigands.

The climax came with the Fourth Crusade when the crusaders captured Constantinople, gave half of it to the Venetians and looted the rest, then proceeded to set up a Latin empire. What was previously a theological controversy with the West became the burning resentment of a whole people against Western Christendom.

From time to time in succeeding centuries attempts were made to heal the schism but they resulted in failure. In the fifteenth century, after long discussions between Orthodox and Latin bishops as to whether the Holy Spirit proceeds from the Father and the Son, a decree of union was signed in 1439 at the Council of Florence and all seemed bright for the future. But the monks and other members of the Orthodox Church were unhappy about the agreement. When the Turks captured Constantinople in 1453, one of the leaders of the opposition, a monk named

Gennadius, was chosen Patriarch and this marked the end of the union.

In Russia, Patriarch Isidore, who had worked for unity at Florence, was deposed and the Orthodox Church in Russia became independent of Constantinople. It viewed itself as the third Rome, judged the first Rome to be heretical, the second Rome (Constantinople) to have fallen under the power of the Turks, and therefore asserted its claim to lead the Orthodox. Today the Russian Orthodox Church is numerically the largest of all the Orthodox Churches. It has over fifty million members; the Church of Rumania is next with sixteen million; the Orthodox Church of Greece is third with about eight million, while the once flourishing Church at Constantinople has scarcely more than one hundred thousand members.

From the time of the fall of Constantinople, the two great sections of Christendom were resolutely divided. Under Turkish rule the Christians of what we call Western Europe had little contact with the Christians in the Turkish Empire (e.g. the Balkans) or in Russia. The isolation was aggravated by the development of theology in the West which caused some of the Orthodox to look with suspicion on these developments as radical innovations. Differences in rite, in language, in cultural ideals also barred the way to mutual understanding. The West, moreover, was influenced profoundly by the Industrial Revolution and by the French Revolution, both of which left the East almost untouched.

The proclamation of papal primacy and papal infallibility by the First Vatican Council in 1870 also tended to harden the walls of division. To the Orthodox the most authoritative voice in the Church is that of an ecumenical council attended by all the bishops of the world. But in 1870 many Orthodox felt that the primacy and infallibility proclamations had threatened the future of all ecumenical councils. They reasoned that the Pope would see no reason to convene a council at any time in the future since he believed that he himself was infallible. They feared that the Roman Church had made the whole idea of a council obsolete and they felt it would be altogether wrong to unite with a Church that held no councils.

The East and West at Odds 19

Moreover, many Orthodox were convinced that Rome had attributed supreme power to the Pope, thus making him an absolute monarch and degrading bishops to the role of papal clerks. In the last hundred years, however, Catholic theologians have tried to explain that Vatican I did not diminish the status of bishops. Now the Second Vatican Council has approved the doctrine of collegiality which holds that the bishops share in the universal government of the Church by divine law. Perhaps the Orthodox are still dubious and therefore await the full implementation of the doctrine of collegiality.

Looking back on history one gets the impression that both Catholics and Orthodox have harbored certain misconceptions of Church authority. The Christians of the East seemed to feel that a bishop or local church could enjoy a pre-eminence, not of jurisdiction over other churches, but only a primacy deriving from superiority in faith, hope, or charity. The Christians of the West, however, thought of the universal Church in terms of jurisdiction, affected as they were by Roman law. Whereas the East thought of a bishop in terms of the spiritual gifts he receives at his consecration, the West thought of him mainly as an administrator with jurisdiction over a certain diocese. Moreover, Roman theologians, attempting to rebut Protestant objections to papal authority, have tended to put a heavy emphasis on the Pope's divinely given powers. They have stressed his primacy and infallibility so much that the Orthodox have come to think we regard the Bishop of Rome as an absolute monarch, a concept that runs counter to their image of the bishop as good shepherd or servant. In short, both Eastern and Western Christians have given to the concept of authority nuances that are false but the unfortunate fact is that they did not listen to each other in the past in order to reconcile their differences. They have allowed nontheological factors, and political considerations in particular, to keep them from getting down to discussion of the theological differences.

Hopes for Catholic-Orthodox unity took a bright turn with the election of Pope John. Because he had developed so many personal friendships with Orthodox laity and clergy during his twenty years as papal representative in the Middle East, he entertained a personal desire to bring about reunion with the Orthodox. He invited the Orthodox Churches to send observers to the Second Vatican Council; and while there was some reluctance at first (the Russian Church alone sending observers at the beginning), other Orthodox Churches sent observers to later sessions.

All the world knows of Pope Paul's historic 1963 visit to Jerusalem where he embraced Patriarch Athenagoras, leader of the Eastern Orthodox Churches. However, the most dramatic event of all occurred at the closing of the Second Vatican Council in St. Peter's on December 7, 1965. Pope Paul embraced a representative of Patriarch Athenagoras after a brief was read which lifted the excommunication imposed in 1054 on Patriarch Michael Cerularius and also annulled the excommunication imposed by the Patriarch on Cardinal Humbert and his associates. The brief was a declaration made jointly by Pope Paul and Patriarch Athenagoras in which both expressed regret for "the offensive words, the reproaches without foundation, and the reprehensible gestures which, on both sides, have marked or accompanied the sad events of this period." They then said that this gesture would not be sufficient to end the schism but that they hoped it would issue in dialogue which would eventually lead both groups to live a common life together again, as in the first thousand years of Christianity.

Patriarch Athenagoras took part in a similar ceremony at Istanbul on the same day. Before leaving Rome, the Patriarch's representative, Metropolitan Meliton, left nine white roses at the tomb of Pope John, symbol of the nine centuries of division now consigned to oblivion by the annulment of the ancient bitterness. The roses bore a ribbon inscribed *"en eirene, en eirene"* (in peace, in peace).

We can afford to be optimistic about the impact and significance of this event but we must be realistic as well. One of the discouraging features on the horizon is a lack of unity among the Orthodox themselves. There is, for instance, a certain amount of rivalry between the Russian Orthodox Church and the Patriarchate of Constantinople, Moscow being quite willing to assert its claim to leadership of the Orthodox Churches. One somber echo of the dramatic event in St. Peter's was a statement made by Archbishop Nikodim of the Russian Church to the effect that the withdrawal of the excommunication by Patriarch Athenagoras was only "a gesture emanating from one local Orthodox Church and not from the whole body of Eastern Orthodoxy."

What about the Orthodox in the United States? There are in the United States about four million members of the Orthodox Churches and these churches agree generally in worship and doctrine. Confession is not as common among them as in the Catholic Church but they accept the seven sacraments. Their priests may marry before they receive the order of deacon but not after. Some churches have introduced English into their worship, others have kept their traditional language of worship but use English in preaching and religious education. In general, it may be said that the trend is toward a laudable degree of "Americanization" in the Orthodox Churches in American and for this reason it seems an anachronism to call them "Eastern Orthodox Churches."

The U. S. Bishops' Commission for Ecumenical Affairs has appointed a subcommission for relations with the Orthodox Churches. The prospects for Catholic-Orthodox dialogue here seem bright, as Archbishop Iakovos, Greek Orthodox Primate of North and South America, has long been active in ecumenical affairs. He is one of the presidents of the World Council of Churches.

In some sections of the United States there is mutual mistrust between Catholics and Orthodox, possibly for purely social or cultural reasons. This aloofness can be melted by the warm sunshine of friendly dialogue but it is imperative that American Catholics get to know more about the Orthodox way of life and thought. Even at the Second Vatican Council, Catholic lack of understanding of the Orthodox was evident. The document on the Oriental Churches was notably Latin and Western in its approach and the great majority of Council speakers on ecumenical subjects were trying to make contact with the Protestant belief and way of life and to answer Protestant questions. Few seemed to come to grips with the questions of the Orthodox and the tendency was to look upon the Orthodox as colorful, quaint, somewhat exotic in their liturgy but hopelessly medieval. If the Roman Catholic Church is to engage in successful dialogue with the Orthodox, it must rediscover them as genuine Christians with a valid Christian way of life even though it is not Western.

Pope Paul summed it all up in a talk he gave on August 18, 1963, in which he urged unity with the Orthodox Churches: "We are all a bit deaf, and all a bit mute. May the Lord open our senses to understanding the voice of history, to understanding the voices of the Spirit..."

III
The Reformation

When Martin Luther nailed his theses to the church door at Wittenberg, Germany, in 1517, he was beginning a movement that would align him against emperor as well as Pope. At first he had no intention of rebelling against either. He was simply announcing his readiness to defend his theses against all comers. What he was objecting to mainly was the manner in which a certain Dominican monk named John Tetzel was preaching indulgences.

Tetzel had been dispensing indulgences throughout Germany since 1504, but in 1517 he was preaching indulgences to collect money for the rebuilding of St. Peter's in Rome. Tetzel's style was high-pressure salesmanship that amounted almost to swindle. He sometimes held up an indulgence certificate before the assembled crowd and announced that the salvation of the soul of the beneficiary was assured, possibly adding a cheery little verse such as: "As soon as the coin in the basket rings, the soul out of Purgatory springs."

Luther, an Augustinian monk, maintained that if Pope Leo knew of the Dominican Tetzel's tactics he would rather see the great Roman basilica burned to the ground than rebuilt out of the flesh and blood of his victimized flock. The young Reformer's protests against abuses perpetrated by Tetzel soon developed into objections to the Catholic doctrine of indulgences. The Pope asked the acting head of the Augustinians, Father John von Staupitz, to admonish the young monk. Staupitz showed Luther the greatest sympathy and consideration.

Even Cardinal Cajetan, the Dominican sent by the Pope to examine the young theologian, dealt tactfully and very gently with him at first, urging him, however, to recant. Cajetan apparently agreed with a number of Luther's complaints, especially those directed at the Roman Curia, but Luther resented his demand for recantation. He wrote to his brethren at Wittenberg: "The Cardinal may be an able Thomist but he is no clear Christian thinker and so he is about as fit to deal with the matter as an ass is to play the harp."[1]

Had other Church officials handled Luther's protests with tact and adroitness equal to that of the kind and fatherly Staupitz, the schism might never have occurred. They should have given him an opportunity to explain his teachings. Cardinal Cushing, speaking to the national Lutheran Laymen's League convention (July 15, 1965) said: "We could have had the reformation without a revolution four hundred years ago if there had been a Pope like John XXIII."

It is true that Luther had a violent temper and was not the most docile of men, yet he was honest and open to reason. The polemics of the Counter Reformation have portrayed him as proud, arrogant, and blustering, but the best modern Catholic historians of Luther reveal him as a deeply sincere and genuinely dedicated Christian.

Unfortunately the wrong papal officials and theologians became involved in the hunting-down of the new heresy and they were unwilling to listen to any prophet. Luther was condemned by the University of Louvain in 1520 without any opportunity to explain his doctrines and was excommunicated by Pope Leo X in 1521. The excommunication, pronouncing him a heretic, subjected him to the death penalty.

There had been many religious dissenters previously in the history of Christianity but Luther's challenge to Church authority was different in that an admired and passionate preacher and theologian had appeared in Europe at a time of almost convulsive social, political, and religious unrest. The German people tended to feel that Luther had been condemned for saying publicly what they thought

---

[1] John P. Dolan, *History of the Reformation* (New York: Desclee Company, 1965), p. 266.

The Reformation

privately about abuses in the Church. Indeed, some of the German bishops were quite unhappy about the excommunication.

The Holy Roman Emperor, Charles V, bogged down in preparations for military expeditions, was unable to give his undivided attention to the controversy in Germany and Luther took advantage of the situation by urging the princes (in *An Appeal to the Nobility of the German Nation*) to take matters in their own hands by executing certain necessary reforms in Germany. Because he was under excommunication, he was granted a hearing by the Emperor. The Reformer appeared before the imperial assembly, the Diet of Worms, in 1521, under an assurance of safe conduct from the Emperor. The upshot of the hearing was that in May 1521 the Emperor declared him an outlaw.

Luther, however, was able to defy the Emperor with impunity because of the many imperial wars that continued to claim the ruler's attention. He was protected by German princes who had little affection for the Emperor or the Pope. The rise of nationalism, the complaints of the peasants, the personal and political scandals among high-ranking prelates—all coalesced to aid the young Luther—though for a time he had his hands full trying to suppress the rebellion of the peasants who translated the Reformer's protests against the Church into demands for social reform.

In 1526 the princes drafted a legal protest against the Emperor's laws against heretics and from this protest came the word "Protestant." The Emperor responded by proclaiming his intention to suppress Luther's heresy by force, the result being a civil war lasting from 1546 to 1555, ending in the Peace of Augsburg. This treaty officially recognized Lutheranism as a religion but specified that each prince, Catholic or Protestant, was free to dictate the religion of his subjects.

It would be wide of the mark to say that Pope Leo X excommunicated Luther simply for his views on indulgences. While the excommunication document did cite his views on indulgences, it concentrated on his errors in regard to the authority of the Church and his teaching on the sacraments.

The central core of the whole controversy, however, was undoubtedly Luther's view of the role of man's free will in his personal salvation. As a monk, he had striven earnestly to advance in the spiritual life, trying all manner of ascetical and devotional exercises, but without achieving any sense of success. One day (the date is uncertain— perhaps sometime in 1513 or 1514) he was reading St. Paul's Epistle to the Romans, when he came across the words, "For in it the justice of God is revealed, from faith unto faith, as it is written, He who is *just lives by faith*" (Chapter 1, verse 17). This struck him with the force of a revelation. Previously he had thought of God's justice as the vindictiveness of the stern taskmaster who punishes every slightest infraction of the divine law. To him, God had seemed all too ready to inflict a penalty for every sin for he was a "just" God. After having been plagued by this sense of guilt, on reading this passage he felt he had discovered a long-forgotten but heart-warming and exhilarating truth, that God is just but that "justice" means the merciful pity he shows us by justifying us through faith. God is good and will save men, if only they have trust in his promises. Luther had a keen sense of the sovereignty of God and he believed in putting all his trust in God rather than in human effort and good works. He insisted that no man could please God by his own efforts, that every man must realize he is a sinful creature whose only hope is that the heavenly Father will deal kindly with him because of the redeeming death of His Son. The word "justice" became, then, like the gates of Paradise for Luther, opening up an entirely new and wonderful horizon in his life.

Luther's denial that good works would entitle a man to merit and salvation was aimed at those popular preachers of his time who were giving their hearers the impression that the mechanical doing of good works would automatically bring rewards. However, his teaching created the false impression among Catholics—even among some of his own followers—that Luther was encouraging Christians to ignore the moral code and to let God do all the work of saving them, without their cooperation. He was insisting on the absolute need of faith (for which good works could

The Reformation

be no substitute) but the impression rampant in Catholic circles for centuries was that he had encouraged immorality. Luther's often misunderstood maxim: "Sin bravely, still more bravely believe," seen in its own context, simply means that the merciful God will forgive the sinner, no matter how bold his sin.

As to Luther's attitude toward good works, he did not condemn them. He held that the justified person will do good works as the natural consequence of being justified but he insisted that good works never precede justification nor do they entitle a person to justification.

For many years the impression in Catholic circles was that Luther's principle of justification by faith alone" was an insuperable obstacle to fruitful dialogue. The Catholic answer was a flat denial of the validity of such a principle. For the justification that Luther was talking about seemed to be a purely external affair. He described the baptized person as "just and yet sinful" (*simul justus et peccator*). He seemed to be saying that God, in forgiving a sinner, was only *declaring* him to be holy whereas he actually remained full of sin, imputing holiness to the sinner but not imparting it, pardoning his sin but not removing it.

In trying to picture Luther's idea of justification, Catholics used to imagine Christ holding his mantle over the corrupt sinner so that the heavenly Father would not see the corruption and would not condemn the sinner. This concept of justification, of course, would not agree at all with the Catholic teaching that the sinner restored to grace is "a new creature," a holy person, a brother of Christ, not merely someone who has been pronounced to be spiritually well but is interiorly sick.

Today, however, many Catholics feel that Luther's words can be interpreted in the Catholic sense of justification. He was stressing the point that justification comes not from within us as a product of human effort but as a free gift from that Other Who is God. "Without Me you can do nothing," says Our Lord in the Gospels. There can be no such thing as self-justification. Says Luther: "If you have received forgiveness of sins, do not on that account be secure. You are just, holy, from outside yourself (extrinsic). It is through mercy and compassion that you are just. It is not my disposition or a quality of my heart but something outside myself—the divine mercy—which assures us that our sins are forgiven."

To say that Luther denied the inner renovation of the sinner through justification is to contradict Luther. For Luther, the Word of God was so powerful that the mere declaration by Him that the sinner has become pleasing to Him makes the sinner really and truly pleasing. Eventually he denied papal infallibility, the teaching authority of the Church, and most of the sacraments, as well as the sacrifice of the Mass. His only authority was the living Word of God. Luther's emphasis was on the living Word of God *speaking* to man. Religious services, the liturgy, and even the text of the Bible itself were important only if they made the living Word of God an authoritative reality apprehended by heart and mind. It was not even the text of the Bible that counted but rather the warmth and inspiration that God communicates to one who reads or hears the Bible in a spirit of faith.

What do we mean by the Word of God? It is a term seldom used by Catholics but frequently by Protestants. Yet the Catholic theology of the Word of God is very close to that of Protestants. The Word of God is the second person of the Blessed Trinity. Just as a written word in prose aims to express the grace and majesty and power of an idea in all its nuances, so the second person of the Trinity is the perfect Word, the perfect expression of all the perfections of the heavenly Father. The Word took flesh and dwelt among us to reveal to us the Father's love, mercy, and forgiveness and His every word and act revealed divinity. He was the living image of the Father. His whole life from cradle to grave was the Word. On all these points, Catholic teaching agrees with Luther but we differ on the means or agency through which we can receive the Word here and now and take it to heart.

In brief, Luther maintained that we receive the Word through the right preaching of the Scriptures and the right administration of the sacraments. Today Catholics and Protestants agree that the ultimate authority for all Christians is the Word of God but we hold that the teaching authority in the Church is, when necessary, capable of

The Reformation

infallibly interpreting God's Word; while Protestants assert that Christians must be content with prayer to the Holy Spirit for guidance, obedience to his direction, and the use of human instruments of research in discovering the meaning of the revealed Word. They acknowledge no infallible teaching office in the Church.

The Reformation spread like a forest fire across Europe, aided by the power of Luther's written and spoken word. He was a master of German style and a powerful preacher who captured the mind and heart of his hearers. He was no demagogue or spell-binder. Rather, he was like a prophet of the Old Testament living in the Christian era and passionately preaching to his audience the wonder of the Word of God. There was a time when Catholics depicted Luther as an immoral person or a megalomaniac. Today we are not ready to canonize him (indeed Protestants do not regard him as a saint) but we are developing a better appreciation of what he was trying to do. His Reformation plunged Christianity into tragic disunity but his original aims were quite different.

Luther was outstanding in his zeal for preaching the Gospel, admirable for his devotion to Christ Crucified, to Mary, to the Eucharist. Undoubtedly it was a painful experience for Luther to depart from his confreres and from his spiritual and scholarly heritage, but he probably felt he was practicing a deeper loyalty to his cherished traditions by denouncing those who, he thought, were debasing them. He seems to have had a love for the Augustinian traditions and at one time condemned certain individualists in the Order who insisted in following their own whims rather than the will of their superiors. Ultimately, however, the Bible was for him the deep and only source of all his devotion and St. Paul was his lodestar.

The Reformer expressed a vehement hostility to the scholastic philosophers. He felt that St. Augustine was his ally in fighting against naturalism whereas he thought the scholastics did not really understand the sin in human nature. He claimed that these philosophers, and the preachers who relied on them, led the Christian faithful down the road to naturalism by encouraging them to do good works while failing to teach them that only God can make us holy.

He called the scholastic theologians "pig-theologians." They failed to point out the monstrous evil of sin, according to Luther, and instead had concentrated attention on good works, "And so they cause people to become proud in thinking that they are already righteous by having outwardly done good works." Luther declared they should have taught that we can be saved only by the action of God, not by our own actions. He did not oppose truly good works but only "proud good works" which do not proceed from God's grace.

Luther betrays a misunderstanding of the official Catholic teaching on justification, even of the teaching of the great scholastics. How did this happen? Some historians explain it on the ground that Luther was chiefly concerned with the preaching of the Word, not with abstract theology. He was concerned with fostering the piety of the people and he felt that popular piety was hollow as a result of popular preaching. He was probably correct to a large degree: this was not one of the golden eras of the pulpit. Moreover, we have to remember that official Catholic teaching on justification was not as clear in Luther's day as in ours. The Council of Trent, which clarified the Catholic teaching, was held after he had made his break with the Church.

Second, Luther's experience was with a distorted and corrupt form of scholasticism, that of nominalist philosophers like William of Occam, Pierre d'Ailly, and Gabriel Biel. He seems to have had almost no acquaintance with St. Thomas. The Protestant liberal theologian Wilhelm Pauck notes that in Luther's *Lectures on Romans* there is not a single reference to Thomas Aquinas. The Reformer detected the false Christianity in the nominalists like Gabriel Biel. Would he not have agreed with the true Christianity of the great Dominican had he been conversant with the works of St. Thomas?

Luther was disturbed not only by the theology he had learned in Germany but also by the theology preached at the grass roots to the faithful of the flock. His *New Testament* was a communication to the people, not an exercise

The Reformation

in meticulous scholarship. He was proud of his Doctorate, feeling it gave him a right to speak out but in the pulpit he was more the preacher than the professor. He saw among the people a great amount of purely external religion and wanted to help them extricate themselves from the delusion that they could save their souls by their own actions. So he tried to counteract what he considered a smug and superficial piety by calling attention to the colossal persistence of sin in human nature, an evil that could be pardoned only by faith in Christ.

With the passing of Luther in 1546 a new Protestant leader emerged. John Calvin was only a boy of eight when Luther nailed his theses to the door of the Wittenberg church. He never met Luther. In 1534 Calvin apparently experienced "a sudden conversion" to the Reform and in 1536 published *The Institutes of the Christian Religion* in its first version. In this work he explained the main principles of the Reformation and his fundamental teachings, which were the same as those of Luther, i.e. justification by faith alone, the corruption of human nature, the inability of man to merit profound respect for the Word of God. He differed notably from Luther in that he denied the Real Presence, i.e. he denied that Christ is substantially present in the Eucharist. The directness of his preaching drew converts from mendicant orders such as the Dominicans and Franciscans, and from the village workers.

In addition to Luther and Calvin there were other noted Reformers but the Protestant tradition flows down through history in two main streams having their source in these two great leaders.

Luther was the prophet of the new religion; Calvin, the formulator and organizer who converted Luther's insights into a coherent theological system. Calvin was an outstanding scholar. He has often been called the Thomas Aquinas of Protestantism, and it is interesting to note how often he quoted the great Dominican in his writings (in contrast to Luther who almost never mentioned him). In fact E. Harris Harbison in his *The Christian Scholar in the Age of the Reformation* points out that Calvin had almost an obsession for "utility" and Harbison links this concern to his scholarship in a surprising relationship.

Calvin repeatedly insisted on the need for every Christian to produce a "profit" in his investment in life, to bear "fruit" in his activities. Every act of a Christian, according to Calvin, must be useful to the advancement of the Kingdom of God. How reconcile this "utility" with Calvin's natural inclination to scholarship? Harbison suggests that he felt guilty about his passion for scholarship. "Only one thing could justify this continual yielding to his early zest for scholarship. This was the idea that the products of his pen could be useful, could bear 'fruit' in thousands of readers miles away in space and perhaps years away in time."[2]

The Puritans, the most Calvinistic of the American denominations, were a picturesque example of this dedication to utility. They wanted to give themselves to the service of God but at the same time renounced anything that might stand in the way of service. Card-playing and dancing they considered a frivolous waste of time, the reading of good literature a rewarding and useful occupation. Their resultant thrift, sobriety and hard work, along with the idea that success was a sign of God's blessing, have lent to the American character a deep sense of personal responsibility.

It is said that no modern man can possibly accept Calvin's doctrine of predestination, which held that God from all eternity chooses some men for damnation. It would be impossible for a Catholic ever to accept it; but are we not surrounded today by a contemporary equivalent to predestination—determinism? Predestination is pessimistic enough but is it any more pessimistic than the prevailing ideologies of psychological or social determinism which assert that men are governed by instinct or environment?

The one great shadow over Calvin was the inhumaneness of his rule over Geneva. He ruled it like a police state until his death in 1564; and his name is therefore forever linked with intolerance, especially with the burning of the

---

[2] E. Harris Harbison, *The Christian Scholar in the Age of the Reformation* (New York: Charles Scribner's Sons, 1956), p. 164.

The Reformation

Swiss Protestant, Servetus, in 1553 for denying the doctrine of the Trinity.

However, we must not forget that intolerance was the order of the day everywhere in the sixteenth century. The assumption in Europe was that there could be no political unity without religious unity and the heretic was considered a public enemy to be burned or sent into exile. Divided Christendom had departed so far from the spirit of the Gospel as to approve the killing of Christians for obeying the voice of conscience directing them how to worship God.

IV
The Church Against the World

The religious wars that broke out in Europe after the Reformation constitute one of the darkest pages in the history of Christendom. Christian murdered Christian in the name of Christ. Ultimately the Western world tired of bloody wars carried on by religious fanatics and exploited by politicians with the result that men and women of the seventeenth century also began to weary of the theologies that were being so grimly defended.

This is not to say that Europe was inundated with a tidal wave of unbelief. In fact, there were innumerable saints in Europe at the time. But the tendency, especially among the educated, was to question the sterner aspects of Christian theology such as the moral law and doctrines of eternal punishment. To the intellectuals of the time the Christian religion began to look more and more like a dismal relic of the dark ages. Inevitably the Age of Enlightenment dawned.

It was a central theme of the Enlightenment that the soft, white light of pure reason could bring about on earth a paradise that Christianity had been unable to achieve. The Catholic Church became the target of this new breed of Reformer. The cynical Voltaire scoffed at the clergy and at religious people generally. The French philosopher Rousseau offered a variation on the theme by claiming that all men are naturally good but have been corrupted by institutions. The Catholic Church, being the oldest institution, came under heavy fire.

The followers of Rousseau looked forward to the time

The Church Against the World

"when the last king is strangled in the entrails of the last priest." The natural religion engendered by Rousseau was a sentimental subjectivism that was utterly irreconcilable with the idea of an organized Church designed to safeguard objective truths. Thus, in the eighteenth century the Enlightenment, flowering in the French Revolution, took a resolute stand against the ancient Church. That Church which had leavened European society finally became isolated from the world of its time.

In the nineteenth century the descendants of the men of the Enlightenment were the liberals. Liberalism saw in the French Revolution the great Day of Liberation for all mankind from bondage to the past. In the early Christian centuries liberalism simply meant the defense of the rights of the human person against tyranny and so liberalism was therefore part of the basic tradition of European civilization. Today the word "liberal" seems to mean "broad-minded" or "tolerant" although some politicians tack "fuzzy" to "liberal" and thus make it an emotional "smear" word.

In the nineteenth century, however, liberalism came to be identified, in parts of Europe, with the rejection of all authority in religion or government except the authority of "the sovereign people." The Catholic Church rightly condemned this type of liberalism but unfortunately, in the heat of the battle, it skirmished with certain genuine liberals along with the spurious, thus alienating some of the finest men of the age. Many conservative Catholics even tended to link liberalism with Protestantism, viewing Luther's rejection of the authority of the Church as the seed-bed of liberalism's rejection of all divine authority.

In all fairness we must admit the liberals treated Pope Pius IX roughly. Cardinal Mastai-Ferretti succeeded the intransigent Pope Gregory XVI and as Pope Pius IX was greeted with a sigh of relief by Catholic liberals. The Italian leader, Rossi, assured everyone that "in the house of Mastai-Ferretti everybody is liberal down to the family cat." The new Pope relaxed censorship in the Papal States, eased restrictions on the press and was generally acclaimed as "the liberal Pope" but the press and the politicians soon betrayed him and he was a disillusioned man. Henceforward he became a reactionary, clinging pathetically to certain ideas that had outlived their usefulness.

In 1860, determined to capture the Papal States which he considered an obstacle to Italian unity, Garibaldi started his guerrilla war in Sicily that culminated in General Cadorna's capture of Rome in 1870. In the meantime, Pope Pius IX was attempting to cope with a multitude of "isms" spawned by the false liberalism. In 1864 he compiled *The Syllabus of Errors*. It lashed out at pantheism, rationalism, naturalism, indifferentism, socialism, communism, and liberalism. The item that roused most criticism was his condemnation of the proposition: "The Roman Pontiff can and ought to reconcile himself to and compromise with progress, liberalism and with modern civilization."

The *Syllabus* was a puzzling document. Some theologians say it had in itself no authority at all because it was unsigned and that it amounted to nothing more than an indexed summary of parts of other encyclicals. To interpret it, one had to read the encyclicals to which it referred. For instance, the above-mentioned condemnation of progress, etc., referred to an encyclical which condemned a political movement at Turin, Italy, that had adopted as its slogan: "Progress, Liberalism and Modern Civilization." At first glance, however, it seemed like a fanatical abjuration of all modern civilization.

At any rate, the *Syllabus* was taken by many Catholics to be a declaration of war on the modern world, and when Rome was captured by General Cadorna's army in 1870, the Pope became a voluntary prisoner in the Vatican and seemed to take the whole Church with him in retreat from the modern world. The liberals became violently anticlerical. In Italy, for instance, the religious orders were persecuted in the latter part of the century and the widesweeping program of secularization engineered by the Italian anticlericals was comparable in ruthlessness to that of Bismarck, who abolished religious orders and manhandled bishops, during his *Kulturkampf* in Prussia in 1873. In short, the Church went into its shell in order to avoid contact with the age. The tendency was to regard any forward-looking ideas as being tainted with the anti-clericalism of Italy.

In this period great Catholic thinkers like the British Lord Acton and the French writer and statesman Montalembert became silent while men of the authoritarian stamp of England's Cardinal Manning and the French Catholic journalist Veuillot welcomed the heavy, paternal hand of Rome shielding the Church from the evils of the age, its errors and heresies. Here was reaction, rock-ribbed and resolute, marching back to yesterday.

This reinforced in conservative Catholics the old animus against Protestantism. When Bishop Strossmayr of Bosnia objected, in the First Vatican Council in 1870, to a document's tendency to blame the Protestants for current evils, he said in the course of his remarks that there were many Protestants who still loved Jesus Christ. He was greeted with cries: "He is Lucifer, anathema, anathema," and "He is another Luther, let him be cast out."

This hostility to the modern world molded and solidified an approach to problems of the modern world that has pervaded the Church to a large degree right down to our own time.

Pope Leo XIII (1878–1903) was influential in creating a more genial attitude. He was receptive to new ideas, and in opening up the Vatican archives to historians he was helping to allay the Catholic scholar's fear and suspicion of modern scholarship. It seems, however, that the new spirit of freedom was practically crushed in the bud by the condemnation of Modernism in 1906 and 1907. Contending that personal religious experience is the heart and essence of religion, the Modernists saw dogmas as mere historical expressions of the evolution of the inner religious sense. Some Catholic scholars were attracted by Modernism, feeling that it was not entirely evil and had something to contribute to Catholic scholarship, especially its methods of research.

Yet, in its extreme form, Modernism was the most destructive heresy in Christian history. Claiming that the Church was simply the collective conscience of the early Christians, it was a denial that Christ founded the Church. However, the sad fact is that genuinely orthodox as well as unorthodox Catholic scholars were treated harshly and the official condemnations were followed by an official program of eagle-eyed vigilance that purged seminary faculties, imposed strict censorship of books, suppressed periodicals and imposed the anti-Modernist oath. Catholic theologians and scriptural scholars thenceforward approached their studies with less than critical honesty and with a reluctance to come into contact with new ideas or to communicate them to the faithful. It was the era of the closed Church.

The atmosphere began to brighten again under Pope Pius XII, who began his pontificate in 1939. His encyclical on Scriptural Studies (*Divino Afflante Spiritu*, 1943), was a go-ahead signal for Bible scholars and he showed a great pastoral concern for adaptation of the Church to the demands of a world in flux and ferment. From 1950 on, however, Pope Pius modified his reforming spirit considerably. He repeatedly warned of dangers to doctrine (viz. the encyclical *Humani Generis*), dangers of social action (condemnation of the priest-workers) and in politics. Says the eminent Belgian Catholic historian Father Roger Aubert: "... the growing rigidity by which the declining years of Pius XII were marked caused disquiet and anxiety lest the Church might be making its way back to the sad days of intolerance."[1] Aubert, nevertheless, admits that this hardening does not seem to have undone much of the adaptation which Pope Pius had carried out in his earlier years immediately after the end of the war. These reforms did prepare the way for the reforms urged by Pope John.

Cardinal Doepfner, Archbishop of Munich-Freising, says that many regard Pope Pius XII's pontificate as conservative or reactionary but that he had the same goals as Pope John: the renewal of the Church and the fruitful encounter of the faithful with the tasks and concerns of the modern world. "His encyclical letters, addresses and other pronouncements on countless important questions opened the door to discussion and reform within the

---

[1] Roger Aubert, "The Church of Rome," in *Twentieth Century Christianity*, edited by Stephen C. Neill (Garden City, New York: Dolphin Books, Doubleday & Company, 1963), p. 35.

Church, or at least paved the way for future developments."[2]

October 28, 1958, marks the beginning of the era of the open Church. It was on that day that Cardinal Roncalli of Venice was elected to the papacy and took the name of John XXIII. He was no stranger to the tensions produced by the hunt for Modernists that began after the condemnations of it in the papal encyclicals. He once admitted that his name had been handed into the Holy Office during this period.[3] In his experiences as papal representative in Bulgaria, Turkey, Greece, and France, he came to see that the closed-door attitude of sections of the Roman Curia was out of line with Christ's command to "go out into the whole world and preach the Gospel to every creature."

In his opening address to the Second Vatican Council, Pope John made it clear to the bishops that this Council was not to talk to itself but to the whole world. When he spoke of unity, he spoke of a triple ray of supernal beneficent light—the unity of Catholics among themselves, the wider unity that should unite Catholics and all separated Christians, finally the unity that should exist between Catholics and the followers of non-Christian religions. He did not deny that errors are rampant in the modern world but affirmed that nowadays the Church prefers to use the medicine of mercy rather than severity in handling these errors. "She considers that she meets the needs of the present day by demonstrating the validity of her teaching rather than by condemnations."

The effect on the bishops was immediate and profound. In their deliberations, they concentrated on renewal but always with an eye to renewal by way of preparation for reunion and mission. No one has expressed as vividly as Pope Paul himself the "outgoing" experience that took possesssion of the bishops after hearing Pope John at the opening of the Council. In his address at the opening of the second session, Pope Paul stated that one of the main

---

[2] Julius Cardinal Doepfner, *The Questioning Church* (London: Burns & Oates, 1964), p. 3.

[3] Francis X. Murphy, C.SS.R., "Pope John XXIII, Pastor and Theologian" (*Catholic World;* August, 1963).

aims of the Council would be to build a bridge of understanding to the modern world. Then he reminisced about Pope John's talk and said: "Indeed, you yourselves, when you were undertaking the labors of the first session, aglow with the opening words of Pope John XXIII, instantly felt the need of opening, as it were, the doors of this assembly and of suddenly shouting to the world a message of greeting, of brotherhood, and of hope."

Anyone who attended the actual sessions of the Council would say that it was, indeed, not so much a dialogue among the bishops as a dialogue of the bishops with the world.

As Pope John said, the Church today prefers to use the medicine of mercy rather than severity in handling errors. So we can well afford to take the cue and look back at our recent Catholic past with mercy rather than severity. Maybe this Pope was too reactionary or that cardinal was too authoritarian. But we must remember that the adversaries facing the Church in the last few centuries were no strawmen. The Reformation was a great challenge to the authority of the Church and the Church's decision to assume a defensive stance against it is altogether understandable. Likewise the threat from the Enlightenment was a grave cause for alarm. In both instances, the Church was faced with disaster. That she ever survived seems like a miracle. "When we reflect," wrote the historian Macaulay, "on the tremendous assaults which she has survived, we find it difficult to conceive in what way she will perish."

The important thing for us is not to criticize our predecessors for the manner in which they responded to challenges but to make the most of the tolerance and freedom that they never knew but which we now enjoy. The task ahead of us is to unite with our separated brethren so that we can more effectively bring the blessings of the Gospel to the whole world.

V

The Catholic Church and Ecumenism in the Past

In previous chapters I have attempted to describe the tragic events that led to the separation of Roman Catholics from Orthodox, the upheavals in religious and social life that divided Roman Catholics from Protestants, and, finally, the developments that tended to isolate the Catholic Church from the modern world. As a result of these divisions, the Roman Catholic Church was content to survive, to remain on the defensive and aloof from other Christian bodies and the contemporary world.

Today the Catholic Church promotes ecumenical dialogues, but in the long centuries before the Second Vatican Council, the Catholic Church made no official overtures to Protestants (except for the fruitless Regensburg Colloquy in 1542 and the Colloquy of Poissy in 1561). In these years prior to the Council, were there no individual Catholics who crossed the battle lines to speak to other members of the Christian family with the hope of achieving reconciliation? Were there no Catholic ecumenists before Pope John?

There were individual Catholics who did engage from time to time in projects designed to further Christian unity but these had no lasting effect. The Dutch scholar Erasmus tried to bring about a reconciliation of Catholics and Protestants by proposing Christian unity on the basis of a number of fundamental articles of the Christian faith. He failed partially because he was suspected of "laying the egg hatched by Luther" and partially because he wanted to reduce the dogmas of the faith to a mere handful. Some modern Catholic historians claim that Erasmus was a grave threat to the Church not only because of his withering criticism of prelates and practices but also because he tended to shrink Christianity to a basic monotheism plus a dash of morality.

The papal delegate at the Diet of Worms in 1521 wrote to Pope Leo X (who admired Erasmus): "For heaven's sake, don't send us any more privileges for Erasmus. The man is doing far more harm than Luther ever can." However, as ecumenism progresses, Erasmus will regain prestige. It is easy to see why Erasmus would antagonize, as an ecumenist, the majority of Church officials and theologians of his day.

The great French bishop Bossuet corresponded with Leibnitz, the famous German philosopher, in regard to a possible reconciliation of Lutherans and Catholics; and there were others as well who engaged in enterprises of this nature. None achieved any permanent results.

An Irish bishop was one of the most remarkable of the Catholic ecumenical pioneers. In 1824 Bishop James Warren Doyle of Kildare sent a letter to the Chancellor of the Exchequer of the British Government. In it, he proposed that the Government support a project to hold theological talks aimed at removing the differences between the Roman Catholic Church and the Anglican Church in Ireland. Bishop Doyle even offered to renounce his episcopal see if it would help toward union. As the Catholic ecumenical scholar Father George Tavard says, "This letter indicates three points which the Catholic ecumenists were due to rediscover since then."[1] First, that most of the differences were nontheological; second, that dialogue was the best method for clearing up the misunderstandings that block the way to discussion of ultimate theological issues; and third, that something like what is

---

[1] George H. Tavard, *Two Centuries of Ecumenism* (New York: Mentor-Omega, New American Library, 1962), pp. 45–46.

The Catholic Church and Ecumenism in the Past 43

now called "spiritual emulation" should be cultivated. In regard to this latter item, Bishop Doyle felt that successful dialogue demands a love for humility, charity, and truth. Father Tavard claims that if the Bishop's proposals had been heeded, the ecumenical movement would today be a hundred years in advance of what it actually is, at least as far as Catholics are involved.

Pope Leo XIII (1878–1903) laid the bases for modern ecumenical thinking among Catholics. His letters and addresses penetrated profoundly into ecumenical problems in dealing with particular episodes which arose during his pontificate and which had ecumenical implications. Father Tavard points out that Pope Leo did not use the terms "heretic" or "schismatic" in referring to Christians outside the visible borders of the Roman Catholic Church. He usually referred to them as "dissidents." He introduced prayers for unity that were not designed to bring about individual conversions to the faith but rather the reconciliation of separated communities of Christians. He drew a sharp distinction between "convert work" and work for Christian unity. His *Praeclara Gratulationis* was the first papal encyclical ever dedicated to the question of unity and in it he appealed not only to the Orthodox Churches but also to the Protestants: "For a long time Catholics all over the world have awaited you, with the anxiousness of a brotherly love, that you might serve God with us in the unity of the same Gospel, the same faith, the same hope, bound by perfect love."

Although he had a special interest in the Orthodox, Pope Leo did not neglect the Anglicans. Discovering that they deemed the Catholic refusal to admit the validity of Anglican Orders a bar to reunion, he responded by appointing a committee to study the question. In 1898 he addressed a letter to the Catholic bishops of Scotland, expressing his desire for unity with the Presbyterians of Scotland that "they may one day be willing to join us in restoring the communion of one and the same faith." He felt that the Scots' love for Scripture might become the bridge to unity. "The Scots deserve the highest congratulations for being assiduous in their study of and love for Sacred Scripture. This high regard for the study of Sacred

Scripture is a kind of relationship with the Catholic Church, so to speak. Couldn't this be the beginning of the unity that is to be regained?"

Other popes built on the ecumenical foundation established by Pope Leo. Benedict XV took a special interest in the Malines Conferences (Malines, Belgium, 1921–26), which were attended by Cardinal Mercier of Belgium as well as by other Catholics and by Anglican ecumenists. Pope Pius XI worked hard for unity with the Orthodox and in 1925 had the satisfaction of seeing a monastery at Amay, Belgium, founded for the purpose of fostering Catholic-Orthodox unity.

In his allocution of January 10, 1927, Pope Pius XI said of the Christian elements in Orthodoxy: "The separated particles of gold-bearing rock themselves contain gold. The venerable Eastern Christian bodies have preserved in their mentality a holiness so worthy of reverence that they not only merit all our respect but likewise our mutual understanding."

On January 6, 1928, Pope Pius issued his *Mortalium Animos* in which he took the ecumenical movement to task for its operational procedures. It seems the movement known as *Faith and Order* (which later became the *Faith and Order* department of the *World Council of Churches,* the department set apart for theological discussion) at that time employed a method of dialogue which consisted mainly in comparing the theologies of the respective churches. The *Life and Work* movement, on the contrary, avoided all theological discussion on the ground that "doctrine divides, service unites" and devoted its efforts to study of and participation in social action. Pope Pius' opinion was that ecumenical discussions should be theological discussions and he expressed a preference for study of the doctrines that Christians share in common rather than the things that divide them. He also asked for study of the theology of the early Church Fathers. The encyclical is not as ecumenical as we might like but yet not as negative as some have pictured it, and its general theme runs close to the accepted policy of the *Faith and Order* meetings of the World Council today.

The Anglican bishops at the Lambeth Conference in

The Catholic Church and Ecumenism in the Past 45

England in 1920 had stated their readiness to agree to a policy of re-ordination in case this was necessary for Christian unity. Their appeal was intended for the Free Churches but Lord Halifax saw in it a ray of hope and arranged with Belgium's Cardinal Mercier the series of Malines Conferences between Anglicans and Catholics to which I have alluded above. The Catholic and Anglican delegates went to Malines as private theologians, not as official representatives of their churches to negotiate a reunion. They simply wanted to discuss in order to clarify teachings. Thus, for five years, top-ranking Catholic and Anglican theologians engaged in dialogue. The deaths of Cardinal Mercier and Abbé Portal in 1926 fore-shadowed the end of the Conferences. The last was held October 11–12, 1926.

What was the result? Father Tavard says that at least it showed that dialogue between Catholics and separated brethren is possible, and that it is advisable to restrict dialogue to a small group. No more than a dozen took part in these conferences.

Father Tavard is notably reserved in his evaluation of the results of the Conferences. Stephen Neill, one of the greatest historians of the ecumenical movement, is likewise guarded in his reaction, to the point of disparagement. He says that the importance of the Conferences has been enormously exaggerated due to the fact that Cardinal Mercier, hero of the First World War, and the indomitable Lord Halifax, doggedly pursuing the will-o'-the-wisp of Catholic reunion, shed a certain air of romance over the meetings. "Nothing was achieved beyond a deepening of personal respect and affection, and when the discussions were broken off, it was agreed that they would not be resumed."[2]

German Catholics have played a very large role in the development of ecumenism among Catholics. There are many reasons for this. First, the German Protestants are

---

[2] Stephen C. Neill, "The Movement for Christian Union," in *Twentieth Century Christianity,* edited by Stephen C. Neill (Garden City, New York: Dolphin Books, Doubleday & Company, 1963), p. 340.

mainly Lutherans with a strong doctrinal orientation and German Catholic theologians feel that in the Lutherans they have found kindred spirits. Second, German Catholics and Protestants were brought closer to each other by their common sufferings under Hitler. Persecution took their eyes off many of the peripheral differences that divided them and focused their attention on the ties that bound them—the great truths of the Incarnation, Resurrection, and Redemption.

The first outstanding German Catholic ecumenist was Father Josef Metzger, who founded the *Una Sancta* Confraternity in 1939. *Una Sancta* prayed for peace among Christians and endeavored to build bridges of intellectual and spiritual understanding between separated Christian confessions, "emphasizing that which unites rather than that which divides."

The Second World War unhappily ended the *Una Sancta* gatherings and Metzger himself was killed by the Nazis in 1944. It is interesting to note that while in prison in 1939 he wrote a letter to Pope Pius XII (whether it was received is uncertain) in which he suggested that the Pope convene an Ecumenical Council, which Metzger saw as the only hope for reunion. "The history of the Church and that of the world as well will raise up a monument to the Pope who starts this work on a large scale and to the one who completes it later on."[3]

After the war, *Una Sancta* revived under Father Matthias Laros and, later, under Father Thomas Sartory, O.S.B., bearing fruit in works such as Karl Adam's *One and Holy*. Today, *Una Sancta* is overshadowed by a galaxy of ecumenical enterprises in Germany such as the scholarly Johann Moehler Institute in Paderborn.

In Holland ecumenical activity flourishes so exuberantly that over a hundred priests have been assigned to the work. Monsignor J. G. Willebrands (now a Bishop and secretary of the Secretariat for Promoting Christian Unity) directed Dutch ecumenical work for many years and established the international *Catholic Conference for Ecumenical Questions* in 1952. This is a group of top

---

[3] Tavard, *op. cit.*, p. 112.

The Catholic Church and Ecumenism in the Past 47

ecumenists from all parts of the Catholic world. (I remember vividly being present at the 1960 meeting at Gazzada, Italy, attended by Cardinals Bea, Alfrink, and Montini.) Perhaps the Dutch ecumenist best known to American Catholics is Dr. W. H. Van de Pol, the author of *Protestantism,* who holds the chair of phenomenology at the University of Nijmegen in the Netherlands.

In France, Abbé Portal (1855–1926) was one of the Catholic ecumenical pioneers. A kindred spirit to Lord Halifax, he collaborated with him on the Malines Conferences and displayed an extraordinary knowledge of Anglicanism. French ecumenism has always paid special attention to the Orthodox Churches and Abbé Portal helped to stimulate Catholic interest in Eastern questions. Dom Lambert Beauduin, friend of Cardinal Mercier, established at Amay, Belgium, in 1925, a monastery which he made bi-ritual, with monks from the Byzantine as well as the Latin rite. Here, in 1927, the magazine *Irenikon* came into existence. Beauduin's idea was that unity with the Orthodox would require profound spiritual preparation, so Amay became a place for prayer and study. It was here that the noted Father Paul Couturier, a priest of Lyons, France, received inspiration for his future work. In 1939 the monastery was transferred to Chevetogne, Belgium.

Abbé Couturier founded the *Week of Prayer for Christian Unity*. The older practice, the Church Unity Octave, was based on the theme of unity through submission to the See of Peter. In this form, Catholics might be expected to pray for other Christians but other Christians could hardly be expected to pray for their submission to the papacy. Father Couturier felt that we must all pray together if we are to have unity, hence a new formula would be necessary. The framework of the *Week* (January 18–25) embraces daily Mass for Christian Unity and an evening of prayer. Father Michalon of the University Seminary, Lyons, edits an annual tract for the *Week* containing a program for prayers and hymns, and *Faith and Order* (World Council of Churches) publishes a similar tract, making a total circulation of several million copies of the *Week* booklet. It has been adopted by many Catholic as well as non-Catholic Churches. In the United States, the National Council of Churches and the World Council of Churches sponsor this prayer booklet of the *Week of Prayer*. It bears the printed endorsement of the U. S. Bishops' Commission for Ecumenical Affairs and can be ordered from the World Council or from the Graymoor Friars.

Father Couturier laid a strong emphasis on the need of prayer, calling his ecumenical method "spiritual emulation." His aim was to stir up the spirit of prayer in all Churches as a means of spiritual development. He did not, however, disparage theology. His approach was simply that prayer is necessary not only to solve the theological problems but even to approach them with the right psychological attitudes, a meeting of hearts being a necessary prelude to a meeting of minds. Father George Tavard suggests that Abbé Couturier possibly did not take sufficient account of the urgent need of engaging in dialogue as soon as possible. "Dialogue should not be postponed until there is a meeting of hearts. We cannot love what we do not know and therefore we should engage in dialogue in order to understand other Christian beliefs before we can really love other Christians."[4]

Among the greatest of the French ecumenical theologians is Yves Congar, O.P., whose *Divided Christendom* appeared in English in 1939. It was a penetrating study of the origins of Christian disunity and a forecast of the ecumenical future. At the Second Vatican Council he was regarded as the grand old man of Catholic ecumenism.

Another Dominican, Père C. J. Dumont, directs the Center called *Istina,* in a suburb of Paris. Its special focus of attention is Orthodoxy, and Orthodox priests and prelates are frequent visitors, usually taking advantage of its well-stocked research library. Père Beaupère, O.P., directs the St. Irenaeus Center at Lyons. The Rev. Jerome Hamer, O.P. (whose book on *Karl Barth* [Newman] is an ecumenical masterpiece) is now Associate Secretary of the Secretariat for Promoting Christian Unity.

---

[4] Tavard, *op. cit.,* p. 125.

The Catholic Church and Ecumenism in the Past 49

In England the ecumenical movement has made slow progress in Catholic circles. It has not known any Father Couturier, Abbé Portal, or Father Metzger but the movement is making headway against built-in obstacles. Baron von Hügel made a profound impression on the Anglicans in the early years of this century but his friendship with Modernists like Tyrrel and Loisy lost him the support of English Catholics. British Catholics generally seem to be hostile to the Established Church and demonstrated in the past no great love for European Catholic ecumenists who came to Britain to form or expand contacts with Protestants. The arrangers of the Malines Conferences tactlessly conducted their sessions as though the British hierarchy did not exist and yet they were involved in a matter of deepest significance for that hierarchy. The tension was aggravated when the English Jesuit, Father Woodlock, assailed Cardinal Mercier in a magazine article.

In view of the British hierarchy's opposition to the Malines Conferences, it was encouraging to read the speech delivered by Archbishop Heenan of Liverpool at the Second Vatican Council expressing the hierarchy's approval of the Ecumenism Schema: "We declare that we are prepared to do anything outside of denying the faith to obtain the union of Christians. We desire fuller and more frequent dialogues with all Christian denominations."

In his talk, he remarked that some consider Catholics in England indifferent to ecumenism; indeed, some British Protestants have had to go abroad to engage in dialogue. Then, in what many journalists interpreted as an echo of the unpleasantness at the time of Malines Conferences, the Archbishop urged the Council to recommend that dialogue be carried on normally "within the region of those taking part in it." After the third session ended, with its enthusiastic approval of the schema, the British hierarchy officially decided to establish an ecumenical commission in every diocese.

At the present time, the prospects for continuing ecumenism in England are growing brighter. We find competent ecumenists like Father Henry St. John, O.P., Dom Columba Cary-Elwes, O.S.B., John Todd (author of a fine work on Luther), and the writers in the *Eastern Churches Quarterly* (now called *One in Christ*), edited for many years by Dom Bede Winslow, O.S.B.

During the Second World War, Cardinal Hinsley founded *The Sword of the Spirit,* a movement intended to unite all Christians in a crusade for "the restoration of order, justice, and peace." It had a phenomenal success during the war but unfortunately it was essentially a temporary body, having been organized to meet a national emergency on the social and civic level. It did not foster theological dialogue. *The Sword of the Spirit* still exists but not particularly as an ecumenical organization.

In the United States the ecumenical movement made even slower progress than in Britain. There were many reasons for this. Persecution of Catholics in the last century and discrimination against them in the first part of this century did not contribute to the improvement of Catholic-Protestant relations. And yet we find some surprising ecumenical voices among American Catholics in the last century. Bishop John England of Charleston, South Carolina, used to preach in Protestant Churches in the 1830's. Father Isaac T. Hecker founded the Paulist Fathers in 1858 for the conversion of America, but in his latter days evinced a unique interest in Christian unity. In April 1888 he published an article in *The Catholic World* entitled "The Things That Make for Unity." He advised Catholics and Protestants to discuss points of agreement rather than disagreement: "Let us cultivate the things that make for unity," he wrote. "There is no reason why a movement toward unity should not set in, under the providence of God in our day, just as in the sixteenth century the perversity of men brought about disunion and sects." Two friends of Father Hecker, Cardinal Gibbons and Archbishop Ireland, participated in the Parliament of Religions at Chicago in 1892.

In 1908 Father Paul (Lewis Wattson) of the Atonement Friars popularized a prayer format for Christian unity whose aim was the corporate conversion of separated Christians to Rome. Father Tavard calls this a form of pre-ecumenism and it did serve the purpose of

The Catholic Church and Ecumenism in the Past 51

developing interest in corporate unity. Today, as I have already mentioned, the Atonement Friars collaborate with the National and World Councils in distributing a thoroughly ecumenical format of prayer—the *Week of Prayer for Christian Unity*. This is striking evidence of ecumenical development in a religious society that began at a time (1908) not at all propitious to ecumenism, an era when the Church was scrutinizing with a cold eye the religious views of other Christians as well as any new ideas in Catholic circles. *Americanism* had been condemned by Pope Leo XIII in 1898 and *Modernism* was also condemned in 1907. In fact, for the greater part of the first half of the twentieth century, Catholic priests were forbidden to appear on public platforms with ministers of other religions for fear of giving scandal by creating the impression that one religion is as good as another. The Catholic Church went about its own affairs quietly and blissfully indifferent to the life and thought of other Christians.

In 1948, Catholics in the United States paid practically no attention whatever to what was then considered to be the greatest ecumenical event of all time, the formation of the World Council of Churches at Amsterdam, Holland. This global organization had its beginnings in a meeting of Protestant missionaries at Edinburgh, Scotland, in 1910. The germinal meeting gave rise to a movement for Christian unity that branched into two sub-movements, *Faith and Order* and *Life and Work,* the first to deal with theological questions and the second to deal with problems of social action. Both groups found they were inevitably crossing and recrossing each other's concerns; so in a meeting at Utrecht, Holland, in 1939, they agreed to form one organization.

The outbreak of the Second World War forced postponement of further action until 1948 when the World Council was born. Composed of members of 148 Churches, the organization had representatives even from some of the Eastern Orthodox Churches. The Russian Orthodox Church, largest of the Orthodox Churches, did not join until 1961. Today there are over 200 Churches in the World Council. Its Central Committee meets once a year and is made up of one hundred members representing the various Churches. Supreme power, however, is found only in the General Assembly which meets once every six years. Dr. Franklin Clark Fry, head of the Lutheran Church in America, was elected head of the Central Committee in 1954 and Dr. W. G. Visser 't Hooft, a Dutch Calvinist, guided the world organization from its beginnings in 1948 as general secretary until he was succeeded by Dr. Eugene Carson Blake, an American Presbyterian, in 1966.

A few weeks before the meeting at Amsterdam, a decree of the Holy Office (1948) forbade Catholic participation in any meetings of Catholics with non-Catholics at which religion would be discussed. Later, an *Instruction* (called *Ecclesia Catholica*) was published by the Holy Office on December 20, 1949. It evinced a positive and encouraging attitude to ecumenical work, entrusting bishops with the task of fostering ecumenical discussions by competent priests. It said that the desire for reunion in non-Catholic ecumenical gatherings has been awakened "under the inspiring grace of God." *Ecclesia Catholica,* however, pertained only to participation in meetings sponsored by Catholics.

As for meetings arranged by non-Catholics, the *Instruction* says tersely: "The Catholic Church takes no part in ecumenical conventions and other assemblies of a similar nature." Thus the door was closed gently but firmly on Catholic membership in the World Council or on any Catholic participation at that time in ecumenical meetings sponsored by other Christian groups.

Possibly this ban on attendance at meetings sponsored by other groups was responsible for the general impression that the *Instruction* was hostile to the ecumenical movement. The fact is, however, that the *Instruction* favored adoption by Catholics of the ecumenical approach and said that it was the Church's duty to give reunion work care, attention, encouragement, and direction. It provided for the establishment of "reunion work" centers in each diocese at the bishop's discretion, the centers to be staffed by priests who were experts in ecumenical work. The *Instruction* concluded with the statement that "reunion work" should assume a larger role in the regular activities of the Church and that every Catholic should pray for its success. It recommended to Catholics and Protestants the practice of joint recitation of the Lord's Prayer.

The *Instruction*, however, was apparently taken by American clergy as a disapproval of ecumenical work because it scarcely ruffled the surface of Catholic-Protestant relations in the United States. No American diocese, to my knowledge, instituted a "reunion work" center.

The World Council of Churches held its General Assembly at Evanston, Illinois, in 1954. On that occasion, Cardinal Stritch of Chicago issued a pastoral letter not only opposing the sending of observers but even forbidding priests as reporters. The pastoral seemed to run counter to the intent of the 1949 *Instruction*.

The *North American Faith and Order Conference* held a week-long meeting at Oberlin, Ohio, from September 3 to 10, 1957. Father Gustave Weigel, S.J., and I were selected as "unofficial observers" with the approval of the Apostolic Delegate and several other prelates. We spent a very interesting week with some four hundred Protestant ministers and about fifteen representatives of the Orthodox Churches. The World Council officials were most hospitable and one evening held an informal dinner in honor of the two Catholic observers. As the head of a Protestant divinity school observed, at Oberlin, for the first time in this century there was a Protestant trend toward a visible, organized Church. Gone was the old idea that "doctrine divides, service unites." The emphasis at Oberlin was on absolute fidelity to the Gospel as the only valid basis of unity.

What was the situation on the eve of the Second Vatican Council? In the June 8, 1959, issue of *Christianity and Crisis* there was an article by Father Gustave Weigel entitled "Inside Roman Catholicism." He said that American Catholics know little about Protestantism and show no desire to know about it. "In such a situation," he wrote, "the American Catholic is totally unprepared for ecumenical dialogue though this is the task that our moment calls for. There is no Catholic hostility to ecumenism. There is just a great ignorance of what it is and why it is important." He said that a few American ecumenists had raised their voices but that their impact had not been wide or deep. He felt that on the whole nothing was being accomplished and that while he hoped that the Council might produce some good fruits, we would have to wait and see. In the same issue William Clancy agreed with Reinhold Niebuhr's statement, "The relations between Catholics and Protestants in this country are a scandal and an offense against Christian charity."

Everyone knows what happened after that. On June 5, 1960, Pope John established the Secretariat for Promoting Christian Unity with Cardinal Bea as its head; on December 2 of that year the Pope received a courtesy visit from the Archbishop of Canterbury. In 1961 the Vatican sent five official observers to the World Council General Assembly at New Delhi, India, and on October 11, 1962, Pope John addressed the opening meeting of the Second Vatican Council.

The Council, at its third session (1964), approved the document on ecumenism and in it urged bishops all over the world to promote Christian unity. The approval of this document as well as the presence of Protestant observers at the Council has resulted in closer ecumenical ties between the Catholic Church and the World Council of Churches, climaxed by the visit of Cardinal Bea to the World Council of Churches' headquarters at Geneva on February 18, 1965. There he formally accepted the World Council's invitation to appoint six Catholic experts to join eight World Council experts on a committee to explore the prospects and possibilities of dialogue between the Catholic Church and the World Council of Churches.

Here in the United States, the ecumenical movement is gathering momentum. Numerous diocesan ecumenical commissions have been created and the U. S. Bishops' Commission for Ecumenical Affairs, piloted by Bishop Carberry of Columbus, Ohio, has launched out into the deep. The Very Rev. Msgr. William W. Baum began his work as executive director on January 7, 1965; his assistant since November, 1966 has been Rev. John F. Hotchkin of Chicago. My guess is that American Catholic ecumenical work will make faster progress than Catholic ecumenism anywhere else in the world. The Commission has been renamed The Bishops' Committee for Ecumenical and Interreligious Affairs.

VI

Ecumenism in the Constitution on the Church

The present policy of the Catholic Church in regard to unity is reflected in two main documents, the Constitution on the Church and The Decree on Ecumenism (Appendix Two of this book). These two documents were formally approved at the third session of the Council and represent a startling change from the previous official policy. In 1954 Cardinal Stritch of Chicago prohibited Catholic observers from attending the General Assembly of the World Council of Churches at Evanston, Illinois, and priests were forbidden to attend even as journalists. Now the Vatican sends observers to World Council meetings.

Yet it would be wrong to assume that the two Council documents were the result of sudden and entirely unexpected decisions by the Council Fathers. Ecumenism, as we have seen in the preceding chapter, were slowly germinating in the mind of the Church for quite a few years before the Council opened in 1962. The official policy of the Church usually lags behind the mind of the Church, and with good reason. Great new ideas usually bud and blossom within the Church itself before receiving approval at the highest level. The policy-making departments of the Vatican do not create new ideas and invent new movements which they proceed to impose upon the faithful. Fasting in Lent and frequent confession, for instance,

Ecumenism in the Constitution on the Church 57

were practices embraced by the ordinary faithful before they were written into the pastoral policy of the Church.

What were the new ideas and movements that prepared the way for ecumenism? I might mention the liturgical, scriptural, and catechetical revivals which had been in progress long before the Council met. These movements seemed to converge toward unity and, in fact, there were liturgical, scriptural, and catechetical movements in Protestantism that ran parallel to the Catholic trends. To imagine the Council as the result of a sudden inspiration that came to Pope John out of the blue is to romanticize it. His decision to call a Council may well have been the result of an inspiration but the Church was waiting for reform. It was in the air. Many bishops went to the Council thinking they had been nurturing new ideas only to find themselves in the company of kindred spirits who had been thinking along the same lines. The enthusiasm for progressive ideas manifested at the Council opening may have been due partly to Pope John's opening address but the more plausible explanation, in my opinion, was the amount of time and consideration bishops all over the world had given to the new ideas.

In parts of the world where the Church was flourishing and attention had to be given to the building of churches and schools, bishops were probably too busy with construction and administration to keep abreast of the latest developments in Catholic thought. The majority of bishops, however, shared the yearning of the scholars for reform and renewal. Like Pope John, they felt that a revitalized Church would present such a vision of unity and truth that separated Christians would desire union with it.

The Constitution on the Church is a tremendously important document from the standpoint of Christian unity. Its basic theology points toward the need of unity, just as The Decree on Ecumenism points back to the Constitution as vindication of some of its recommendations.

The Constitution on the Church clarifies the Catholic concept of the Church. The essential core of the Catholic-Protestant controversy is the concept of the Church. Protestants disagree with us on our concept of the nature and structure of the Church even though they do agree with us on the great concepts of the Incarnation and Redemption. One might think that the Catholic Church would have no need to clarify its idea of the Church. Have we not held on doggedly to the traditional teaching on the Church in the face of challenges from false teachers for twenty centuries? Did not the seventeenth- and eighteenth-century Roman Catholic theologians describe the nature, constitution, and membership of the Church in sharp, clear definitions much more precise than the concepts offered by Protestant theologians?

The fact is, however, that the Council Fathers felt that the existing doctrine on the Church needed further elaboration in view of the fact that our knowledge of doctrine had expanded since the seventeenth and eighteenth centuries. Pope Paul himself said that the main purpose of the Council was to clarify the Church's concept of herself. He declared that Pope Pius XII, in his encyclical on the Mystical Body (*Mystici Corporis,* 1943), had shed a strong light on the nature of the Church but had also stimulated the Church to give a still more penetrating description of herself.

True, the Church must ever remain a mystery. We will never fully understand it. But we can partially understand it and we must keep increasing that partial understanding, especially if the new insights help to further Christian unity. Pope Paul stated at the second session that the chief concern of the bishops in Council should be to re-examine the doctrine on the Church in preparation for unity: "This integral doctrine can receive many noteworthy developments which even may be carefully considered by our separated brethren. We ardently hope that this doctrine will make easier the path toward common agreement."

The Constitution refers in Chapter I to "The Mystery of the Church." This very term has ecumenical implications. For centuries Protestants have felt that Catholic theologians, with their precise definitions and distinctions, have been trying to rationalize what must remain a mystery. They considered these precisions to be "vain subtleties," to a large extent. One could describe the institutional features of the Church, said the Protestants, but how is it possible to describe the presence within it of the invisible God Who hides Himself and is known only by faith? It is interesting, then, to note that the Constitution begins with the serene affirmation that the Church is a mystery, the presence of God among men.

However, the document goes on to say that "the kingdom of Christ now present in mystery, grows visibly through the power of God in the world." The Church of Christ is a visible body in which the visible assembly and the spiritual community are combined in one reality. As Christ's visible humanity was united to his divinity in one person, so the visible structure of the Church serves the invisible Spirit of Christ who vivifies it.

We have, then, in the Church, a divine and a human element. In the wording of the Constitution we can notice a deliberate attempt to be precise in describing the visible elements of this complex reality but also a reluctance to apply to the divine presence in the Church any words that might give the impression of weighing, measuring, and testing this invisible presence.

The Constitution states that a person is incorporated into the society of the Church by baptism. It does not use the term "member" or "membership in the Church." Possibly the reason for this is that Pope Pius XII, in his Mystical Body encyclical, was unclear as to "membership in the Church," and the present Council did not want to take sides in the controversy over the meaning of the Pope's words. Those words are as follows: "Actually only those are to be included as real members of the Church who have been baptized and profess the true faith and who have not been so unfortunate as to separate themselves from the unity of the Body or been excluded from it by legitimate authority for serious faults committed." [1]

Some theologians say this passage means that Pope Pius did not consider Protestants members of the Church. Others claim he meant simply to exclude from membership only those who have detached themselves willfully

---

[1] Pope Pius XII, *Foundations of Renewal* (Glen Rock, New Jersey: Paulist Press, 1961), p. 14.

and deliberately from the Church but that he did not desire to exclude those Christians who are simply born out of the visible Church.

The Constitution describes the Church as communion of life with Jesus in the Spirit and, under another aspect, as a visible social structure or institution. In the Church "as communion" we share, with all those who have received the gifts of redemption, all those invisible spiritual riches that came to us from Calvary. All validly baptized persons are sharers in this communion. Thus baptized Protestants and Orthodox share in the Church as communion. However, according to the Constitution, only those Christians are fully incorporated into the Church who accept all the teachings of the Church. "They are fully incorporated in the society of the Church who, having the Spirit of Christ, accept her entire system and all the means of salvation given to her, and are united with her as part of her visible bodily structure and through her with Christ, who rules her through the supreme pontiff and the bishops (Chapter II, Article 14).

Note the word *fully*. The degree of incorporation into the Church depends on the degree to which Christians accept what the Catholic Church proclaims as the full doctrine of Christ. The members of the Orthodox Churches, sharing with us more of the essential elements than do the Protestants, would be judged to enjoy a higher degree of participation in the Church. Protestants generally would look askance at this whole formula of incorporation into the Church. They would say that if full incorporation means full acceptance of the whole Roman Catholic system, with papal primacy and infallibility and all that, they would prefer not to be considered fully incorporated.

In brief, Catholics, Protestants, and Orthodox are sharers in the Church as communion. Roman Catholics are incorporated into the Church as communion and also as institution. Our ecumenical hope is that some day all Christians will share fully with us all those means of salvation that we believe Christ established for all Christians as a common heritage. To us Catholics, our separated brethren are far more than members of the same human family. Like us, they are adopted members of the family

Ecumenism in the Constitution on the Church

of the Blessed Trinity and co-heirs with Christ, our Brother. No matter what differences of language, culture, or history may divide us we are united with them in the body of Christ. We cannot look upon them as strangers. "Therefore, you are now no longer strangers and foreigners, but you are citizens with the saints and members of God's household . . ." (Ephesians 2:19).

After the Reformation, the tendency on the part of Roman Catholic theologians was to emphasize the Church as a visible institution, a visible organization. The reason for this was that the Reformers challenged the visible, organizational features of the Church. Both Catholics and Protestants admitted Christ was the invisible head of the Church but Protestants denied the Pope was the visible head. They spoke insistently about the *invisible* Church. Apparently Luther, for instance, did not mean to contrast a desirable invisible Church as against an undesirable visible Church when he used the term "invisible Church" but referred rather to two aspects of the same Church.

The Protestant theologian Karl Barth said that according to Protestant doctrine, the visible and invisible Church are one and the same, two predicates of the same subject. At the time of the Reformation, however, Protestants constantly referred to the *invisible* Church and probably meant that their Church was "spiritual" in contrast to the worldly Roman Catholic Church against which they protested. Their Church was not in unity with the Roman Catholic, but they claimed it was in continuity with the *invisible* Church which had been invisible since Emperor Constantine corrupted the then existing Church.

Because the Reformers emphasized the invisible Church so prominently, the Catholic theologians responded by emphasizing the visible features of the Church. Cardinal Bellarmine said that the Church was as visible as the Republic of Venice. The result was that Protestants came to think of the Catholic Church almost exclusively in terms of external organization and formal dogmas while Catholics, busily engaged in defending the visible and external features, tended somewhat to overlook the invisible presence of the Holy Spirit in the Church.

This was one of the most unfortunate results of the

controversy. Roman Catholics did not deny the invisible, spiritual element in the Church: they never really lost sight of it. But they gave it less attention than they gave the visible organization and did not give much explicit emphasis to the indwelling presence of the Holy Spirit. Indeed, they looked with suspicion on Protestant teaching which claimed that a Christian could have direct access to God rather than through the Church, and they abhorred Protestant extremists who used "Christian liberty" as a pretext for rejecting all visible Christianity. The Catholic Counter Reformation distrusted mysticism for being too spiritual, hence it was suspect of rebellion against the visible Church of authority. The Inquisition arrested even St. Ignatius and St. John of the Cross. In the seventeenth century there was a temporary reaction in the direction of mysticism and away from the cut-and-dried system of formal meditation then prevalent but, by and large, Catholicism in the Counter Reformation subjected to cold scrutiny any spiritual writer for fear his teachings might lead to personal delusion, hallucination, heresy or disobedience to authority.

This was certainly an abnormal situation, for Catholic life is normally spiritual rather than one-sidedly institutional, and yet it is perfectly understandable that the Church, in state of siege, should man the outer battlements. Today, however, the Catholic-Protestant war is over and we can resume our normal Catholic way of life. So we find the Constitution on the Church placing a heavy emphasis on the invisible as well as the organizational features of the Church. The faithful share in the invisible spiritual realities no matter how unprepossessing the externals of the Church edifice: in the lowliest chapel as in the great basilica of St. Peter's, they can gather in worship and receive the invisible Body and Blood of Christ. "In these communities, though frequently small and poor or living in the diaspora," says the Constitution, "Christ is present, and in virtue of His presence there is brought together one, holy, Catholic and apostolic Church."

In Chapter III the Constitution deals with the collegiality of bishops. This too has enormous ecumenical significance. After the First Vatican Council in 1870 (as mentioned in Chapter II) the non-Roman Christian world tended to think that the Roman Catholic Church had deliberately chosen to become a papal monarchy. The Council had defined the primacy and infallibility of the Pope and separated Christians felt that this decision had demoted the bishops of the Church to an insignificant role in the Church. The Orthodox and the Anglicans, in particular, have great respect for their bishops and therefore assumed that reunion with Rome was henceforward quite unthinkable. But the fact is that the Council had not deliberately thrust the bishops into the shadows of papal power. The Council agenda had included a discussion of the role of bishops in the Church but unfortunately the Franco-Prussian War (1870–71) had broken out before the Council could get to this item on the agenda and the Council came to an abrupt end.

The Constitution says that the bishops of the Catholic Church share with and under the Pope in the universal government of the Church by divine law. This does not diminish the papal power but it does dissipate the fable of an absolute papal monarchy. Just how the bishops will share in the government of the Church will be worked out as the years go on. The first meeting of the World Synod of Bishops took place September 29, 1967.

The doctrine of collegiality is expected to infuse a spirit of collegiality—a sense of collective responsibility—into the Church at every level. It will not only bring the Pope closer to the bishops but the bishops closer to their priests, the priests closer to the whole universal Church. It is anticipated, for instance, that collegiality will stimulate the interest of the ordinary American parishioner in the whole missionary program of the Church. He will be concerned not exclusively about his own personal salvation or the welfare of his parish but about the welfare of the whole universal Church. In short, collegiality should result in dialogue at all levels in the Church, thus helping to dispel the clerical authoritarianism that dismays our separated brethren and is an obstacle to unity. All persons in authority in the Church must now consult their subjects before making major decisions.

Often times the Protestant concept of a "priest-ridden"

Catholic laity whose clergy do all their thinking for them is a caricature but there is enough truth in it to embarrass Catholics. The doctrine of collegiality, in the strict sense, applies only to relations between Pope and bishops as regards a sharing in Church government but in the wider sense it can be applied to clergy-laity relations in general. In this sense it means closer contacts between priest and layman. This will help immeasurably to dissipate the non-Catholic's idea of a "priest-ridden" laity and an authoritarian clergy. With this in mind, the Constitution on the Church (Chapter IV) urges "familiar dialogue" between laity and their pastors. It states that laity should openly reveal to their pastors their needs and desires with all the freedom and confidence that is fitting for brothers in Christ. At times, according to the Constitution, laity are even obliged to express their opinions on those things that concern the good of the Church and the document admonishes pastors: "Let pastors recognize and promote the dignity as well as the responsibility of the laity in the Church. Let them willingly employ their prudent advice ... Attentively in Christ, let them consider with fatherly love the projects, suggestions, and desires proposed by the laity."

Collegiality implies two-way communication and lay-clergy communication in the Church will help to make Catholic obedience seem more reasonable and Catholic authority less of a stumbling block on the road to Christian unity.

In Chapter III of the Constitution (which treats of collegiality) there is also a section which proclaims that bishops at the time of their consecration receive a sacrament. They receive the fullness of the sacrament of holy orders. They are bishops, therefore, not because of appointment by the Pope but by virtue of spiritual powers given them by Christ Himself in the sacrament. Some Catholic theologians declare that this teaching on the sacramentality of the episcopate will widen the gap between Catholics and Protestants, for the latter hold for the priesthood of all believers and reject the doctrines of episcopacy and apostolic succession.

What is needed is a fuller and richer theological explanation of the sacrament of holy orders in order to allay the Protestant fear that exaltation of the bishop's role will tend to belittle the dignity of the Protesant pastor's function. At the same time we must remember that while this section of the chapter may enlarge the gap between Catholics and Protestants, it will probably bring us closer to the Anglicans and Orthodox who greatly revere their bishops and hold for the need of apostolic succession.

Viewed in its entirety, the Constitution can be said to be the basic theological foundation for the refinements of The Decree on Ecumenism. In the Constitution the Church is describing herself in rich biblical language, not as an army on the march to slay heretics, but primarily as the People of God on pilgrimage through time, all essentially equal with the hierarchy existing for the People of God— not the People for the hierarchy.

In its emphasis on the baptismal bond uniting all Christians, in its approval of collegiality which dissipates the notion of the Church as a papal monarchy, in its teaching on the sharing of all baptized in the grace of Christ, the Constitution on the Church leads us directly to the ecumenism document which will give us more specific information about relations with our separated brethren.

VII
The Decree on Ecumenism: General Principles

When the Second Vatican Council approved The Decree on Ecumenism, there were Protestants who greeted the document as "superb," "memorable," "momentous." Some went so far as to say that it was so inspiring as to constitute a call to all Christians for renewal through the Holy Spirit. Some felt confident that the ecumenical movement was at long last in full stride and that the handling of obstacles to reunion would be only a mopping-up operation. Others, of a more cautious bent, denied that the Decree radically changed the situation since the Catholic Church, in the Decree, was still insisting it was the one true Church. Edmund Schlink, professor of theology at the University of Heidelberg and Council observer for the Evangelical Church in Germany, warned that the Decree must play second fiddle to the more conservative Constitution on the Church since a Constitution bears more authority than a Decree. For these and other reasons, it is wise to read The Decree on Ecumenism (our Appendix Two) in the light of the Constitution.

But what does the Decree say? Before taking up its actual contents, I think it is reasonable to say that the wording of the Decree is of less significance than the ecumenical impulse the Decree has released in the Council itself and throughout the world. To appreciate the spirit behind The Decree on Ecumenism, one would have had to be present at the Council itself when the Decree was being discussed. The cold text of the document does not adequately reflect the vehemence of the breakthrough into ecumenism. In fact, bishops who had previously been considered indifferent to ecumenism showed a surprising enthusiasm for it in their Council speeches. Of course, the wording of the document had to be cautious in order to win the votes of the more conservative bishops for the document, and Schlink is not far from the truth when he writes: "Thus the cautious phraseology and the great reserve of the decree are to be explained by the fact that the Fathers of the Council were concerned to win over the whole Roman Church to the new ecumenical ideas."[1]

Chapter I of the Decree deals with "Catholic Principles on Ecumenism." There is an interesting story behind the title. The original version was entitled "Principles of Catholic Ecumenism" but this wording seemed to create the impression that there was a special Catholic Ecumenical Movement, independent and apart from the great world movement that has its most vital center at Geneva in the World Council of Churches. This would mean, if the impression were correct, that the Roman Catholic Church was starting up a rival movement in competition with the World Council to win the affiliation of other Christian Churches. Even as late as December 1963, when Pope Paul went to Jerusalem to visit Patriarch Athenagoras, the leader of the Orthodox Churches, rumors of a Catholic ecumenical movement were springing up. Was the Roman Catholic Church fanning the flames of religious competition while it was talking about eliminating such competition?

On August 26, 1963, Dr. W. A. Visser 't Hooft, then general secretary of the World Council, in a talk at Rochester, New York, expressed his satisfaction at the increase in ecumenical activity throughout the world but warned against a competitive spirit: "This danger arises, for instance," he said, "when the impression is created that

---

[1] Edmund Schlink in *Dialogue on the Way*, edited by George A. Lindbeck (Minneapolis, Minnesota: Augsburg Publishing House, 1965), p. 192

the Second Vatican Council is the most comprehensive center of ecumenical activity..." The title "Catholic Principles on Ecumenism" therefore helps to dissipate the false notion of a rival Catholic movement engaged in "Catholic ecumenism."

The Decree then goes on to present the Church's concept of her own unity. It states that Christ gathered together the people of the New Covenant into his Church, which is one and permanent, and entrusted to His twelve Apostles the task of teaching, ruling, and sanctifying His people. To Peter He gave the keys of the Kingdom but Christ was to be forever the invisible shepherd of souls. The unity of this Church has its source and exemplar in the unity of the three persons of the Trinity. The Decree cites Ephesians 4, verses 4–5, in which St. Paul teaches us: "There is one body and one Spirit, just as you were called to the one hope of your calling: one Lord, one faith, one baptism."

It was the Holy Spirit who was to bring about this wonderful communion of the faithful; yet rifts arose within the Church even in St. Paul's time, schisms which he had to condemn. In later centuries, says the Decree (Article 3), more serious dissension arose and "quite large Communities became separated from full communion with the Catholic Church." This refers in the main to the Eastern schism which culminated in 1054 and to the Reformation in the sixteenth century. Who was at fault? The text says "... often enough, men of both sides were to blame." This represents a change in the Catholic style. Formerly the Catholic custom was to put all blame on the dissidents without admitting Catholic faults. This derived from what is called the spirit of triumphalism, the feeling that the Church is forever in the right and forever winning triumph after triumph because it is right.

Note that the text (Article 3) puts the finger of blame on the men actually involved in the schisms. It does not blame their descendants for the schism (yet it does not forget that some may be at fault in continuing it). "... one cannot charge with the sin of the separation those who at present are born into these Communities and in them are brought up in the faith of Christ, and the

Catholic Church accepts them with respect and affection as brothers." The basic reason for this affection is the sacred tie of baptism that unites all Christians. Even though they may have only an imperfect communion with the Catholic Church, yet they do have real communion. They may lack belief in Catholic doctrines or structures but the fact remains that they have been baptized and are incorporated into Christ. This approach is a large step forward from the day when Catholics tended to think of Protestants as heretics to be avoided, unregenerate rebels who could not be saved.

In the past Catholics used to concede that an individual Protestant could please God by his desire to worship Him but that he pleased Him in spite of, not because of his Church. They would explain by way of analogy that a friend might give another friend a tie as a Christmas gift and that the other might like the friend's inner intention while disliking the tie itself. So we claimed that Protestants at worship pleased God by their good intentions but that the external form of the worship was not pleasing to God because it was heretical and false. Now all that elaborate canonical condemnation has disappeared as a result of Pope John's plea to the bishops to use the medicine of mercy rather than severity in discussing doctrine.

Not only does the Decree recognize the baptized Protestant as a brother incorporated into Christ but it also recognizes as good and laudable many elements in the other Christian Churches, stating (in Article 3) that many of the elements that give life to the Church can exist outside the visible boundaries of the Catholic Church, such as the written Word of God, the life of grace and the interior gifts of the Holy Spirit. The separated brethren, according to the text, use many liturgical actions which "can truly engender a life of grace, and, one must say, can aptly give access to the communion of salvation." Therefore, these Churches have by no means been deprived of significance in the mission of salvation. "For the Spirit of Christ has not refrained from using them as means of salvation which derive their efficacy from the very fullness of grace and truth entrusted to the Catholic Church."

No longer then do we regard Protestants as being saved in spite of their Churches: the text says that God uses these Churches as means of saving their members. No longer do we speak of modern Protestants as "heretics." Cardinal Bea has frequently asserted that the New Testament's harsh words for heretics were addressed to Christians who had deliberately and maliciously rejected what they knew to be the truth. These terms cannot be applied to contemporary Christians whose only offense is that they are loyal to the spiritual heritage transmitted to them by their ancestors. Says Cardinal Bea: "In the same way that it is no credit of ours to have been born and educated in a family belonging to the Catholic Church, neither is it to their discredit that they are the sons of parents separated from our Church" (*Civiltà Cattolica,* January 14, 1961).

Nevertheless, the text does not hesitate to assert the traditional doctrine with regard to the fullness of Catholic unity. It goes on to say that our separated brethren, "whether considered as individuals or as Communities and Churches, are not blessed with that unity which Jesus Christ wished to bestow on all those to whom He has given new birth into one body, and whom He has quickened to newness of life." Only in the Catholic Church can they benefit fully from all the means of salvation. Protestant theologians say they are grateful for the frankness with which the Church is here stating its position, but at the same time they cannot accept it. Some consider it arrogant, most consider it a claim that prevents genuine and successful dialogue. For they contend that dialogue presumes a basis of equality among the participants but this is a high-and-mighty stance that the Church is taking that will permit of little more than monologue. They feel that the Church is saying, "The only real Christian unity is in the Catholic Church and if you want unity, you will have to join the Catholic Church."

Is the Roman Catholic position an insuperable obstacle to dialogue? The claim of some Protestants is that they simply cannot accept the Catholic Church as the center of ecumenical discussion, as the criterion of full unity, the goal toward which all other Christian Churches must

The Decree on Ecumenism: General Principles 71

strive. Some deny that the Catholic Church possesses the fullness of unity but the controversy pertains more to procedure than to doctrine. How can there be dialogue if one partner insists his Church is the only true Church? This is such an important question that I have preferred to deal with it at length in a separate section, "The One True Church," in Chapter Twelve, "Obstacles to Unity."

Article 4 of the Decree takes up the ecumenical movement. "Today, in many parts of the world, under the inspiring grace of the Holy Spirit, many efforts are being made in prayer, word and action to attain that fullness of unity which Jesus Christ desires. The sacred Council exhorts, therefore, all the Catholic faithful to recognize the signs of the times and to take an active and intelligent part in the work of ecumenism."

The text goes on to sum up the main features of ecumenical work. First, a mutual endeavor to avoid expressions and actions which do not fairly and accurately describe the religious positions of the separated brethren, thus making relations with them more difficult. Second, dialogue between experts from various Churches to present their Churches' teaching in depth and clarity. Third, cooperation in projects designed to aid the common good. Finally, the text cites common prayer and rigorous self-examination as preludes to renewal and reform.

These ecumenical activities, according to the text, promote the spirit of brotherly love and unity: "The result will be that, little by little, as the obstacles to perfect ecclesiastical communion are overcome, all Christians will be gathered, in a common celebration of the Eucharist, into the unity of the one and only Church, which Christ bestowed on His Church from the beginning."

While the text looks forward to the blessed day of Christian unity, it does not discourage individual conversions. It says that this type of reconciliation is distinct from ecumenical action but that there is no opposition between the two since both proceed from "the marvelous ways of God." Some ecumenists have asked for a moratorium on "convert work" for the duration of the ecumenical movement, since individual conversions, so they affirm, mar the smooth progress of ecumenism.

Recently there has been a drop in the number of conversions to the Catholic Church and it may be due to the fact that certain priests no longer strive for conversions but consider that type of activity obsolete. Yet the Catholic Church must hold itself ready to receive into its ranks individuals who believe in conscience that the Holy Spirit is leading them to take the step. Probably those who oppose individual conversions do so because they are critical of old-fashioned methods of convert-making or convert instruction. We must by all means abandon Counter Reformation apologetic and the polemic it employed. Emphasis on proofs from reason, the use of Scripture texts as weapons to drive home a point, the knock-down and drag-out tactics of debate—all these are methods of an age that is no more.

Article 4 of the Decree goes on to say that the primary duty of Catholics at present is not to inform other Christians but to reform the Catholic household. We must clean our own doorstep before asking others to clean theirs. For the sad fact is that the members of the Church fail to live up to the grace and truth entrusted to the Church. This dims the radiance of the Church and retards the growth of God's Kingdom. The text asks every Catholic, therefore, to aim at Christian perfection and to play his role so that the Church may daily be "more purified and renewed." As Catholics, we claim to have all the means of salvation left by Christ. We make colossal claims but the mediocrity of our behavior is a sad contrast to the claims we assert.

We hope that Catholic unity will continue to increase as the years go on but in preserving our unity we must not destroy the liberty we enjoy. Article 4 says that everyone in the Church should preserve freedom "in the various forms of spiritual life and discipline, in the variety of liturgical rites, and even in the theological elaborations of revealed truth. In all things let charity prevail. If they are true to this course of action, they will be giving even richer expression to the authentic catholicity and apostolicity of the Church."

Protestants pride themselves on their freedom which

The Decree on Ecumenism: General Principles 73

results in diversity in rite and theological expression and they tend to feel there is too much uniformity in the Catholic Church. Indeed, there are Catholics who confirm the suspicion of excessive uniformity and take pride in the present uniformity in so many features of Church life. We have all heard the Catholic who used to boast that he could hear Mass in Latin everywhere in the world. (Someone has said: "As though the Church were running a service for tourists.") The fact is, however, that the Church is universal and all peoples should feel at ease in it. In speaking of freedom in the variety of religious rites, the Decree here is urging Latin rite Catholics to cultivate a sympathetic understanding and appreciation of the Eastern rites, especially of the fact that these rites constitute a whole way of life.

Among less informed Catholics there is a tendency to regard Eastern rites as hybrid forms of Catholic worship, tolerated but not encouraged. Yet the Eastern rites are just as sacred and holy as the Latin rite. We should expect people of different regions and traditions to worship God in a fashion that fits in with their way of life. This is at least the liberty of the sons of God, free to worship not only according to conscience but also according to custom. The trend at the Council was away from Latinized forms and Roman policies and toward greater diversity. As Methodist observer Albert C. Outler said, "The *Roman* Catholic Church is beginning to be the Roman *Catholic* Church" (*Trends,* March 1965, p. 9). All this is in line with the old Catholic maxim, "as much unity as necessary, as much diversity as possible."

The Decree, after extolling diversity, goes on to say that Catholics should acknowledge and esteem truly Christian values that are found among our separated brethren. God is wonderful in his works whether He works through Catholics, Protestants, or Orthodox. In fact, Christian disunity prevents the Church from possessing those many valid expressions of Christianity that have sprung up in Christendom outside the visible orders of the Catholic Church. Many bright flowers of the Christian faith have blossomed among other Christians. God speed the day when they will be found in the Catholic Church.

As Article 4 of the Decree says, we must never forget that anything wrought by the grace of the Holy Spirit in the hearts of our separated brethren can contribute to our own edification. This is true of the renewal movement that seems to be active in Protestantism ever since the Second Vatican Council began. Catholics should not claim credit for inspiring it, nor should they attempt to instruct Protestants on the reform and renewal of Protestantism. It is more important for us to be grateful to the Holy Spirit for His work among Protestants.

J. Lester Harnish, president of the American Baptist Convention, says that Baptists should "keep those windows open that were thrown open by little Pope John, the peasant." He cites the readiness of Catholics to adopt the vernacular at Mass and even to publish in their hymnbooks Martin Luther's Reformation hymn. "Now, we can say it is about time they are reforming their church and straightening up and flying right because they have been wrong all along. But wait a minute! Can we Baptists, can we American Baptists, equal, in renewal, in updating, in shaking off some shackles of the past, what the Roman Catholics are doing?"[2]

Even more significant was the article that the great Swiss Protestant theologian Karl Barth wrote in *The Ecumenical Review*. In it he pointed out that both the Roman Catholic and the non-Roman Churches are living by the same dynamics of the evangelical Word and Spirit. The big question for both is precisely this dynamic movement and Barth affirms that the movement of the Spirit at the Council puts a question to the Protestant Churches: "We are not asked whether we could, should or would wish to become Catholic but we are asked whether, in view of the spiritual motion that is taking place there, something has been set in motion—or not set in motion—on our side." Contemplating the spiritual renewal that is in process in the Roman Catholic Church, should not Protestants pray that "something new might occur among us—a new

---

[2] J. Lester Harnish, "Keep Those Windows Open," in *Christianity Today* (January 29, 1965), p. 39.

attentiveness to the Word of God among us—a new outpouring of the Holy Spirit among us?"[3]

The moral is not that Catholics should lecture Protestants on the need of renewal. The Decree says that Catholics should be *concerned* about their separated brethren. "But their primary duty is to make a careful and honest appraisal of whatever needs to be renewed and done in the Catholic household itself..." (Article 4).

The mutual interaction should serve to make Catholics more aware that there is a co-partnership of Catholics and Protestants animated by the one Holy Spirit. Priests and ministers who have made a retreat together have experienced this awareness but it will take time for such an awareness of unity to filter down to every corner of the Church.

---

[3] Karl Barth, "Thoughts on the Second Vatican Council," in *The Ecumenical Review* (July 1963), p. 363.

VIII
The Decree's Practical Recommendations

In lecturing to groups of Catholics or Protestants on ecumenism, I find the audiences anxious for a bill of particulars. They are not content to hope for Christian unity but want to do something practical to achieve it. A speaker on ecumenism is usually greeted with this query in the question period after the lecture: "What can I do here and now to promote ecumenism?"

The Decree outlines the answer to this question by devoting Chapter II to the "practice of ecumenism." It is obvious, however, that the Council Fathers were in no position to draw up detailed formulas for effective ecumenical work everywhere in the world, for the practice of ecumenism will vary according to local needs and problems. What will be practical for an American, university-educated parish group will not necessarily answer the needs of a group in Zanzibar or Zurich. Article 5 of the Decree says that the ecumenical task extends to everyone in the Church, according to his talent, whether it be exercised in daily Christian living or in theological or historical studies.

The suggestions offered in the Decree are therefore rather general and tentative. We are only at the beginning of the ecumenical movement and we have much to learn by way of experimentation, and trial and error. The United States Bishops' Commission for Ecumenical Affairs has presented to the American bishops a set of guidelines for

The Decree's Practical Recommendations

ecumenical activity but these are intended simply as *recommendations* to the bishops in their supervision of ecumenical work, and are not intended as permissions for parishioners. Appendix Two of this book is the text of these "Interim Guidelines for Prayer in Common and *Communicatio in Sacris.*" (The Secretariat for Promoting Christian Unity has also published a set of guidelines but they too are intended for bishops. (See Appendix Three.) Of necessity they are quite general as the Secretariat would not want to impose a rigid uniformity upon the Church but would prefer bishops to adapt their methods to local conditions.)

Ecumenism is basically an attempt to renew the Church in order to make it more perfectly what Christ intended it should be. The first requisite, then, is to admit that the Church needs reform. This is frankly admitted in Article 6 of the Decree: "Christ summons the Church, as she goes her pilgrim way, to that continual reformation of which she always has need, insofar as she is an institution of men here on earth." This statement helps to remind us that the Church is not a church of angels but of men and that the human element in the Church is forever falling short of the perfection at which she aims. Scripture says that Christ wearied from the journey and rested at the well of Jacob. So too, the human element in the Church grows weary in well-doing. We have the best of intentions and soaring spiritual aspirations but something within us betrays our most high-minded resolutions. "Proud man, dressed in a little brief authority ... plays such fantastic tricks before high heaven as make the angels weep," says Shakespeare in *Measure for Measure.*

The need of reform is obvious, of course, in the moral conduct of members of the Church as well as in Church discipline. Catholics have never been reluctant to admit that there is chaff along with the wheat, bad fish along with the good in the Church. Some of our great Catholic literary works, like Dante's *Inferno,* in *The Divine Comedy,* have not hesitated to condemn even certain popes. Christ's institution of the sacrament of penance was an implicit admission that sin would defile His Church.

But the Decree goes beyond the need of moral reform.

Article 6 says that there have been deficiencies in the *manner* in which Church teaching has been formulated and this is a startling departure from the Counter Reformation style. The theologian of that time tended to take it for granted that Catholic doctrine was clearly and adequately stated and he resented objections to Catholic formulas and catechism definitions quite as vehemently as he resented objections to the doctrines themselves. Article 6 says that the expression of Catholic teaching must be carefully distinguished from the deposit of faith itself and here it is following Pope John's reminder to the bishops at the Council to remember the distinction between the substance of doctrine and the manner in which it is expressed.

In short, the Catholic position is that no human words can possibly exhaust the full majesty, power, and glory of divine revelation. Like garments, words grow old and need to be adapted to the changing circumstances of time and place. For instance, we say that Christ descended into Hell. The word Hell once meant simply the abode of the dead. Today Hell means the state and place of the damned, but Christ could not have gone to the place of the damned. The Decree says that defective formulations of doctrine should be "set right at the opportune moment and in the proper way" (Article 6).

This problem of rectifying formulas of doctrine does not concern the ordinary parishioner as he will not be given the official task of altering doctrinal formulations. But he should be prepared for new developments in the sacred sciences, and not be shocked or surprised at new ways of expressing Catholic teaching. He should be ready in conversation moreover to express doctrines in understandable language. In fact, he can interpret new terms as good omens of the progress of ecumenism, signs that the Church is trying valiantly to live up to its vocation as the People of God.

In Article 6, too, the Decree cites developments such as the biblical and liturgical movements, the revival of preaching and catechetics, the renewal of the lay apostolate, religious life and marriage, spirituality, social teaching and social action. These developments are usually expressed in

The Decree's Practical Recommendations 79

new terminology and reflect new approaches to old problems.

In the Decree's scale of values in renewal, personal renewal comes first. "There can be no ecumenism worthy of the name without interior conversion." Catholics should pray to the Holy Spirit "to be genuinely self-denying, humble, gentle in the service of others and to have an attitude of brotherly generosity toward them" (Article 7). St. Paul asked his Christians at Ephesus to lead a life of humility and meekness and patience, "forbearing one another in love, eager to maintain the unity of the Spirit in the bond of peace." The Decree, citing these words of the Apostle, calls attention to the fact that St. Paul addressed his words especially to those in sacred orders so that they might continue the mission of Christ who came "not to be served but to serve."

In calling the attention of the clergy to the need for humility, meekness, and patience, the Decree does not exempt the laity from "interior conversion." The clergy can provide good example in this direction by way of encouraging the laity but all of us must shake off the old idea that the clergy is the Church. The fact is that great movements in the Church have come not from the top down but from the bottom up.

For many Christians it is a painful experience to become meek, humble, and patient. The Spirit seems to drag the cross through the heart in order to imprint the image of Christ Who was meek and humble of heart. By nature most of us are ready to admit we have all the answers but unready to admit our faults. Cocksureness spawns sectarian quarrels but the ecumenist must be open-minded, ready to listen.

In addressing this special appeal to those in sacred orders, the Council probably had in mind the ancient distrust of the Catholic clergy as masters rather than servants of the people. Clericalism has been a reality in the Church. Pope Boniface VIII, in the thirteenth century, said that the laity have always been hostile to the clergy. May we not infer that the laity may have had their reasons? Like so many public officials in our own country at present, there have been priests who felt they should rule their subjects with a very heavy hand. My Protestant friends assure me that some of their clergy can be quite officious and bureaucratic at times but the devout Protestant, accepting "the priesthood of all believers," finds any form of clerical domination particularly un-Christian. Who will ever forget Pope John's remarks at the time of his election when he said he would not be a skilled diplomat, a statesman, a scholar, or an organizer, but simply a good shepherd? He exercised his papal authority not as a magnificent ruler like the Roman *pontifex maximus* or like a stately Jewish high priest of ancient times, but as "a servant of the servants of God." Hans Küng speaks of Pope John's "vast, unassuming humility." In a true sense he was an evangelical Pope.

The humility of heart needed for renewal of the Church forces us to admit that Catholics have committed sins against unity. In the past the Catholic tendency was to deny any blame for Christian disunity and to shift all the blame to the "rebel" Reformers. In the Counter Reformation when we were living under martial law, as it were, this psychology was understandable. In a nation under siege, a citizen who criticizes his government raises many an eyebrow and will probably be considered a traitor. We were at war with the Protestants for four centuries, and while we conceded that some individual Catholics had misbehaved, we claimed the whole Reformation was a sham and the Reformers enemies of God and His Church. This was especially true of the English Reformation. We saw it as the brainchild of a lecherous king's lust and a shabby pretext for plundering the British monasteries. Luther and Calvin, we felt, were tragically in error but we considered the English Reformation nothing more than a racket. With relish we quoted a British historian who cynically asserted that the English Reformers, scandalized by the Church's wealth, melted down the sacred vessels of gold and silver so that they could fit the loot into their pockets.

Today, however, if we are really serious about Christian unity, we must get the facts and develop a more sympathetic attitude toward the aims of the Reformation, more aware of Catholic faults in causing it, and more

The Decree's Practical Recommendations 81

ready to assume the good faith of the Reformers even if we cannot agree with their teachings.

Of course genuine humility can degenerate into ostentatious breast-beating and in some places today there are Catholics who make quite a show of denigrating their Catholic past as if the Catholic Church had been a snake pit before 1960. An "ecumaniac" has been defined as a Christian who thinks every Church is better than his own, and some Catholics sound that way. The trouble is that they are beating someone else's breast rather than their own.

The Decree (Article 7) sums up this need for "interior conversion" by quoting St. John's Gospel: "If we say that we have not sinned, we make Him a liar, and His word is not in us" (1 John 1:10). The Decree then applies this text to sins against unity: "Thus, in humble prayer we beg pardon of God and of our separated brethren, just as we forgive them that trespass against us." This is like an echo of the act of contrition made by Pope Paul at the second session of the Council when he asked pardon of God and of the separated brethren for Catholic offenses against unity.

Nor should we forget the opening words of the prayer *Adsumus* (We are present...) which the Council Fathers said at the beginning of each day's deliberations. The prayer starts, "We are present, Holy Spirit of God: we are present, conscious indeed of the burden of sin, but gathered together especially in Thy name." The Protestant observer Robert McAfee Brown has said that he was impressed by the prayer's recognition of human failings and its exclusion of "triumphalism."

This change of heart resulting in holiness of life should find expression in public and private prayers for unity. The Decree describes these factors as the "soul" of the ecumenical movement and states that they deserve the title "spiritual ecumenism" (Article 8). This term refers to the type of ecumenism praised by Father Paul Couturier, the French abbé who has been called "the apostle of ecumenism." He laid special emphasis on prayer as a means of achieving unity and this emphasis is needed as there are Catholics who tend to think of unity almost exclusively in terms of theological dialogue and there are Protestants who think of it in terms of bigger and better mergers. The fact is that unity will come when the Spirit desires it, and it is obvious, therefore, that prayer will be a major factor in arriving at unity.

Article 8 of the Decree says that in certain special circumstances, such as prayer services for unity and during ecumenical gatherings, it is allowable and in fact desirable that Catholics should join in prayer with their separated brethren. For some reason many American Catholics have been strangely reluctant to participate in joint prayers with Protestants even though the Holy Office in its 1949 Instruction gave permission to Catholics to join with Protestants in saying the Lord's Prayer. Some bishops still hesitate to grant permission for participation in joint prayer services if they are held in a church, whether Catholic or Protestant. Yet it would seem that the most logical place for a joint prayer service would be a church, not a hall or auditorium. Pope Paul set the precedent when he himself took part in a prayer service with Protestant and Orthodox observers at St. Paul's Outside the Walls on December 4, 1965, just a few days before the end of the Council. (The program for this joint prayer service is included at the end of this chapter.)

The Decree however makes clear that participation in common worship is a more complex problem than that of participation in joint prayer services. Common worship is the technical term for participation in the sacred liturgical rites of another Christian Church. As the Decree says: "Yet worship in common (*communicatio in sacris*) is not to be considered as a means to be used indiscriminately for the restoration of unity among Christians" (Article 8). Why does the Decree speak so cautiously about participation of Catholics and Protestants in sacred rites but so enthusiastically about participation in joint prayer?

Take the Catholic Mass as an example of a sacred rite. It is a Eucharistic rite in which Catholics express their unity by receiving the one Body of Christ. The Eucharist not only is a real cause of unity but according to Catholic teaching is also the sign and symbol of perfect unity. Many theologians contend that if a priest were to give

The Decree's Practical Recommendations

Holy Communion to a Protestant he would be bearing false witness to a unity that does not exist between Catholics and Protestants as yet. Other Catholic theologians are somewhat dubious about this. May not some Protestants be actually closer to the Church of Christ than are certain Catholics, especially lax Catholics who attend church perhaps once a year? As for perfect unity, even the Catholic Church itself does not possess it as yet. The Catholic Church will possess it only when there is full Christian unity.

Cases may arise in which the resolution of the problem can prove very difficult for a bishop. There is, for instance, a high degree of unity between Catholics and Orthodox because they share so many of the same doctrines, and the spiritual benefit to be gained from reception of the Eucharist would counterbalance the disunity factor. The Decree however, emphasizes that the final decision in each case, for Catholics, must be left to the prudent judgment of the local bishop, unless the national episcopal conference, or the Holy See, should decide otherwise (Article 8).

A special commission for the revision of canon law is hard at work in Rome but until the Pope approves its recommendations, the traditional rules regarding common worship (*communicatio in sacris*) are still in force. The trend is in the direction of relaxing them. The guidelines issued (May 26, 1967) by the Secretariat for Promoting Christian Unity allows separated Christians access to sacraments in a few special cases.

Some years ago at an ecumenical meeting, Archbishop Nikodim of the Russian Orthodox Church told me that it is the general practice in Russia today for Orthodox priests to administer sacraments to Roman Catholics, Catholic priests being absent. The Catholic Church, of course, recognizes the validity of sacraments administered by Orthodox priests. This principle would not hold good in the case of a Protestant minister unless he were ordained by a bishop enjoying apostolic succession.

However, the bishop, in considering a request for common worship, will take into account not only the possible good results of common worship but also possible dangers. The great danger is that the separated Christian might begin to think he is fully united with the Roman Catholic Church, or the sight of non-Catholics receiving sacraments might lead Catholics to think one religion is as good as another, thus promoting indifferentism. Many Protestants who long for unity feel that Catholic priests or ministers of other Protestant Churches who refuse them communion are doing something that is thoroughly un-ecumenical. I have heard other Protestant ecumenists say, however, that the very anguish of Christians in not receiving the Eucharist from separated brethren can help to foster unity while indiscriminate intercommunion would only harm the cause. The Decree states the problem succinctly when it says: "The expression of unity very generally forbids common worship" (Article 8). Of great significance is the fact that the joint Anglican-Roman Catholic Commission (meeting at Milwaukee, May 24–26, 1967) agreed that the doctrine of Eucharistic sacrifice is no longer a major obstacle to Anglican-Roman Catholic unity.

We must get to know the outlook of our separated brethren. Getting to know them requires some study but the study must be pursued with respect for the truth and with good will. It is futile to read up on Protestantism if we read with suspicion and hostility. Granted a receptive and open mind, Catholics who have some background in the matter should acquire, according to the Decree, "a more accurate understanding of the respective doctrines of our separated brethren, their history, their spiritual and liturgical life, their religious psychology and cultural background" (Article 9).

How little we Catholics know of Protestant history, especially of American Protestant history. What do we know of the Circuit Riders? Of writers such as Barth, Brunner, Bonhoeffer or of Evelyn Underhill, C. S. Lewis, Farrar? The fact is that there are many Protestant writers who can be read with profit by Catholic readers. Naturally I don't recommend such reading for ill-informed Catholics. They had better get acquainted with their own literature first; but Catholics grounded in their own faith can derive inspiring new insights from Protestant literature.

More important, however, than study, is personal contact. The Decree says: "Most valuable for this purpose are meetings of the two sides—especially for discussion of theological problems—where each can treat with the other on an equal footing, provided that those who take part in them under the guidance of the authorities are truly competent" (Article 9). From such an exchange of viewpoints, each partner in dialogue will find his own viewpoint clarified, and will be better able to present his own belief.

The importance of this personal contact cannot be overstressed. Father Yves Congar says: "... in the ecumenical dialogue the new worlds opened up to us are spiritual worlds inhabited by other Christians. We have to get to know these worlds. Books tell us of these things but we cannot appreciate the validity of what they say except in the light of personal experience. This experience has something more to contribute than books; nothing can take the place of direct contact with living reality."[1]

Dialogue is not to be restricted to scholars in the top echelons of theology and Scripture study. The constant concern of the World Council of Churches is to get ecumenism down to the grass-roots and the conviction is growing that the laity must be drawn as soon as possible into dialogue groups. The notion of restricting dialogue to the specialists is a form of clericalism, for the specialists are generally members of the clergy. Every member of the Church, according to his ability, must help the cause of unity.

The format of the dialogue meetings should be flexible. It is impossible to lay down cut-and-dried rules for the organization of groups since the local situation, the convenience of the participants, and the spirit of the group will dictate differing arrangements in different places. Some groups meet once a month. At the beginning of a series of meetings, they choose the topics for discussion during the following meetings. Usually it is advisable to

---

[1] Yves Congar, O.P., "Ecumenical Experience and Conversion: a Personal Testimony," in *The Sufficiency of God,* edited by Robert C. Mackie and Charles C. West (Philadelphia: Westminster Press, 1963), p. 73.

have someone in the group prepare a brief paper outlining the main points of the evening's discussion. Should the clergy be on hand? This depends on the clergy, their ecumenical concern, availability, and cooperation. Informal meetings need no official approval any more than you need approval for a bridge circle. The probability, however, is that the priest or minister will be of help in unraveling some of the technical problems and can certainly aid in shedding light on the technical terms of theology. *Living Room Dialogues* by William B. Greenspun, C.S.P. and William Norgren (National Council of Churches and Paulist Press) is a mine of information on such dialogues.

How we conduct ourselves in discussion is more important than the structure of the meeting. Here is the heart of dialogue—when Catholic and Protestant engage in that personal contact that Congar cites as indispensable. The Rev. Gregory Baum, O.S.A.,[2] has offered an outline of the differences between the convert-making approach and the ecumenical approach and from his suggestions I have drawn up a list of suggestions for Catholics to help them develop the proper ecumenical approach in dialogue:

1. The Catholic ecumenist readily acknowledges the Christian elements in other Christian Communities. He shows an appreciation not only of the personal virtues of Protestants, but also of the specifically Christian practices, doctrines, and sacraments in Protestant Churches. As Catholics we have always recognized the validity of Protestant baptism but have we had proper respect for certain elements of their liturgy?

2. The ecumenist listens rather than argues. He wants to understand the positive teachings of Protestantism and the motivation behind its negative teaching. Why did Luther view faith as necessary for justification (which we accept) and why did he deny that good works were necessary for salvation? It is imperative in understanding Protestant teaching to go behind the wording of Protestant doctrine to find out precisely what the doctrine really

---

[2] Gregory Baum, O.S.A., *The Catholic Quest for Christian Unity,* (Glen Rock, New Jersey: Deus Books, Paulist Press, 1965), Chapter 5.

The Decree's Practical Recommendations 87

means. Otherwise we will not have an appreciation of the deep intentions of the Reformers.

Words can be deceptive. One word, such as "ecumenical," can have two different meanings and two words, such as "faith" and "belief," can have the same meaning. Father Baum points out that often the errors of the Reformation were "exaggerated expressions of legitimate concerns." We should try to discover what the Reformers were trying to do by means of a certain doctrine. When Luther preached justification by faith alone, was he not reacting by way of protest against the Catholic preachers of the time who gave the impression that sinners could be saved by good works alone, even by money contributions? In rejecting the liturgy, for instance, were not the Reformers reacting against too much formalism in medieval Catholic worship?

3. The ecumenist avoids needlessly offensive language. We need not become Mr. Milquetoasts but we can avoid imputing unworthy motives to the Reformer.

4. The ecumenist takes Protestant objections seriously. Only the closed mind refuses to listen to criticism. Instead of dismissing objections as the product of prejudice, we study them, and in the past this study has led us to the realization that we have neglected certain essential Catholic teachings which the Protestants have preserved. For instance, how lamentably we Catholics have neglected the doctrine of the indwelling Holy Spirit.

5. The Catholic ecumenist feels that a humble confession of his faults will ultimately benefit the whole Church. The Council Fathers made a humble admission of their sins at the beginning of each Council meeting as did Pope Paul in his speech at the opening of the second session. Constant attempts at self-justification are not convincing. Father Baum says that it is precisely because we are so sure of the infallible rightness of our essential teachings that we can afford to be frank about our human failings.

6. The ecumenist does not take pleasure in Protestant defeats or failures, but regrets the waning of Christian faith and influence wherever it occurs.

7. The ecumenist has no desire to compromise or

gloss over differences between Catholic teaching and the teaching of the separated brethren. Neither they nor we will ever discover what is keeping us apart if we hide from Protestants what the real Catholic teaching is. By blurring differences we only betray the ecumenical movement, based as it is on a frank and honest airing of differences.

8. We should not expect some tangible form of quick results. As a matter of fact, dialogue often removes the fog enveloping our differences and enables us to see that some of our differences are greater than we realized.

9. We should try to collaborate with, not clobber, our partner in dialogue. The debater wants to win a victory over his opponent and inflict as much harm as possible while emerging unscathed himself. But what doth it profit a man if he wins a victory and loses a friend? The old-style apologist girded for battle with his quiver full of ready-made answers to old questions and his aim was to devastate Protestant arguments with irresistible and irrefutable logic. Our Lord's words to the Apostles are apt here: "If any man wishes to be first, he shall be last of all, and servant of all." (Mark 9:34). In dialogue, the aim is not slaughter but service.

10. We should speak a language the Protestant understands. Though we don't realize it, there is a Catholic language that we acquire from sermons, reading, and Catholic education. Protestants have their language and Orthodox theirs but ours is often quite incomprehensible to other Christians. I remember explaining infallibility to an uneducated Protestant woman one day and she replied, "What is this inflammability you mention?"

What shall we discuss? The topics for discussion should be selected with considerable care. The field is so vast that the possibilities are almost unlimited but I might make two suggestions.

1. That dialogue begin not with things that divide Catholics and Protestants but with those doctrines that we share. From these topics the discussion can eventually broaden out to the differences. When we are getting to

The Decree's Practical Recommendations

know each other is not the time to discuss our differences.

2. It seems to me that the topics of discussion should be the doctrines that Catholics and Protestants believe today. Robert McAfee Brown some time ago said to a Protestant audience, "Things are going on in the Catholic Church you would never dream of." The essential doctrines have not been changed but there has been an amazing development in certain doctrines. Consider, for instance, the teaching of the Second Vatican Council on the nature of the Church in contrast to the state of Catholic doctrine on the Church four centuries ago. Consider the developments in the theology of the Presbyterian Church which has decided to update its teaching by means of a new Confession of Faith (to supplement the old Westminster Confession) plus six additional documents. In brief, it seems to me that we should discuss not the points that are of interest to the historian of theology but rather the present beliefs of separated Christians.

The Decree makes a strong recommendation for the reform of teaching in seminaries. Theology and other branches of knowledge, especially those of a historical nature, must be taught with due regard for the ecumenical point of view "so that they may correspond as exactly as possible with the facts" (Article 10). There is just a slight touch of humor here. Seminary teaching in the past did not always conform to the facts. Often seminary professors were too ready to pass along, without questioning, pious fables and impious libels on other Christians. Luther was a notable casualty in our seminary courses. It is sadly true that we priests learned our theology against the Protestants in the old days. The seminaries of tomorrow will teach Catholicism rather than condemn Protestantism.

If ecumenism is ever to succeed, it will have to be conveyed by priests to their people but there will be precious little ecumenism if the old polemic style is employed in the pulpit. The seminarian of today is the priest of tomorrow and what he learns in the seminary now will profoundly influence his future attitude toward the separated brethren. This ecumenical approach should be adopted especially in seminaries where missionaries are trained. For it is in the mission field that religious bias and a spirit of competition are most destructive. For this reason, young missionaries should be informed of the benefits and problems which affect their apostolate because of the ecumenical movement.

It is possible to state Catholic belief correctly and yet in such a manner as to antagonize unnecessarily the partner in dialogue. The Decree says that the manner of expressing our belief should never become an obstacle to dialogue (Article 11). It insists that doctrine must be presented clearly and that we must guard against the ever-present temptation to lapse into false irenicism, that is, the danger of concealing or withholding truth for the sake of making a favorable impression on our partner in dialogue. Article 11 goes on to point out that nothing is so foreign to the ecumenical spirit as false irenicism because it harms the purity of Christian doctrine and obscures its real meaning.

There are Catholic ecumenists who seem to think that we should promote unity by taking the sting out of Catholic doctrine and demoting certain major doctrines to a position of secondary importance in the hierarchy of values. When the Protestant bewails the Catholic proclamation of the doctrine of the Assumption we may be tempted to tell him that one can get along happily in the Church without holding that as an infallible doctrine. The eager beaver who tampers with truth in this fashion is doing a great disservice to ecumenism because ecumenism lays heavy stress on the need of absolute fidelity to what one believes is the Word of God. We have long ago emerged from the era when it was said that "doctrine divides, service unites." Those were the days of sentimental ecumenism when fellowship was considered a greater good than fidelity to the eternal Gospel.

Today, however, the Protestant has killed and buried the maxim "Doctrine divides, service unites." He wants to know the truth, the whole truth, and nothing but the truth about Catholic teaching. If the truth is going to be a hard one for him to accept, he wants to face up to it rather than be led down a back alley in order to escape from it.

In an address on November 21, 1965, at a general weekly audience, Pope Paul warned against the temptation

The Decree's Practical Recommendations

to hide, modify, or deny Catholic teachings which are not today accepted by separated brethren. "We say this is an easy temptation because it can seem unimportant to minimize and get rid of certain truths and certain dogmas which are the object of controversy so as to attain comfortably the so greatly desired union." Such temptations affect not only the uninformed but also the experts "who seek, often in good faith, some expedient rationale for smoothing out the way of coming together with the separated brethren. The intention is good. The method is not."

On this occasion Pope Paul commended the attempt to present the essential aspects, leaving aside the debatable and unessential or to recognize the good still found in other Christian Communities or to discuss controversial points in terms that can be understood by other Christians. "This is brotherly patience . . . this is charity at the service of truth. But to pretend to resolve doctrinal difficulties by seeking to discredit or disregard or conceal affirmations which the teaching authority of the Church declares binding and definitive is not a good service." This sort of thing, according to the Pope, creates false hopes or perhaps rouses the fear that unity is being sought at the price of truth.

The ideal is to explain our doctrines in depth but with clarity and in such a fashion that the separated brethren can understand what we are trying to say. When Pope John reminded the bishops that he wanted them to pay special attention to this question of the manner of expressing doctrine, he meant something more than mere vocabulary. He meant they should use a type of language, thought patterns, and psychological approach that contemporary Christians can understand. An abstract and metaphysical approach would be outside the mental reach of our contemporaries in these existential days when people are very much concerned about the here and now. Moreover, we have to keep in mind that Americans are frightfully down to earth in their approach to problems. Europeans, especially the French, like to speculate about a problem in abstract, general terms while the American likes to know its practical facets and its practical possibilities.

We have to keep in mind that the man we talk to in

dialogue is to an extent the product of his environment. Walter Lippmann, that highly perceptive journalist, once said that if you told him the financial and educational background of a correspondent he could predict to you the "slant" or perspective in which the correspondent would present the news. Just as we form a habit of dressing in a certain fashion, so too we dress our ideas in a certain fashion. For that reason we are wise not to present our ideas in an outlandish fashion that is quite incomprehensible to the other person. What a delight it is to hear words that seem like fresh-minted coins rather than worn-out nickels and dimes. Christ accommodated himself to his hearers by speaking to them in parables, the literary form his contemporaries loved. He even used their favorite figure of speech, the hyperbole—stressing a point by overstressing it.

We Christians must not speak in a vacuum but in the language of the man to whom we are talking. One of our difficulties, of course, is to convince ourselves that the Protestant or Orthodox has no idea of what we are saying when we use the pious language of our prayerbooks or the technical jargon of our theology books. We imagine that everybody speaks our language but it is not so. The scholastic terminology that springs so readily to our lips often sounds medieval to Protestants.

In Article 11 the Decree says that Catholic theologians should remember that there exists a "hierarchy" of Catholic truths, that is, that not all Catholic doctrines are of equal importance. This is particularly true in regard to natural law teachings. Obviously the Church holds tenaciously to the primary principles of natural law, to do good and avoid evil. But when it comes to a matter of deducing implications from the primary principles, there is less authority in these applications of the primary principles. Moral theologians are certain that one must not steal but they speak with much less conviction when they attempt to tell us how large a theft constitutes a mortal sin. Again, it may happen that popular preachers may put as heavy a stress on a papal teaching as on a dogma. Some have done this in regard to the teaching on birth control with the result that some hearers got the impression that

Catholic birth control teaching was of equal status with the dogmas of the Incarnation and Redemption. In brief, we have to remember that Catholic teaching is not a deposit of doctrines all having precisely the same identical authority.

One of the most important fields of ecumenical work is cooperation in social affairs. All men have a responsibility to work for the welfare of the local and national community but believers, and especially Christians, have a greater responsibility. By the very act of cooperation Christians bear witness to their baptismal ties and give expression to their desire to serve, in imitation of Christ Who came not to be served but to serve. The Decree asks that this social cooperation be developed to a higher degree among Christians, especially in areas where social and technical evolution is taking place (Article 12). Cooperation on the social scene will contribute to a just evaluation of the dignity of the human person. This has been dramatically expressed in the civil rights campaign in the United States. It is true that secular humanists have played a leading part in this movement, yet the movement has had a strong religious tone. The demonstrators have been led in most cases by churchmen, meetings have been held in churches, the great marches were led by religious leaders like Martin Luther King, Jr.

This cooperation means not only going about doing good in imitation of Christ, raising the standards of social life, relieving misery and illiteracy, but Christians engaged in it will also get to know each other better and, through shoulder-to-shoulder cooperation, come to understand and appreciate each other, thus breaking down the walls of misunderstanding that bar the way to unity. Because this cooperation is becoming a major form of ecumenism in America, it will be discussed in detail in the next chapter.

BIBLE SERVICE FOR CHRISTIAN UNITY

The following is the program of the common service of worship celebrated in the Basilica of Saint Paul Outside the Walls, Rome, on December 4, 1965, with the participation of Pope Paul VI and the Fathers of the Council together with the

Orthodox, Protestant, and Anglican observer-delegates and guests of the Council.

1. Entrance chant—psalm 26 with verse, *Dominus illuminatio mea et salus mea,* as refrain.

2. Introductory prayer—invitation to prayer, period of silent prayer, collect.

3. Readings.

(a) I Chron. 29:10-18, followed by the hymn "Now thank we all our God."

(b) Romans 15:1-6, followed by verses of psalm 122 with three-fold Alleluia as refrain.

(c) Matthew 5:1-12.

(d) Homily (by the Holy Father).

4. Litany—

One of the participants: My dear Brethren, let us pray to the God of our fathers, that he may be pleased to preserve the wonders of his power and his mercy in his Church.

1. For peace from on high and for the salvation of our souls, let us pray to the Lord.

Response: Kyrie eleison.

2. That his holy Church may be preserved from every evil and be made perfect in his love, let us pray to the Lord.

Response: Kyrie eleison.

3. That the pastors of every Christian communion may be faithful servants of the Gospel of Christ, let us pray to the Lord.

Response: Kyrie eleison.

4. For all who are gathered here, for those from all over the world who pray with us that we may devote ourselves to the works of peace, of love, and of justice, let us pray to the Lord.

Response: Kyrie eleison.

5. For all who bear the name of Christ, that the word of the Lord may be fulfilled and their unity may be perfect, let us pray to the Lord.

Response: Kyrie eleison.

6. For all Christians suffering trials and afflictions, for all who have need of the mercy and assistance of God, and for all who are seeking the light of Christ, let us pray to the Lord.

Response: Kyrie eleison.

Prayer: May our prayer rise to your glorious throne, O Lord, and may our request not return to us unheeded. Unite our lips and our hearts in praise and repentance, so that one day, in the fullness of the community of your Church we may advance together towards your kingdom, which has no end. Through Christ our Lord.

All: Amen.

The Decree's Practical Recommendations

5. The Lord's Prayer.

6. Final invocation ("Gratia Domini nostri Iesu Christi et caritas Dei Patris et communicatio Sancti Spiritus sit cum omnibus vobis. *All:* Amen."), followed by the Magnificat.

(The three scriptural lessons were read by Protestant and Orthodox observers. The Holy Father recited the introductory prayer, the invitation to the Lord's Prayer, and the final invocation.)

Reprinted with the kind permission of the NCWC's NEWSLETTER: Bishops' Commission on the Liturgical Apostolate (Dec. 1965; Vol. 1, No. 4).

IX
The Decree and the Orthodox

One wall of misunderstanding that must be broken down is that which prevents the Christians of the West from realizing their close spiritual relationship to the Christians of the East. They seem so very different from us and yet they share the same baptism, the same spiritual life, the same heritage of saints and martyrs. They seem different mainly because they have experienced the same faith in a different way and this variant experience has expressed itself in rites, customs, and traditions that are deceptively picturesque. These differences however should not blind us to the fact that Eastern Orthodox and Roman Catholics share substantially the same faith.

"Oh, East is East, and West is West, and never the twain shall meet," wrote Rudyard Kipling. The historical fact is that the Christians of the East and of the West did meet at least occasionally in the early years of Christianity. They met often enough to realize that their doctrines were identical because they had received them through the Apostles from Christ Himself.

To many American Catholics the Eastern Orthodox are a mystery. One of the reasons is that there seems to be little uniformity in the names applied to them. Sometimes called Eastern, they actually are dispersed throughout the world at the present time. Sometimes they are called Oriental, and to Americans Oriental usually means Asiatic. They are also often called the Greek Orthodox, yet that seems to restrict them to the Orthodox Church of Greece which is only a small part of Orthodoxy. And inevitably

The Decree and the Orthodox

some American Catholics confuse them with the Catholics of the Eastern Rite (Uniates).

The term Eastern Orthodox is properly applied to descendants of the Christians who constituted the Church of the old Byzantine Empire (330–1453). At the Council of Chalcedon (451) some of these Christians rejected the doctrine taught by the Council to the effect that Christ had one nature, not two. These Christians broke away from the others and have generally been called "non-Chalcedonian" Orthodox Churches. Today they are holding dialogues with the Eastern Orthodox and it seems that there will be a reunion of the two groups in the immediate future. In this chapter, however, I will focus attention mainly on the Eastern Orthodox who acknowledge Athenagoras, the Ecumenical Patriarch of Istanbul, as their leader. There are at least 175 million Eastern Orthodox in the world and about 4 million in the United States.

After a brief introduction (Article 13), the Decree on Ecumenism takes up "The Special Position of the Eastern Churches" (Article 14) among the various Churches that are separated from the Roman Catholic Church. Note that the Decree refers to them as *Churches*. In papal documents in the past, the Eastern Orthodox Churches have always been referred to as Churches, probably because of their hierarchical and sacramental nature. On the other hand, official Catholic documents in the past have not referred to the Protestant bodies as Churches.

In dealing with the special position of the Eastern Orthodox Churches, the text says that the Churches of East and West "went their own ways" in the early years of Christianity though they did continue to enjoy a brotherly communion of faith and sacramental life. In the East the Christian Church, therefore, formed a family of Churches among which the patriarchal Churches held first place.

This brings up the question of the relation existing between these Christian Churches of the East and the Bishop of Rome. Was the Church at Rome merely a sister Church on a basis of equality with the Churches in places like Antioch and Alexandria? Or did the Bishop of Rome have supreme authority over all other Christian Churches in the East and in the West? History does not provide us with a clear answer. The Church in the East was vexed from time to time by heretics such as the Gnostics who wanted to mix Greek culture with the Christian religion, and someone had to act as arbitrator in these quarrels. Unquestionably the Bishop of Rome served in this capacity but history does not give us many instances of such intervention by the Pope.

As early as A.D. 107, St. Ignatius of Antioch referred to Rome as "presiding in love" over the other Christian Churches and even the patriarchs of the East looked with deference to the patriarch of the West, the Bishop of Rome. As the years went by, the prestige of the Bishop of Rome increased but many Orthodox historians claim that the Roman bishops inflated what was intended as a primacy of love or honor into a primacy of authority and jurisdiction. The Orthodox theologian Alexander Schmemann says: "Thus very early we see both acknowledgement of the universal significance of Rome as the first Church to express the common consent and the common unity but also a reaction against a specifically Roman interpretation of this significance."[1]

The Orthodox position, generally, is that the supreme authority in the Church is the college of bishops, the bishops united in the Ecumenical Council. The controversy over the primacy of the Pope was the core of many East-West quarrels but some Catholic historians are inclined to take the point of view that this was a pretext to cover up purely human antagonisms of a political, cultured, or psychological nature. Today it seems that these cultural, political, and historical differences are more formidable obstacles to unity than is the question of papal primacy. For instance, the memory of the shameful behavior of the Crusaders in Constantinople has left a strong imprint on the psychology of the Orthodox. However, the Melkite Metropolitan of Beirut, Philip Nabaa, writes: "When it comes to defining the true nature and

---

[1] Alexander Schmemann, *The Historical Road of Eastern Orthodoxy* (New York: Holt, Rinehart & Winston, 1963), p. 84.

extent of the Roman primacy, many Orthodox writers deny that it is one of ordinary jurisdiction, applying directly and universally. Others, however, are more reticent on the point. Others again are in favour of admitting all the Catholic demands because they see the need for them in governing and saving the divided Christian Church."[2]

The Decree urges ecumenists not only to study the origin of the Eastern Churches and their relation to Rome before 1054 but also to develop and appreciate the heritage of faith and traditions shared by Catholics and Orthodox (Article 14). By historical accident the Christians of the West had to rely on the Church of the East for liturgy, spiritual tradition, and jurisprudence. For centuries the East was the cultural light of the world while Europe was in the darkness of the Dark Ages, overrun by barbarians.

It was in the East that the basic dogmas of the faith regarding the Trinity, the Word of God, the Blessed Virgin, were defined in ecumenical councils. The West has also borrowed from the liturgy of the East and underneath the external differences we can see in both liturgies the same essential doctrine and worship. The Decree says: "Everyone knows with what love the Eastern Christians celebrate the Sacred Liturgy, especially the eucharistic mystery, source of the Church's life and pledge of future glory" (Article 15).

In the magnificence of the Eastern liturgy we Roman Catholics find the same essential Mass we have in our own parish church. For the Orthodox priest can validly consecrate the bread and wine. In their worship the Orthodox pay high tribute to the Blessed Mother whom an Eastern synod proclaimed to be the Mother of God. Here, incidentally, is an ecumenical problem area. Some Catholic ecumenists, anxious to smooth the road to unity, discourage exuberant popular devotions to the Blessed Mother, but such caution may be sadly misdirected as the Orthodox

---

[2] Metropolitan Philip Nabaa, "Diversity in Unity," in *The Eastern Churches and Catholic Unity,* edited by Maximos IV Sayegh (New York: Herder & Herder, 1963), p. 82.

are as fervent in their devotion to Mary as the Protestants are unresponsive. The Orthodox are ardent in their prayers to the saints, giving special veneration to the Church Fathers who are saints. (I remember vividly the first time I visited the Valley of the Saints in Lebanon and how impressed I was to hear of the unflinching faith of these revered Eastern martyrs who suffered incredible privations during the Muslim persecutions.)

Because the Orthodox bishops have received their sacred powers in a direct line from the Apostles by the traditional laying on of hands, they can confer a true priesthood when they ordain. Thus, although divided juridically from Orthodox priests, Catholic priests are joined to them in a close sacramental intimacy. Intercommunion with the Orthodox, given suitable circumstances and the approval of the proper authorities, is encouraged by the Decree (Article 15). However, it seems that the Orthodox bishops are not quite so ready from their side to permit or encourage intercommunion. In the United States the Orthodox bishops forbid intercommunion between Catholics and Orthodox. Their reason is not reluctance to recognize the validity of Catholic sacraments but probably a fear that intercommunion might lead Orthodox to join the Catholic Church.

Another facet of our common heritage is monasticism. As the faith itself was brought to the West by missionaries from the East, so monasticism came to us from the East. Long centuries before the great European monasteries flourished, the monks of the East lived saintly lives in communities apart from the world.

In the West our Christian way of life is expressed in the code of canon law. It embraces all the customs, practices, and regulations that have been accepted by the Western Church after centuries of experience. The Churches of the East have also had their own discipline, sanctioned by the Fathers of the Church, by synods and even by ecumenical councils. "Far from being an obstacle to the Church's unity," says Article 16 of the Decree, "such diversity of customs and observances only adds to her comeliness, and contributes greatly to carrying out her mission..." The Council here proclaims that it has no desire to impose Roman Catholic canon law on the Eastern Churches but affirms that these Churches can govern themselves according to their own disciplines, "since these are better suited to the character of their faithful and better adapted to foster the good of souls." Moreover, the Council says that this principle is a prerequisite for the restoration of Christian unity.

Again we have an exemplification of the maxim "As much unity as necessary, as much diversity as possible." Variety is the spice of religion as of life. God never duplicates in nature: every robin is different from every other robin. So too in the spiritual life: every saint is different from every other. In religious practice, then, we should expect a dazzling variety of reflections of the beauty and majesty of God; not an assembly line but a garden. The Decree therefore in Articles 16, 17, and 18 is assuring the Eastern Churches that they need not Westernize or Latinize in order to achieve unity. Would that this principle had been observed in the past. All too often Roman Catholics have attempted to impose Latin customs on the Eastern Churches. Cardinal Maximos, the Melkite Patriarch of Antioch, reflected centuries of Eastern resentment when he declined to speak Latin at the Council and spoke in French.

What has been said about legitimate variety in religious customs and practices can be said about differences in theological expression. Sometimes the Eastern style has brought out more effectively certain aspects of doctrine, sometimes the Western style has been more successful. The Decree says that in such cases varying formulations are complementary rather than conflicting (Article 17). The Council has nothing but praise for authentic Eastern traditions in theology.

The reader may wonder how Catholics and Orthodox can possibly differ. Both accept the same original deposit of faith; both accept the first seven ecumenical councils. It is human to imagine that our way of doing things is right in every respect and yet some other way of doing things may be very different and quite as correct. No two paintings of Christ are identical. Our temperament intrudes into everything we say or express in our actions. The old proverb is that the optimist looks at a milk pitcher and says it is half full while the pessimist says it is half empty. Both may be absolutely right and yet radically different in expressing the fact. Neither can deny the legitimacy of the other's observation or the essential truth of what he says.

So the Western Christian may describe the Church as an organization while the Eastern Orthodox may describe it as a mysterious meeting place where man shares the life of the Trinity. Both are right. Nowhere is this difference in viewpoint more obvious than in the Eastern and Western concepts of moral law. The Orthodox feel that we in the West are legalists, making exact calculations of sins which, by their very nature, cannot be measured precisely. An old Yankee once said that he became a Catholic because the Catholic Church tells one not only to behave but also how to behave. An Eastern Orthodox is not a Yankee. He thinks of behavior not so much in terms of sharply defined and very specific do's and don'ts, as in positive terms of love of God.

The temperament of the Eastern Orthodox is contemplative, that of the Western Christian, active. In the East the parties receive the sacrament of matrimony from the priest. In the West the spouses confer the sacrament on each other, the priest attending only as official witness for the Church. In the liturgy of the Orthodox, Christ is remote in His majesty and the Host is hidden. In the Western Church, the Host is fully exposed to the gaze of the faithful. The important thing for us is to respect these differences and to thank God for what we share in common with the Orthodox.

There are, of course, Eastern Christians who belong to the Eastern rites of the Catholic Church, e.g., the Ukrainians, the Maronites, the Melkites. The Orthodox sometimes call them contemptuously "Uniates" but they are proud of their Eastern traditions, many of which go back to the beginnings of Christianity. They are children of the East in the best sense and yet they recognize the Pope as having a primacy of jurisdiction. Their situation, however, is not entirely a happy one. Orthodox tend to consider these groups as traitors who have united with Rome ("Uniate") and so they judge their Eastern liturgy to be a camouflage for Latinity. The existence of the Eastern rites, however, is a salutary fact for us Catholics of the Latin rite. It serves to remind us that the Latin rite is not the whole Catholic Church.

It is very important that the Eastern rite Catholics show themselves profoundly Eastern, not Latin. Some have taken on Western influences and as one Eastern rite bishop said, "All they know is scholastic philosophy, Carmelite mysticism, or Sulpician asceticism." It is part of their role in the ecumenical movement to become more deeply immersed in Eastern theology, art, literature, and philosophy. The Eastern rite Catholics should not be different from Western Catholics merely in liturgical ceremonies. In the East, rite means a way of life, and if the Eastern rite Catholics are to bring about closer relations between Catholics and Orthodox they will have to become fully Eastern. True, the Orthodox are reluctant to mix with these Catholics but it is the task of Eastern rite Catholics to break down this disaffection and prove that one can be a good Catholic without being Latin.

There is no caste in Catholicism. There can be no totalitarian uniformity that washes out national, cultural, and historical differences and characteristics. Variety enriches the Church. Pope Pius XII insisted that Christians of the East should enjoy legitimate freedom and should be assured that they will never be forced to change their own rites and ancient institutions for Latin Rites and institutions.

Article 18 of the Decree quotes a text taken from the Acts of the Apostles, "impose no burden beyond what is indispensible" (Acts 15:28). This was the criterion applied to Gentiles who asked for admission to the Church in the days of the Apostles. This, therefore, is the Catholic Church's approach to the Orthodox. They are asked to surrender nothing that is authentically Eastern. Stated positively, they are asked only to accept the true and full doctrine of Jesus Christ, and Latinism is not part of the full doctrine.

To all pastors and faithful of the Roman Catholic Church, the Council urges closer relations with their Orthodox friends in their home areas so that friendly collaboration with them may increase in a spirit of love without any bickering or rivalry (Article 18).

X
The Decree and the Protestants

Under the heading "The Separated Churches and Ecclesial Communities of the West," Article 19 of the Decree discusses the relations between the Catholic Church and the Protestant Churches. (The title obviously embraces other Churches of the West as well but for the sake of brevity I will restrict my comments to the Protestant Churches.) Some of the Bishops at the Second Vatican Council demanded that the term "Church" be applied to the Protestant communities as well as to the Orthodox bodies while other Bishops insisted that Protestant communities do not constitute a Church in the strict sense, especially because of lack of episcopacy. The Council, in Article 19 of the Decree, circumvented the difficulty by referring to "The Separated Churches and Ecclesial Communities in the West." (It is notable that Article 13 says: "Among those in which Catholic traditions and institutions in part continue to exist, the Anglican Communion occupies a special place.")

Catholics are related to the Protestant Churches through those long years of association when our common ancestors in the faith lived in ecclesiastical communion. The Decree makes no attempt to describe in detail the agreements and disagreements that broke out at the time of the Reformation but focuses attention mainly on the features of Protestantism today which deserve our respect and admiration.

Nevertheless Article 19 points out that there are "very weighty differences," not only of a historical, sociological, and cultural character but also important differences in the interpretation of revealed truth. As an aid in facilitating dialogue on the agreements and disagreements, the Council offers some brief considerations.

The Decree does not address itself to those who regard Christ as a merely human person but to those Protestants who confess Him as God and Lord and as the only mediator between God and Man. There are wide differences between Catholic and Protestant theology in regard to the doctrines of the Incarnation and Redemption as well as the nature of the Church; but the important fact is that both Catholics and Protestants look to Jesus Christ as the source and center of the life of their Churches. It is the longing of our separated brethren for union with Christ that impels them to seek Christian unity.

One of the most admirable Protestant characteristics, according to Article 21 of the Decree, is their reverence for Holy Scripture.[1] The Council says that with them this reverence is "almost a cult" that leads them to constant study of the sacred text. While calling upon the Holy Spirit as they read, they seek God speaking to them in Christ in the pages of the sacred books, especially in the mysteries of His death and resurrection. However there is a great difference between Catholic and Protestant teaching on the relation of the Scriptures to the Church. The Catholic teaching is that the Church is the final and only authentic authority in expounding the meaning of the Word of God in Scripture. This the Protestant theologians do not accept. Catholics, however, are adamant that the Church is the only infallible interpreter of Scripture.

There are two common Catholic misconceptions I might mention here; first, that Protestants hold that no Church can interpret Scripture with authority; and second, that the individual Christian is the only authority. The Reformers believed that the true Church was able to interpret Scripture but they denied that the Catholic Church was the true Church. They felt it had divorced

---
[1] The original version of the Decree said that Protestants "find" God in Scripture. They were painfully disappointed when Pope Paul asked that "seek" be substituted for "find."

The Decree and the Protestants

itself from Scripture and was teaching its own man-made doctrine. Luther went so far as to describe the papacy as the Anti-Christ. Yet the Reformers held that the true Church did exist and that it could be found wherever the Word of God was rightly preached and the sacraments rightly administered. Luther maintained that the true Church was visible but visible only to the man of faith. Who knows what is pure doctrine and pure sacraments? Only the man whose faith is enlightened on these points. As Father George Tavard points out, the Lutheran Church was visible—according to Luther's criterion—only to Lutherans and this vicious circle became obvious even to the most radical Protestants.

Many Catholics imagine that the Reformers taught the doctrine of private interpretation of the Scriptures. This is false. Probably we derived our misunderstanding from the Protestant emphasis on the Gospel as the living Word. Catholics tend to think of the Bible as a sacred tome or arsenal of texts to be interpreted with objective accuracy only by the teaching Church. We think of it as an objective reality outside of us and we hold that it is a dangerous form of subjectivism to try on our own to interpret the Gospel.

The Reformers contended, on the contrary, that the Bible is a source of living faith, God speaking to the heart of every Christian. Said John Calvin: "It is necessary that the same Spirit who spoke by the mouth of the prophets should enter our hearts and pierce them to the depths..."[2] Such statements, however, do not mean that Protestants can believe as they please. They must follow conscience and they believe that a Church can help them to educate conscience. But in forming conscience they believe they must not accept as final any human authority whether it be the Augsburg Confession, Calvin's *Institutes,* or the Westminster Confession. These may be used as aids to interpretation but are not to be regarded as the ultimate authority. The only absolute authority for the Protestant is the Word of God. How can he be sure that his interpretation is the true Word of God? He has the "terrifying

---

[2] John Calvin, *The Institutes of the Christian Religion,* 1. I, Ch. 7, no. 4.

responsibility" of trusting in the Holy Spirit Who, he believes, will help him to find the right interpretation just as He has always guided Christians who walk by faith in Him. Thus the Protestant feels that he avoids the Scylla of subjectivism by not trusting himself and the Charybdis of authoritarianism by refusing to depend entirely on any human institution. To depend on himself or on any human authority would be for him to mistrust or deny the promise of the Holy Spirit.

All this assumes, of course, that Christ, founder of the Church, has not delegated to His Church an infallible authority in interpreting the Bible. Here is the central point of difference between Catholic and Protestant teaching on the Bible: Did Christ as a matter of historical fact grant such infallibility to the Church? Both Catholics and Protestants hold that the Word of God is the only absolute authority.

Catholics, accustomed to the teaching authority of the Church in biblical interpretation, are not prepared for the diversity of views on the inspiration of the Bible to be found in Protestant circles. The Protestant fundamentalist accepts the verbal inspiration of the Bible whereas Luther handled the Bible with a high degree of selectivity. For him the Bible was true revelation only when it spoke to the heart of the Christian in his joys and sorrows: It contained the living Word only when the message of salvation through faith came alive in the heart of the believer. So Luther threw out certain books that are found in Catholic versions of the Bible, belittled the Epistle of St. James, and denied that the Bible was always infallibly correct.

In later centuries, however, Protestants tended to look to the Bible as an authoritative voice more trustworthy than the authoritative voice of the Catholic Church. So there were many Protestants who held tenaciously to the verbal inspiration of the Bible. Today the conservative evangelicals hold that the original Bible was free from error and that although errors have been made in copying, God has protected the translators from errors that endanger salvation.

The Decree and the Protestants

Many conservative evangelicals, however, object to "higher criticism" of the Bible. They refuse to accept the idea that the research methods successfully applied to other ancient writings can be used to find the meaning of the books of sacred Scripture. The conservative feels that "higher criticism" proceeds on the false assumption that the Bible is not a supernatural revelation and that miracles are impossible. He contends that religion must defend itself by rational methods but that the higher critic's rejection of the supernatural is irrational. The conservative evangelical is often labeled "anti-intellectual" and reactionary but the fact is that some excellent theology is being published by conservative Protestant theologians today.

After Scripture, the Decree takes up (Article 22) the great question of baptism. Probably the most important statement in the whole Decree is this: "By the sacrament of baptism, whenever it is properly conferred in the way the Lord determined and received with the proper dispositions of soul, man becomes truly incorporated into the crucified and glorified Christ and is reborn to a sharing of the divine life . . ." This is, of course, a restatement of the teaching of the Constitution on the Church in regard to baptism and this teaching is the very base of our ecumenical hope—baptism is the tie that binds Christians together.

It is ancient Catholic teaching that baptism is valid whenever it is properly conferred. Anyone may confer baptism in an emergency and if he does it correctly, the baptism is valid no matter what his religious belief may be. As early as A.D. 255 Pope Stephen condemned the false notion that baptism conferred by heretics was null and void and by the time of St. Thomas it was universally held that even the unbaptized can baptize validly. When a priest receives into the Church a convert from another Christian Church, he investigates the original baptism and if he finds it has been properly conferred, he cannot rebaptize even at the request of the convert. Other Christian Churches resent the rebaptism of such persons as a reflection on the validity of baptism performed according to their rites. If a priest, however, has investigated and remains dubious about the validity of the original baptism, he will baptize conditionally.

The reception of Princess Irene of Holland and of Luci Baines Johnson into the Catholic Church occasioned considerable unpleasantness and a stir of ecumenical uneasiness. Members of the Protestant clergy protested the Catholic "baptism" in each case. In the case of the conditional baptism of the President's daughter, Episcopal Bishop James A. Pike labeled the Catholic ceremony "sacrilegious," "an insult," "a direct slap at our Church." Later he seemed to have second thoughts and said that the incident had made a distinct contribution to the ecumenical movement in that it evoked statements from Catholic officials re-emphasizing the Catholic teaching. The Rev. Thomas F. Stransky, C.S.P., of the Secretariat for Promoting Christian Unity, for instance, declared that American priests customarily rebaptize converts without investigating the first baptism, a violation of clear rulings of the Holy Office. It was particularly unfortunate in the case of Luci Johnson since Episcopal teaching on baptism is so clear, definite and distinctly in line with Catholic teaching. The Unity Secretariat's guidelines forbid "indiscriminate conditional baptism" of converts.

The Decree goes on to say, in Article 22, that baptism is the beginning of the Christian life but is only a beginning, a point of departure in the ecumenical quest, a gateway to the other sacraments. It points toward the acquisition of the fullness of life in Christ and is oriented toward a complete profession of faith. If baptism is the gateway to other sacraments, cannot a baptized Catholic and baptized Protestant confer the sacrament of matrimony on each other—even if the marriage takes place in a Protestant Church? This is one of the thorny questions involved in the problems of mixed marriages now under scrutiny by Catholic scholars.

The Council leaves other Christians under no illusions that baptism is sufficient in itself for Christian unity. Rather it is oriented, as Article 22 points out, toward "a complete incorporation into the system of salvation such as Christ Himself willed it to be, and finally, toward a complete integration into eucharistic communion." The

The Decree and the Protestants

Eucharist is the seal and symbol and cause of perfect unity and the ecumenical quest will be ended only when all Christians are fully integrated into all the means of salvation left by Christ and are gathered together in one faith around the table of the Lord.

The Decree does not disparage the present forms of eucharistic worship in Protestant Churches. It says that although these Churches have not preserved the reality of the eucharistic mystery in its fullness (especially because their ministers do not have a valid sacrament of holy orders), yet their liturgy is not without significance. "When they commemorate the Lord's death and resurrection in the Holy Supper," Article 22 says, "they profess that it signifies life in communion with Christ and await His coming in glory." This approach stands in sharp contrast to that of former days when we dismissed Protestant eucharistic services as ceremonies in which parishioners received nothing but bread and grape juice.

The Decree extols the Protestants for their Christian way of life, nourished as it is by faith in Christ, the grace of baptism and the hearing of the Word of God (Article 23). This way of life is not a secular or merely humanitarian way of life. It expresses itself in private prayer, in meditation on the Scriptures, in Christian family life and in community worship. As to this worship, the article points out that it sometimes displays "notable features of a liturgy once shared in common."

Many Catholics first grasped some idea of the common liturgical heritage of separated Christians when they viewed the coronation of Queen Elizabeth II on television. Here they saw a ceremony that closely resembled the Catholic Mass. In fact, the English coronation ceremony developed historically along the lines of the consecration of a Catholic bishop. As a result of the liturgical movement in Protestant circles, the services in many of their churches are coming to approximate Roman Catholic services ever more closely.

The Decree lauds the Protestants also for their lively sense of justice and their genuine charity. "This active faith has been responsible for many organizations for the relief of spiritual and material distress, the furtherance of education of youth, the improvement of social conditions of life, and the promotion of peace throughout the world" (Article 23).

In medieval Christendom the faithful set their sights on the other world. The pious Christian considered himself a pilgrim on his way through the wilderness of this world to his heavenly home and for that reason he feared to become absorbed in this world "for we have not here a lasting city." The ideal was life in a monastery and it was felt that the monastery was almost the beginning of heaven.

Luther, on the contrary, held that every man was a priest and that he should serve God wherever he finds himself but it was Calvin who gave to the world of commerce and finance a new dignity. He claimed that every phase of social as well as private life could be utilized to give glory to God, especially in the form of homely virtues such as thrift, sobriety, integrity. The new capitalism was beginning to develop in Europe and Calvin looked upon it with a kindly eye. Contrary to the teaching of the Catholic Church which had banned usury, Calvin allowed the taking of interest. Some historians have suggested that there was a close relation between the rise of capitalism and the rise of Calvinism. Eventually, as a result of the new attitude toward commerce, Protestantism in places began to identify itself with the status quo.

Toward the end of the last century there was a reaction among Protestants against this tendency to justify the existing social order and in America the reaction was called "the Social Gospel." Protestant leaders came to lend new emphasis to the social teaching of the ancient Jewish prophets and to look askance at unrestricted commercial competition. The social action ferment crystallized in 1948 in the World Council of Churches, which took as the theme for its first meeting, "Man's Disorder and God's Design." The meeting resulted in statements that contained acid criticism of laissez-faire capitalism as well as of Communism.

Today the main thrusts of the Social Gospel are still found in Protestantism though Protestant social crusaders today are less romantic about their causes than previously,

The Decree and the Protestants 113

except those who crusade for peace. Roswell P. Barnes, the longtime executive secretary in the United States for the World Council, says that it is impossible for a Protestant consistently to hold to an extreme individualism which regards religion as a purely private affair. He points out that while Protestants maintain that acceptance or rejection of Christ is a solitary decision, acceptance of Christ means acceptance of the call to do His work in the world. Christians individually and as a Church must work for the neighbor's welfare. "No aspect of the life of society or the individual's experience is outside or beyond the rule of God and therefore not outside or beyond the concern of the Church, which is committed to seek, to interpret, and to do His will." Barnes contends that the Church has no choice but to be concerned with what men do as groups, as nations, labor unions, chambers of commerce, patriotic organizations, garden clubs, or political parties. It cannot evade involvement in public affairs.[3]

Conservative Protestants, however, are generally opposed to Church involvement in social action. One reason for this is that the "Social Gospel" was at one time tied up with liberal theology. Today it has shaken these old-fashioned liberal nuances but conservative Protestants are often reluctant to go along with Christian social action. Many opposed the United Nations, the Welfare State and some protest the Civil Rights Act.

In Article 23 the Council Decree extols Protestants for their fidelity to Christ's Word as the source of Christian virtue and observes that the ecumenical dialogue might well start from the moral application of the Gospel. In this century the Catholic Church has taken strong positions on the moral problems of contemporary society. Pius XI stated the Catholic position on marriage and the family in *Casti Connubii* (1931) and Popes Leo XIII, Pius XI, and Pius XII have issued strong pronouncements on the economic and social problems. The encyclicals *Rerum*

---

[3] Roswell P. Barnes, *Under Orders: the Churches and Public Affairs* (Garden City, New York; Doubleday & Company, 1961), p. 25.

Novarum and *Quadragesimo Anno* are well known to all students of the social question.

Pope Pius XII was outstanding in his concern for the problems of the modern world, especially the need for international order as a basis for peace. One tragically picturesque evidence of the Catholic Church's interest in social problems was the ill-fated "priest-workers" experiment in France in the 1950's. In its original form it failed, but it has led to a widespread desire on the part of priests to become closely involved in the problems of people under their pastoral care and the French hierarchy have now restored the experiment in a different form.

Pacem in Terris offers solutions similar to those offered by the World Council of Churches in the area of problems such as world peace; but the encyclical approaches a problem from a natural law viewpoint while the World Council approaches the problem from the vantage point of Scripture. Will the approaches begin to converge? Let us hope so. At least it can be said that theologians are not at ease with their respective approaches. Some Protestants feel that the moral precepts found in the Bible are too general to apply with vigor to contemporary situations. Moreover, in this new one-world society, Scripture has no persuasive force in dealings with non-Christians. Catholic authorities, on the other hand, feel that natural law must be brought up-to-date, that it can be more dynamic than is generally believed but needs a thorough overhauling. It is felt that certain Catholic moralists in the past have been too ready to make finely detailed deductions from its very broad principles.

In Article 24, looking forward to the ecumenical future, the Decree warns against frivolousness or imprudent zeal on the part of the Catholic faithful in their ecumenical work. It reminds them that they must be "loyal to the truth we have received from the Apostles and Fathers, and in harmony with the faith which the Catholic Church has always professed." This is a necessary caution but also a helpful one where conservative Protestants, such as the Southern Baptists, are concerned. One of their reasons for reluctance to participate in the ecumenical movement is the suspicion that ecumenists are all

The Decree and the Protestants 115

to ready to barter away traditional Christianity. They repeatedly affirm that they are also concerned about Christian disunity but that truth is more important than unity.

At the end of Article 24 the Decree asks that there be no prejudging of the future inspirations of the Holy Spirit. Barriers to unity may seem insuperable to us but we cannot forbid the Holy Spirit to breathe where He will. This is His work and we should not impede it from a narrow perspective. Admittedly the unity of all Christians is a humanly impossible task but we place our hopes in the prayer of Christ for his Church, in the Father's love for us and in the power of the Holy Spirit.

Now that we have seen some of the most admirable features of Protestantism, I would like to try to gather the threads into a more unified picture of Protestantism. There is a broad Protestant consensus but I would like to preface the consensus by considering certain wrong views of Protestantism we should reject. In the following conspectus I have relied largely on a comprehensive Protestant work by John Dillenberger and Claude Welch.[4]

First, Protestantism is not anti-Catholicism. At times Catholicism has stated its doctrines by relating them to opposite Protestant doctrines and Protestantism has contrasted its teaching with that of Catholicism. But it is utterly wrong to think of Protestantism as a religion which lives a sort of parasitical existence by protesting against Catholicism and which would die if Catholicism did not exist. Second, Protestantism is not the Reformation. It cannot be identified with any particular period or any particular Church, whether Lutheran, Calvinist, or nonconformist.

There are, however, certain fundamental principles common to all periods and groups in Protestant history and they can be summarized under six headings. They are not really "Protestant principles" in the sense that they are to be found in Protestantism alone; rather it is the Prot-

---

[4] John Dillenberger and Claude Welch, *Protestant Christianity Interpreted Through Its Development* (New York: Charles Scribner's Sons, 1954), Chapter 14.

estant contention that these principles are found in any Church when that Church is truly Christian. Dillenberger and Welch call it a Christian perspective which has repeatedly been lost and recovered in the Church.

1. *Prophetic criticism*. The Protestant feels that he must, out of respect for the sovereignty of God, protest every human claim to finality and absoluteness. Therefore he protests against the Catholic claim to infallibility. Likewise he protests against any claims in Protestantism to absoluteness or finality. Yet he maintains that this protest is not negative but creative, that God is forever meeting man in new situations and therefore the Gospel forever needs new interpretations. For that reason no single form of Protestantism can ever be considered final. In brief, Catholicism also subscribes to this general principle. It holds for the principle of development and believes strongly in *aggiornamento*.

2. *The sovereignty of God*. God takes absolute precedence in our lives in every way. Without Him we can do nothing. He is at the beginning of all our good thoughts and acts. He justifies and sanctifies us. He alone is Lord and free. His merciful hands cannot be tied. This too is Catholic teaching.

3. *The living Word*. Because Jesus is the living Word, He must be free to speak directly to men in their life situations. Nothing should be allowed to stand in the way of His communication of Himself to men. He is not a figure of the past but the living Lord Who encounters man in the present. In this way He alone is the head of the Church for He is the source of life in the Church. This too is basic Catholic teaching. The difference is that the Reformers claimed that that the Church was not an aid but an obstacle to the communication of the living Word whereas Catholics hold that the Church and its teaching can be the means to salvation.

4. *The response in faith*. The Word of God can come alive in the Christian only insofar as he personally believes something to be true. No one else can believe for him. He must accept the Word—no Church or institution or group or society can accept the Word for him. Luther

The Decree and the Protestants

said, "Every one must do his own believing as he will have to do his own dying." This does not mean the right of private judgment (to believe as one pleases) but rather the personal obligation to believe what the Word says. The phrase "priesthood of all believers" does not mean that every person is his own priest and can whimsically pick and choose what he wants to believe, but rather that all Christians enjoy an equal status in the eyes of God and each one must wrestle with the Gospel for himself while acting as servant of his neighbor. This stress on the need of personal response in faith has enabled the Protestant Churches to insure personal confrontation between Christ and the Christian. This is evident in the emphasis on preaching, on the use of the vernacular, and on many other devices to help the people to make personal commitment. This too is Catholic teaching, though at times in the past we have not paid proper attention to personal conscience and personal commitment.

5. *The common life.* There are no second-class citizens in Protestantism. There is no "religious vocation" or "holy orders" putting one Christian in a superior status. The minister has merely a functional role. He is only one among equals. Clergy and laity are on the same level. Any man in honest and useful work is equal to any Church official. The Council document, the Constitution on the Church, states that the Catholic clergy are servants of the People of God and that all members of the Church are equal in that they share the same faith and hope, are fed by the same sacraments, and have the same eternal destiny.

6. *The Church.* It is a historical community of faith seeking to bear witness to the Gospel. It is a congregation of believers in which the Word is truly preached and the sacraments rightly administered. It is a community of grace and yet sin remains within it, so that reform is often demanded. It finds its unity in common loyalty to Christ. The Catholic Church holds all this and yet insists that the Lord Jesus established one visible organization as His Church and that He would be with it till the end of time.

XI
American Protestantism

The American Catholic, in spite of the progress of the ecumenical movement, is still unacquainted with American Protestantism. He does not hate it as his forefathers hated Martin Luther but he does not understand it. He admires his Protestant neighbors but probably feels that they derive little sustenance from their Churches. His picture of American Protestantism is a picture of a congeries of Churches, none of which demands much of its members or has much to give them. Most Catholics, I venture to say, regard Protestant Church membership as an affiliation that is sincere and loyal but less vital and intense than a Catholic's devotion to his Church.

To attempt to describe American Protestantism in a few pages would be to attempt the impossible. The field is too vast and complex.

Some two hundred and thirty denominations in the United States are commonly regarded as Protestant and it is not unusual to find greater diversity of belief within one denomination than between it and another denomination. Mergers, moreover, are constantly in progress. Any report on the ecclesiastical or theological status of American Protestant Churches would have to be a tentative and very general description of a wide variety of Christian doctrines and practices.

Yet there is among these Churches a broad unity which derives from their acceptance of the main Protestant principles, although each denomination assigns a different priority to the principles.

Sometimes it is said that the different Protestant Churches have a fundamental variety in unity that is similar to the variety found among Roman Catholic religious orders. This is too facile a comparison. For the Catholic orders share the same theology, the same liturgy, read substantially the same religious press and literature, and differ only in theological nuances, community esprit de corps, and customs.

Perhaps it might be said, with some degree of accuracy, that the variety among Catholic orders resembles the variety that exists among different territorial groups of Protestants. For instance, the many American Protestant Churches bear a family resemblance to each other that marks them off as a group distinct from European Protestants. Among American Protestants you will find an activism, a pragmatic approach to theology, and a sense of fellowship that are distinctively American. Seldom will you find these features to the same degree in European Protestantism.

Instead of cataloguing the two hundred and thirty Protestant denominations, I would prefer to relate the history of the conflicting trends of thought that have agitated the Protestant Churches here in the United States since the beginning of the country. Two main trends, the conservative and the liberal, have crisscrossed denominational lines. At any one moment of American history one might find conservative and liberal tendencies working against each other in practically every denomination. Sometimes it was a quiet exchange of opinions, sometimes a struggle of monumental proportions.

At the beginning of the last century, almost all the old Protestant denominations (and a few native additions) were represented in the United States. There were Lutherans, Presbyterians, Congregationalists, Episcopalians, Baptists, Disciples of Christ, the Reformed Churches. Groups like the Episcopalians stressed liturgy and the sacraments but most of the Protestant Church members at that time were Bible-centered, revival-minded Christians.

After the Civil War, and increasingly so after the turn of the century, the Protestant seminaries were swept by a wave of new ideas that came from the Continent. The new teachings were called "biblical criticism" or "modernism." The thoughtful Protestant wanted to be as modern and up-to-date as possible without renouncing the Bible as the authoritative source of his religious life and thought. He sensed that fundamentalism and revivalism were out of line with modern science and research and he felt that he had to come to terms with the latest biblical research and physical science if he wished to retain his intellectual integrity.

Only a small segment of American Protestantism was affected by the new biblical studies but it was a highly influential segment. It was made up of men who had no desire to become iconoclasts by mocking traditional Christianity but little by little they discovered that "biblical criticism" was gnawing at the edges of their traditional beliefs, blurring the sharp lines dividing the natural from the supernatural and emphasizing the humanity of Christ over His divinity.

What was "modernism" as it appeared to American Protestants? It was not really a theology but simply an approach to Christian thought which aimed to make Christian teaching relevant to modern man. The modernist tried to interpret traditional Christian Scripture and tradition by applying scientific knowledge and historical criticism. While the modernist wanted to hold on to the essential content of Christian doctrine, he felt that its supernatural elements could be dispensed with so as to bring Christianity into line with modern man's natural experience.

The German Protestant theologian F. D. Schleiermacher has been called "the father of modernism." In his *Glaubenslehre* (1821) he attempted to show that Christian doctrines are reflections and expressions of a natural religious sense. Later Protestant modernists applied the theory of evolution to this concept of a religious sense and affirmed that theological creeds have no finality about them but simply represent a stage in the evolutionary development of man's religious sense.

There were a few Catholic modernists who went further than their Protestant counterparts. They claimed that Catholic dogmas are only symbolic expressions of truth and therefore can and must be interpreted in a different way by different generations. Pope Pius X condemned this type of modernism in the encyclicals *Pascendi* and *Lamentabili* in 1907. The Protestant modernists, however, were generally less radical than Catholic theologians such as Alfred Loisy. The former aimed to establish the right of Scripture scholars and theologians to use the latest methods of research and were generally reluctant to elaborate any kind of new theology or philosophy.

In the early years of this century, liberalism began to displace modernism as the subject of conversation among American Protestants. It exalted man, humanitarian ideals, and democratic society. The liberals wanted a democratic God whose religion could be tested in daily life, not by exegesis in lecture halls. The tendency of the liberals was to pay little attention to the origins of the Christian religion but to judge religion by its fruits rather than by its roots. It has been said that modern sociology was born in the Protestant seminaries, to be forced out some years later.

Liberals like the noted Harry Emerson Fosdick demanded that Christianity become less theological and more human. Others urged that it "Christianize" the world not be preaching the traditional Christian faith but by preaching the social democratic faith. They spoke of social sin and the need of the liberal democratic outlook. Individualistic piety they abominated. Most liberals seemd to reject Hell and the devil, claimed that St. Peter had distorted the figure of the Man of Galilee by divinizing Him and insisted that man can make himself better by improving his environment.

The liberal gospel had as its prophet a great social reformer named Walter Rauschenbusch (1861–1918). He was the outstanding promoter of what was called "the Social Gospel," that is, the building of the Kingdom of God on earth through enlightened democratic collectivism. One of the themes of the Social Gospel was that the Christian Church is a community designed for the collective salvation of the world. Rauschenbusch however was not a true-blue liberal. Basically a traditional Christian, he accepted the inspiration of the Bible and the doctrines of

Sin and Redemption but he was a liberal in his rejection of personal piety and in his views on the reconstruction of society.

After the First World War the Protestant conservatives declared war on both the liberals and the modernists. In almost every denomination conservative members demanded more rigid fidelity to the fundamentals of Christianity. William Jennings Bryan became their voice but the conservative cause lost steam at his death in 1925.

We might ask why liberalism, with its casual approach to the Bible, should have exerted such a strong influence on Protestantism, a faith based on the Bible. By way of explanation the Protestant theologian W. M. Horton says that there were three issues that disturbed the Protestant in the early days of the century: (1) biblical and historical criticism as it affected Christian revelation, (2) science as it affected the Christian doctrines of Creation and Providence, and (3) social problems created by the Industrial Revolution as they affected Christian ethics. "Liberalism grew and spread, at the turn of the century," says Horton, "because it had clearer answers than Orthodoxy to these three urgent issues".[1]

What the American conservatives were unable to accomplish was accomplished by the great depression of 1929. That economic catastrophe ended the liberal dream of a heaven on earth. The dream of inevitable progress and human perfection was shattered. European Protestantism— and the European economy—had been deeply affected by the First World War with all its bloodshed and devastation but the American economy flourished after the war and many American Protestant liberals felt America would spread the blessings of reconstruction to Europe and the world. But the depression of 1929 made painfully clear the fact that America could not even control its own destiny and optimism went out the window.

In the middle '30s even liberals began to desert liberal-

---

[1] Walter M. Horton, "The Development of Theological Thought," in *Twentieth Century Christianity*, edited by Stephen C. Neill (Garden City, New York: Dolphin Books, Doubleday & Company, 1963), p. 255.

ism. In 1935 the great Baptist preacher Harry Emerson Fosdick in New York's Riverside Church, the site of his liberal triumphs, renounced certain tendencies of liberalism and said that it "has watered down the thought of the divine and, may we be forgiven for this, left souls standing like the ancient Athenians, before the altar to an unknown God."[2]

Another Protestant leader who dealt a mighty blow to liberalism was Reinhold Niebuhr, of Union Theological Seminary, New York. Educated as a liberal, he began as early as 1932 to restore the Bible, the Christian faith, and human sinfulness to their place in the Protestant perspective. Neither the resources of human nature nor the logic of history would save man, according to Niebuhr. Only the religion of grace and of a transcendent God could bring help to the human spirit "in its inevitable defeat in the world of nature and history." The new school of theology was called "neo-orthodoxy." European theologians of this line of thinking flocked to America with their prophecies of coming doom and their message of human sinfulness or made their influence felt through their published books. Greatest of these was Karl Barth and perhaps the origin of "neo-orthodoxy" was the publication in 1933 of Barth's commentary on St. Paul's Epistle to the Romans.

This new conservatism was largely a return to Luther and Calvin with emphasis on Scripture—especially on the epistles of St. Paul who had been the target of the liberals. These neo-orthodox theologians, however, did not share the American conservatives' hostility to biblical criticism and scholarship and they took to their bosom all the good elements of the Social Gospel. One of the main reasons for the impact of neo-orthodoxy was the fact that so many of its proponents were scholars of the first rank.

Today this "neo-orthodoxy" seems to be losing its grip. W. M. Horton speaks of "post-Barthian liberalism."[3] He refers to a new form of liberalism that is on the rise and

---

[2] Quoted in Herbert W. Schneider, *Religion in 20th Century America,* rev. ed., (New York: Atheneum, 1964), p. 145.

[3] Horton, *op. cit.,* p. 275.

which is quite different from the old liberalism that flourished before Barth re-examined Protestant thought. Perhaps the new liberalism is not yet a school of theology but it does seem to be assuming the proportions of a genuine trend. It objects to Barth's "revolt against reason." This new liberalism, with its sincere respect for human reason, can be found among Anglican theologians like Neill and Casserly as well as in the writings of the Swiss Protestant theologian Brunner and the Germans Bultmann and Tillich. It reveres the Bible and endorses existentialism. Horton says that the new liberals have much in common with Catholic theologians such as Erich Przywara, Hans von Balthasar, Jerome Hamer, O.P., and neo-Thomists like Jacques Maritain. Who knows what will be its relation to Catholic thought after a decade of ecumenical conversations between the new liberals and Catholic ecumenists? (I have not discussed the Protestant theologians whose talk about "the death of God" as "Christian" atheism fits awkwardly into the ecumenical spectrum.)

The American conservatives, however, still constitute a large and powerful section of Protestantism. Sometimes they are called "conservative evangelicals," though many prefer the term "fundamentalists." They have a deep reverence for the Bible and generally hold for its literal interpretation though some are not hostile to the higher criticism. They hold strongly for the need of being born again though most feel that regeneration precedes baptism. That is, they believe they are baptized because they have been regenerated, not regenerated because they have been baptized. They have a deep loyalty to religious freedom and the independence of the local church, contending that the local church is the highest tribunal of Christendom.

For this reason many conservative Protestants fear centralization of Church power. They are not ashamed of denominational disunity. In fact, they feel that it has brought vitality to Protestantism. Because of their fear of centralization they tend to shy away from affiliation with the World Council of Churches and the National Council of Churches. Though there seems to be a gradual diminution of their hostility to the ecumenical movement (with a resultant timid participation in ecumenical dialogue), they look with a cool eye on ecumenism lest it reverse the Reformation and "turn the clock back to medieval Catholicism." Roman Catholic dependence on priesthood and sacrament they regard as a factor that weakens dependence on Holy Scripture.

Conservative evangelicals seem anxious to erase the last lingering traces of the old liberalism from Protestantism but they make clear that they are not attempting to stifle the free conscience of other Protestants. They acknowledge the liberal's freedom to believe and worship but they refuse to acknowledge his right to propagandize his views as an official of a Christian Church whose creed he is undermining with his "modernism." The typical conservative is not at all pro-Roman (indeed he is quite as hostile to Rome as to liberalism), and yet the Catholic finds a certain kinship in his respect for fundamental Christianity and his insistence on the divine inspiration of the Bible.

In any panorama of American Protestantism the Anglicans deserve special attention especially in view of the fact that the ecumenism decree singles them out for special consideration. Anglicanism is much closer to Catholicism than is Lutheranism or Calvinism but yet it adheres to the main thrusts of Protestantism, especially in regard to the teaching authority of the Pope.[4] After the Reformation had swept over England, the Convocation of Bishops in 1563 established a criterion of faith for men in holy orders, called the Thirty-Nine Articles. The Articles asserted that Scripture contains all that is needed for salvation, that the Church of Christ is not infallible in teaching, that general councils have erred, that bishops and priests may marry, that government of the clergy and laity is the province of the Queen, who is not subject to any foreign power, that the Bishop of Rome has no jurisdiction in England.

---

[4] Benson Y. Landis in *World Religions,* rev. ed. (New York: E. P. Dutton & Co., 1965), p. 85, has a footnote saying: "Many Anglicans request that they be not included among Protestants. But in the U.S.A., the Anglicans (the Protestant Episcopal Church) are in most reference works so classified."

American Anglicans do not accept the article which acknowledges the Queen of England as head of the Church.

The Articles deny the doctrine of Transubstantiation, describe the sacrifice of the Mass as a blasphemous fable and affirm that the only sacraments ordained by the Lord are baptism and the Lord's Supper.

Yet in spite of the anti-Roman tendencies in the Articles, Catholic values are dominant in Anglicanism and in the World Council the Anglican Church is regarded as a "Catholic" type of church. The Anglicans have a very definite concept of the Church as an organized community and firmly believe that Christ intended that certain rites be practiced in official worship.

The historic meeting of Pope Paul and Dr. Ramsey, the Archbishop of Canterbury, on March 24, 1966, when they embraced and exchanged the kiss of peace, has raised hopes of Catholic-Anglican reunion. It can be said that Anglicanism could well serve as an ecumenical bridge between Catholicism and the Churches of the Reformation.

In 1789 American Anglicans composed a constitution for a new Church which was called "The Protestant Episcopal Church." At various times attempts have been made to remove the word "Protestant" from the official title but with only partial success. While retaining a relationship with the Church of England, the Protestant Episcopal Church in America shows a great variety in belief and worship. Members do not feel bound to follow the Thirty-Nine Articles closely and harbor few of the anti-Catholic antagonisms that may still be found in England. The Anglo-Catholics among them are very similar to Roman Catholics in belief and forms of worship but many other Episcopalians are thorough-going Protestants.

Like the progressive Roman Catholic Scripture scholars, the American Anglican biblical scholars employ form criticism. While there is a certain degree of authoritarianism in the government of the Protestant Episcopal Church there is no doctrinal authority similar to that in the Roman Catholic Church. Bishop Pike has boasted that the Episcopal Church is as Catholic as the Catholic, as Protestant as the Protestant, and as liberal as the liberals.

American Protestantism

What is the present status of American Protestantism? First, it is very much alive and has disappointed the undertakers who planned to bury it in the 1930s. It is alert to social needs even though the old liberalism that first proposed the Social Gospel is moribund. It is Bible-centered and Christ-centered. Being Bible-centered, it looks for an ethical code deduced from the Bible rather than from natural law, convinced that natural law is too static. (Anglicans, however, retain a respect for natural law.) American Protestantism is mission-minded. One Protestant minister recently told me that one half of his struggling parish's budget goes to the missions.

One of the most attractive features of American Protestantism is fellowship. The minister shakes hands at the door of the church on Sunday, welcoming newcomers or comforting the troubled. (How seldom this happens at the door of the nearby Catholic church.) Fellowship is one of the main themes of the New Testament and we hope our Protestant friends never lose it. Ecumenism and neo-orthodoxy have brought a resurgence of vitality to Protestant theology at the present time and we must not overlook a new theological adroitness emerging among conservative evangelicals. It is imperative, however, that Christianity should not nourish the mind at the expense of the heart. Perhaps the dialogue of the future will study the concept of fellowship to find its fullest implications.

May we not find that Luther rejected an ordained priesthood as a factor that might militate against fellowship? Even today some Protestants view the ordained priesthood as a barrier to the equality that makes for fellowship. As mentioned before, the average Protestant minister is no higher up in a hierarchy than is the laity. "There is differentiation of functions," says Karl Barth, "but the preacher cannot stand any higher than the other elders, nor the bellringer any lower than the professor of theology."

The Second Vatican Council, however, seemed to respond to this demand for fellowship by emphasizing the "brotherhood" of priest and laity. The Constitution on the Church, Chapter IV, Article 32, says in reference to the laity: "They also have for brothers those in the sacred ministry who by teaching, by sanctifying and by ruling with the authority of Christ feed the family of God so that the new commandment of charity may be fulfilled by all. St. Augustine puts this very beautifully when he says: " 'What I am for you terrifies me; what I am with you consoles me. For you I am a bishop; but with you I am a Christian.' " The total context of this passage makes clear that in the priest the laity have for their brother Christ who came not to be served but to serve.

The constant anxiety of American Protestantism in recent years seems to be that it might fall into secularism. The Protestant believes firmly in the need for participation in the affairs of the local and national community but he tends to be somewhat too tolerant of the scale of values of his community. An unquestioning acceptance of community values, a ready conformity to community customs, can be more deadly than the seven capital sins. And if the local minister adapts too readily to the prevalent class values and prejudices he becomes not God's prophet but a false prophet crying "Peace, peace," when there is no peace.

By secularism I do not mean a laudable sense of respect for the secular realm as contrasted with the realm of the sacred. Rather, I mean a corroding force that ravages religious belief by using religion for utilitarian purposes such as peace of mind, community harmony, or national security. In Protestantism (and to a degree in Catholicism) secularism increased with startling suddenness after the Second World War. Strangely, this increase of secularism was accompanied by an increase in Church membership. The American people in the early 1950s were on the march as never before and this mobility, along with a flourishing prosperity, for some unknown reason got people to church. There they prayed for mental security, job security, peace of mind, relief from fear of the Bomb. One writer called it justification by faith in faith. Billy Graham has often been linked with this spurt of religiosity but it seems that his message had an underlying theology that was much more substantial than that of the preachers of Positive Thinking. At any rate, neo-orthodoxy or fundamentalism are good antidotes to such selfish piety.

Occasionally we hear it said that the United States is too pluralistic ever to expect the numerous American Protestant denominations to achieve Christian unity. It is alleged that diversity gives more glory to God than does uniformity and some ecumenists, while working for unity, hope that this unity will prove to be only a form of federation rather than organic union. Yet the signs of the times all point in the direction of greater and greater unity.

One of these signs is the amazing growth of the National Council of Churches, a powerful unifying force. Another indication is the large number of Church mergers achieved or in progress: notably the Blake-Pike plan for merging the United Church of Christ, the Evangelical United Brethren, the Disciples of Christ, and the Methodist, Episcopalian, and United Presbyterian Churches. The avowed aim of this proposed merger is to "establish a united church truly catholic, truly reformed, and truly ecumenical."

In certain sections of the United States, one can find Protestant ministers who are hostile to ecumenism but each passing day finds more and more Protestant clergy delivering sermons which reflect the conviction that Jesus Christ wants all His Christians to be united in one universal community.

XII
Obstacles to Unity

Once the true spirit of the ecumenical movement is understood and accepted as a personal commitment by every Christian, attention can be directed to those features of Catholic life or belief which are serious stumbling blocks to our Protestant brethren. These points represent major obstacles to unity. Yet obstacles can be overcome, and to this end there is no more important aid than accurate information on the part of all concerned. For it is here, in these areas, that misunderstanding and misinformation stifle the very purpose of ecumenical dialogue. Too often the Catholic himself is found wanting when asked pertinent questions on some of these points. Basic to the effectiveness of any dialogue between Christians of all faiths is a sure knowledge of that which divides, as well as that which unites them.

There are five factors which I judge to be major obstacles to unity: the defamation of Luther by Catholics; the Catholic Church as the one true Church; the primacy of the Pope; Papal Infallibility; and Catholic belief in Mary, the Mother of God.

This chapter's five sections are devoted to the fuller understanding of these factors.

A. THE DEFAMATION OF LUTHER

If the ecumenical movement is to prove successful, if Catholic-Protestant dialogue is to be fruitful, it is necessary for Catholics to have a true picture of Luther. It is necessary, first, because his main themes are still the central themes of modern Protestantism and, second, be-

Obstacles to Unity 131

cause Protestant admiration for Luther will baffle us unless we know what kind of man he was. Most Catholics, I dare say, have an ingrained and almost instinctive hostility to the Reformer precisely because the Reformation rent the seamless robe of Western Christian unity.

Our temptation is to admit that the Catholic Church was rampant with all manner of abuses in Luther's era but to ask the question: Why did he not stay in the Catholic Church and reform it from within rather than break away from it? Might he not have accomplished more for the Gospel by purifying the Church humbly, quietly, and undramatically rather than by precipitating the revolution that divided Western Christendom into two armed camps?

To answer these questions, we must know the true Luther in all his prophetic impulsiveness and uncompromising sincerity. To know Luther is to know something of the mysterious inner compulsion that drove him on. To know Luther is to know what elements of his personality caused Catholics to misunderstand him and why he, in turn, misunderstood certain Catholic teachings. To learn the truth about Luther is to learn why he was psychologically driven to a parting of the ways which he lamented. Much as he loved unity, so much the more did he love what he firmly believed to be the truth.

The French Dominican, Yves Congar, has said that Luther has a bad reputation among Roman Catholics, except perhaps in Germany, and that this reputation does not do justice to Luther's basic intentions or to his religious thought. "In fact, I know that nothing really worthwhile with regard to Protestantism will be achieved so long as we take no steps truly to understand Luther, instead of simply condemning him, and to do him historical justice. For this conviction which is mine I would gladly give my life."[1]

Congar feels so deeply on this point because the Catholic record in calumniating Luther is so bad. The

---

[1] Yves Congar, O.P., "Ecumenical Experience and Conversion: a Personal Testimony," in *The Sufficiency of God*, edited by Robert C. Mackie and Charles C. West (Philadelphia: Westminster Press, 1963), p. 74.

earliest Catholic biographer of Luther, John Cochlaeus, published in 1549 a vicious work filled with vituperation and libel. He packed into his book a mine of explosive defamatory material that has kept popping up in Catholic writings on Luther for four centuries. (Our one consolation in the whole messy business is to know that a Catholic historian, Adolf Herte, in 1943 pinpointed Cochlaeus' writings as the fountain-source of all the old wives' tales about Luther found in Counter Reformation polemics.)

The noted Catholic historian Heinrich Denifle, a Dominican subarchivist at the Vatican, in the early 1900s presented Luther as a grossly sensuous person who devised his doctrine of justification by faith alone (without good works) to cover up a life of sexual passion. And biographer Hartmann Grisar [2] made the Reformer out to be a pathetic megalomaniac, more to be pitied than condemned.

The turn came with Joseph Lortz, a German Catholic historian of the Reformation, who in 1939 portrayed Luther as a man of God, exemplary in his obedience to the Gospel, his zeal in preaching Christ crucified, his love for the Blessed Mother and his devotion to the Eucharist. The Reformer, according to Lortz, "was a great and fervent believer, filled with the faith that moves mountains. He burned with love for the Lord Jesus and his zeal for preaching the Gospel was unquenchable."[3] Today Catholic scholarly writing on Luther does not attempt to canonize him or gloss over the disunity he precipitated (nor do modern Protestants) but tries to be absolutely fair to him.

Catholic scholars now refuse to accept the flip interpretations of Luther's writings that are found in most Counter Reformation tracts. If we are ever to have unity, we must re-examine Luther's own writings, for his main themes are still found in Protestant theology. Second, we must re-examine the charges against his personal life (though these are not nearly as important as his writings, from the standpoint of Christian unity today). Luther in

---

[2] Hartmann Grisar, *Martin Luther, His Life and Work* (Westminster, Maryland: The Newman Press, 1960).

[3] Joseph Lortz, *The Reformation; a Problem for Today* (Westminster, Maryland: The Newman Press, 1964), p. 148.

Obstacles to Unity

the flesh is no longer with us and his personal character and conduct are of importance to us only insofar as they throw some light on the meaning of his writings. As to his personal virtue, or sinfulness, we leave all that to the merciful Judge.

The key theme of his writings is, of course, the doctrine of justification by faith alone. In his early years as a monk, Luther had thought of God as a righteous God forever punishing sinners. To him, God's justice meant God's punitive justice and therefore the good news of the Gospel was bad news to him. How he acquired this wrong idea of God is a long story too complex to discuss here.

Between 1513 and 1519 Luther had an extraordinary mystical experience in the tower of the monastery of Wittenberg which revolutionized his thinking and led him to interpret Romans 1:17 as speaking not of God's punitive or vindictive justice, but of his *saving* justice, the free gift of grace through faith. Luther now realized that Christ had paid the penalty for the sins of humanity, that Christ was offering the free gift of pardon and that all he needed to do was to grasp the gift through faith. In the monastery tower, the idea of a merciful, loving God seems to have struck Luther with irresistible force while he was reading Romans 1:17 and he felt that it "opened the gates of Paradise" for him.

This discovery was the seed of the Reformation. Luther now felt that Catholic theologians for years had led him astray. (It must have been some of his Catholic contemporaries who led him astray, not the classic Catholic theologians like St. Thomas who focused a strong light on the love and mercy of God and who also interpreted Romans 1:17 comfortingly.) At any rate, he succeeded in ridding himself of his guilt feelings and he cast them on the medieval theologians, like Christ sending the evil spirits into the swine. Luther never forgave these theologians. His rancor was bitter: "What others have learned from scholastic theology is their own affair. As for me, I know and confess that I have learned nothing but ignorance of sin, righteousness, baptism, and the whole Christian life. I certainly did not learn there what the power of God is, and the work of God, the grace of God, the righteousness of God, and what faith, love, and hope are... Indeed, I lost Christ there but now I have found him again in Paul."[4]

Lortz maintains that the Reformation was to a great degree the result of a mutual misunderstanding, the Church misunderstanding what Luther was trying to do and Luther misunderstanding the theology of the Church. This is no place to enter into a controversy that needs volumes for proper treatment but suffice it to say that Luther's main concern was theological and pastoral. He was concerned not merely about what the theologians were saying in the lecture halls but also about the practical influence of theology as it seeped down into popular piety. He felt that the popular preachers of the day were doing an immense amount of harm, giving the sheep of the flock the impression they could save their souls by good works and at the same time ignoring the need of solid, vital biblical faith. "All I have done," he wrote, "is to advance, preach, and teach the Word of God; otherwise I have done nothing... I have done nothing but let the Word of God do its work."[5]

Luther wanted the Christians of his time to take religion seriously instead of paying it lip service and buying indulgences. He contended that popular preachers were not good shepherds but hirelings inducing a false righteousness by emphasizing good works. To take religion seriously the people would have to take sin seriously but how could the faithful take sin seriously when the preachers did not? Instead of promising the people cheap salvation, according to Luther, the preachers should tell the people they were to be saved not by money but by throwing themselves unreservedly on the mercy of God.

Gordon Rupp, Methodist observer at the Council and Church history scholar, says that the bad reputation of

---

[4] *Luther: Lectures on Romans,* translated and edited by Wilhelm Pauck (Philadelphia: Westminster Press, 1961), p. xxxix.

[5] E. Harris Harbison, *The Christian Scholar in the Age of the Reformation* (New York: Charles Scribner's Sons, 1956), p. 135.

Obstacles to Unity

Luther rests on an insufficient consideration of the historical facts but that unfortunately very few of Luther's voluminous writings have been available in English translation. The collection of anecdotes called *Table Talk* is available and much of the real Luther appears in these garbled reminiscences by friends and admirers; but Rupp says that the material is so diverse that quotations can easily be lifted to support very diverse viewpoints.[6]

What seems to be crystal clear from all the available evidence is that Luther was fundamentally honest. He lived vigorously and spoke forthrightly. He said what was on his mind. Yet scores of Counter Reformation polemicists claimed he was a liar. He did contradict himself at times and not rarely his impulsiveness drove him into making charges about Catholic doctrine and history that were objectively incorrect. And he did lie in the case of the second marriage of Philip of Hesse, consenting to Philip's bigamous union, then denying he had sanctioned it. However, to label Luther a chronic liar because of one lie would be like calling St. Peter a constitutional liar because of his lie to the portress.

Like Peter, Luther was a man of impulse. Rupp says that the Reformer was given to tantrums in his last years "but some of his best as well as worst writing was done in the heat of righteous anger. When his blood was up, he would charge into battle, and when he did, his pen was not so much a sword as the spiked club with which Holbein pictures him as the Hercules Germanicus."[7] He called a spade a spade and in his polemical writings there is much that repels and disgusts, and Catholic polemics has made the most of it. It would be quite unfair, however, to judge him exclusively on his polemical writings and utterances. He had another side to him that was more reticent, compassionate and kind.

It is hard for a Roman Catholic to understand the Reformer's vehement hatred for the papacy. He hated it with no mealy-mouthed acerbity but with a loathing and

---

[6] Gordon Rupp, *The Righteousness of God: Luther Studies* (New York: Philosophical Library, 1954). p. 6.
[7] Rupp, *op. cit.*, p. 7.

detestation that was gargantuan. "Living I was thy plague, dying I shall be thy death, O Pope," was his epitaph, the lines deriving apparently from Luther himself. In 1520 he wrote: "I have hardly any doubt left that the Pope is the very Anti-Christ himself . . ." Pope Leo X was scarcely a monster of these proportions. He was a humanist, a worldly prelate, a playboy Pope who had chosen as his motto, "Let us enjoy the papacy, for God has given it to us." But there was nothing preternatural about Pope Leo; he was simply too much the man of his own time.

To understand Luther's maledictions, we have to realize that he believed he was living in the last age of the world and he was convinced that the papacy was doomed to a terrible fate it richly deserved for perverting its spiritual power into tyranny. He was not afraid of its tyranny. He felt that its glory was hollow and its threats only bluffs. He regarded it nevertheless as something more than a garden variety of tyranny. It was a blasphemy, a tool of the devil, a filthy thing which he did not hesitate to describe in coarse language.

Rupp admits that the reputation of Luther presents some genuine problems for Catholics. "For Luther was a religious who apostatized, renouncing the most sacred vows and he married a runaway nun. He initiated the most disastrous series of events in the history of the Western Church and he attacked the most revered authorities, the most hallowed rites with outrageous and insulting vehemence."[8]

Rupp is right, especially insofar as his statement applies to the Catholic who is not a professional theologian. The ordinary Catholic is ready in these golden ecumenical days to listen sympathetically to Luther's criticism of the Roman Curia. As for his doctrine of justification by faith alone, the ordinary Catholic could hardly care less: he is more mystified than perturbed by a term that may be valid currency in theological circles but obsolete in popular usage. The Catholic regrets that Luther did not remain in the Church to reform it from within rather than divide Western Christendom into two warring factions.

---
[8] Rupp, *op. cit.*, p. 19.

Obstacles to Unity

The one feature of Luther's life, however, that the ordinary Catholic condemns unequivocally and utterly is his marriage to the ex-nun, and he is disconcerted to find Protestants taking it so casually. The old canard about Luther leaving the Church precisely in order to marry is no longer accepted by Catholics: as late as a year before the marriage he wrote a friend that he did not intend to marry because he expected the death decree for heresy. Nor is the modern Catholic exactly squeamish about the matter of clerical celibacy as though it were a divine law. In the Catholic press we find free and open discussion of the merits of clerical celibacy. But the Catholic does regard the solemn vow of celibacy as a vow made not to the Church but to God Himself and to be dispensed from only by the Pope as Vicar of Christ. It is no light matter to violate a solemn vow. I suppose the Protestant might feel that the vow had been imposed upon Luther and therefore was involuntary. From all accounts of his seminary days, however, there is no reason to believe he was coerced into celibacy.

When the former Catholic caricature of Luther is unmasked we find a man who was a genius. To say with the Catholic historian Denifle that Luther was an ignoramus is to fly in the face of the facts. When he first came upon the scene, Luther was already a man of academic status and during his later years he poured forth an incredible number of writings of high competence. Gordon Rupp remarks that Emperor Charles V was reluctant to believe at the Diet of Worms that the pile of Luther's works before him could have been produced by one man in a few months. Yet Luther produced almost one treatise every two weeks for the next twenty-five years.

Even more surprising is the sustained quality of the writings. Luther was a highly original thinker, not in the sense of creative imagination, but in Chesterton's sense of seeing old things from new angles. One of his difficulties, as Lortz points out, was that he was a man of many talents and found difficulty keeping all the talents in equilibrium. For instance, his tendency was to concentrate his profound intelligence so intently upon one phase of a doctrine that he at times formed an unbalanced picture of the total doctrine.

Luther had his faults: intemperateness in expression, a joy in polemics, a tendency to hyperbole, a temptation to subjectivism. But first and last he was a truly religious man who hated any form of religious hypocrisy and sought for God with painful anxiety. One thinks of him in reading the verse, "More than sentinels wait for the dawn, let Israel wait for the Lord" (Psalm 129:6–7).

It is therefore a sad experience to read hostile judgments upon the Reformer written by men of absolute integrity and Christian devotion. Jacques Maritain's *Three Reformers* is an example of a book that Maritain admirers might wish had never been published. The great Catholic philosopher, relying on historians Grisar and Denifle, makes Luther out to be a self-centered individualist.

During the Second World War, there were well-meaning Catholic authors who pointed the finger at Luther as the begetter of the superpatriotic Germanism that had caused two world wars. It is true that Luther was a German patriot who loved his country and had no great love for Rome but it would be absurd to blame him for the excessive nationalism that spawned the two holocausts. Rupp remarks that Scandinavian countries have been far more loyally and consistently Lutheran than Germany and yet they have shown no evidence of excessive nationalism.

Other writers have attributed to Luther every conceivable evil. Some of the charges are: he was his own priest, the maker of his own revelation, the creator of religious individualism, the archpriest of pessimism, the idolator of the state, the apostle of secularism, the foe of the common people, the destroyer of European unity. Name the abomination and you will find it ascribed to Luther. In the last four centuries he was generally the whipping boy or the idol of each age. In fact, among Lutherans themselves in the last three centuries, the portraits of Luther in art and literature have revealed a surprising diversity. Many of his biographers seemed to take the manner or ideals that were popular at the time and invest their hero with these characteristics in the maximum degree.

Luther's memory and writings make the deepest and

most lasting impression when he is speaking to hearts as a man of prayer and a man of God.

There is that unforgettable entry in the Journal of John Wesley for May 24, 1738, in which he tells how he was "converted": "I went very unwillingly to a society in Aldersgate St., where one was reading Luther's preface to the Epistle to the Romans. About a quarter before nine, while he was describing the change which God works in the heart through faith in Christ, I felt my heart strangely warmed. I felt I did trust in Christ, Christ alone for my salvation; and an assurance was given me that he had taken away my sins, even mine, and saved me from the law of sin and death."

B. THE ONE TRUE CHURCH

In ecumenical dialogue, emotional antagonisms based on distortion of history must eventually disappear as they are subjected to the strong white light of historical fact. Theological disagreements, however, have deeper roots than emotional antagonisms. Rooted in faith, they will not disappear overnight. Among the theological disagreements, one of the most important is that which revolves around the Catholic teaching on the one true Church, a perennial source of division between Catholics and Protestants. It takes on, however, a slightly new appearance as a result of the Ecumenism Decree's treatment of the goals of ecumenism.

Certain Protestant and Orthodox ecumenists are not at all happy over the goal of ecumenism as set forth by the Second Vatican Council. That goal is to gather all Christians into visible unity in order to enable them to share in all the means of Salvation Christ gave to the Roman Catholic Church. To the separated brethren this sounds frightfully unecumenical and pompously arrogant. The Roman Catholic Church seems to be looking down its nose at other Christians and saying, "Would that you were like us!" The Council, both in the Constitution on the Church and in the Decree on Ecumenism, declared that full incorporation into Christ can come only when other

Christians accept the entire system of salvation found in the Catholic Church. The Roman Catholic Church is saying there must be one fold and one shepherd but the Protestants are saying we will have no papal primacy or infallibility.

Nor does it help much to point out that the Council documents are speaking of a renewed Church, not the Church as it was in the time of the Reformation. There is no indication that the Catholic Church is going to push renewal to the point of revoking the Acts of the Council of Trent and the dogmas of the Immaculate Conception and the Assumption as well as various objectionable decisions of the First Vatican Council. The burning question therefore is: Does the Council's insistence that the fullness of means of grace can be found only in the Catholic Church, the one true Church, bar the door to any possibility of dialogue?

It has been said that Protestants should take this Catholic position with a grain of salt as there are Protestant Churches that also claim to be the holy, Catholic and apostolic Church. However, these Churches do not exclude the possibility that other Christian Churches might also possess as many of the means of grace as themselves. Some of these Churches feel that Christian unity will come in the form of a fellowship of Churches, not in absorption of smaller Churches by what they call a "superchurch." They are striving for unity but retain the conviction that God works through all Christian Churches and that every Christian can encounter Him in his own local church. They deplore any statement that casts doubt on the radiance of the divine light shining in other Churches. They are dismayed, therefore, by these Council documents making exclusive claims for the Catholic Church.

The Decree on Ecumenism, for instance, says: "For it is through Christ's Catholic Church alone, which is the all-embracing means of salvation, that the fullness of the means of salvation can be obtained" (Article 3). It might seem then that Catholic-Protestant dialogue is out of the question as Protestants not only have no intention of becoming Roman Catholics but also resent the imputation that theirs is an inferior religion.

The statements on the uniqueness of the Catholic Church, however, ought to be read along with the Council statements on the role and merits of the other Churches. The Decree says that God uses these other Churches as "means of salvation." This recognition of spiritual significance in Protestant Churches should at least make Protestants pause before they relax their ecumenical efforts. Here the Catholic Church is at least according Protestant Churches more honor than traditional Catholic theology has ever done and this advance in itself is encouraging. Again, the section of the Decree which extols the other Christian Churches for their praiseworthy Christian teachings and practices is another hopeful sign.

Unquestionably the Catholic Church in these documents does hold itself up as the criterion and goal of unity and it is understandable that Protestants should be disappointed but I do not believe that this Catholic stance should put an end to Catholic-Protestant dialogue. If the Catholic Church were to join the World Council of Churches, I see no reason why it could not play an important role in this ecumenical forum.

Edmund Schlink in *Dialogue on the Way*[1] has a section entitled "Comparison between the Ecumenism of the Roman Church and the Ecumenism of the World Council of Churches." A German Protestant theologian who was an observer at Vatican II, Schlink points out that the ecumenism of the Second Vatican Council had the same origin as the ecumenism of the World Council of Churches, an awakening to a sense of guilt over Christian disunity. Second, both the Catholic Church and the World Council agree in method, i.e. renewal through repentance, prayer, and mutual understanding. In fact, the practical directives in the second chapter of the Council Decree on Ecumenism are very similar to those followed in the World Council. Schlink notes, however, that the goals of the two world bodies are quite different. The World Council leaves wide open the question of the precise form of unity to be

---

[1] *Dialogue on the Way*, edited by George A. Lindbeck (Minneapolis, Minnesota: Augsburg Publishing House, 1965), pp. 225–230. This volume is an excellent compilation of Protestant reports on the Second Vatican Council by observers.

achieved, while the Catholic Church explicitly sets up its own unity as the goal.

Schlink questions the practicality of the Catholic criterion which assumes that the Catholic Church alone has all the means of grace left by Christ. He claims that it really amounts to a *quantitative* comparison of the means of grace in the separated Churches with the means of grace found in Catholicism. The World Council deems such a quantitative method futile since it leads nowhere. The World Council years ago tried such a method of comparing theologies but soon discovered that it came out nowhere, the result being that World Council theologians decided to take the ancient Christian Church and the Bible as criteria of the unity desired.

Schlink, however, advances the opinion that Catholic thinking on the ecumenical goal, in spite of the Council documents, is not yet clear. There are striking ambiguities in the Decree on Ecumenism that have brought joy to some Council observers but alarmed others. Some Protestants seem to think that the Roman formula for unity is just a round-about way of proclaiming that Rome intends to convert the Protestants. If so, queries Schlink, why did the Council lavish praise on so many features of the Protestant and Orthodox Churches? Why did it abandon terms like "heretic" and "schismatic"?

Schlink, therefore, feels that it would be wrong to take a negative view of the Decree's assertion that "the fullness of the means of salvation can be found" in the Catholic Church. He points out that any Church can open its doors to other Churches only insofar as her teaching permits and no one should ask more than that of the Roman Catholic Church. Even the Toronto Declaration of the World Council of Churches (1950) assured every Church the right to hold its own teaching while a member of the World Council and to continue to judge other Churches on the basis of that teaching. The important thing is not to find out how exclusive a Church is in its teaching but how intensely that Church is working for unity.

Schlink feels that there is a real ecumenical dynamism in the Roman Catholic Church: "When we look at the

Obstacles to Unity 143

Second Vatican Council in this way, we will notice a remarkable breakthrough of the ecumenical impulse in the Roman Catholic Church. This breakthrough is even more impressive if we take into account the dogmatic and canonical restrictions which this church had imposed upon herself. She is ecumenical in spite of her dogma and canon law. No matter what our final judgment may be, the Decree on Ecumenism of the Second Vatican Council is so important that no church can pass it by... Every church will have to study it carefully and will gratefully acknowledge the possibilities which this Decree opens up for the future."

Other Protestant theologians, I fear, will not take quite as sanguine a view of the Catholic position. Lukas Vischer asks questions similar to those posed by Schlink but gives different answers.[2] (Vischer acted as observer for the World Council of Churches at the Vatican Council.) He notes that the Roman Catholic Church today is in the ecumenical movement but he wonders how there really can be a dialogue between that Church and the other Christian Churches on the ecumenical basis found in the Council documents. He sees no reasonable hope for unity in the near future, urges dialogue and cooperation between the separated Churches but is not at all sure that the Roman Catholic Church will be able "to fit into a community of equal partners" and still be faithful to the Second Vatican Council position. He is heartened by the fact that the Decree on Ecumenism states that the principle of equality must be safeguarded in the confrontation with other Churches. He is not convinced, however, that statements such as this will overcome the Catholic point of view that the Roman Catholic Church must constitute the focal point of the ecumenical movement and must occupy the center of the ecumenical stage.

An American Protestant, the Rev. Harold Schomer, expressed his reservations in somewhat similar terms in a talk he delivered after the second session of the Council

---

[2] Lukas Vischer, "The World Council of Churches and Christian Unity: a Protestant View," in *The Church and Ecumenism,* Vol. 4 of *Concilium,* p. 100 et seq.

at which he was an observer for the International Congregational Council.[3] He said that Anglican, Protestant, and Orthodox observers made clear to the Secretariat for Promoting Christian Unity their disappointment with the theme of the Council documents which assumes that the Roman Catholic Church stands at the very center of God's dealing with mankind. He asserted that even a few of the bishops questioned, in their speeches, how this exclusive claim of the Catholic Church to possess the fullness of means of salvation could be reconciled with the recognition of the fact that the Holy Spirit works in other Churches. He expressed the hope that Christ Himself might be recognized as the center of our ecumenical encounter, for the ignorance and sin in our Churches, according to Schomer, makes all our Churches somewhat eccentric.

It seems to me that the Constitution on the Church and the Decree on Ecumenism while holding up the Catholic Church as possessing the fullness of grace, do make Christ the center. The text of the Constitution begins with the statement, "Christ is the light of nations" and then goes on to praise Him in many ways. "The head of this body is Christ and it is He who sustains His Church and strengthens his members at the holy table with His Body. He is the source of their salvation, their unity, and their peace and they must remember that their exalted status is to be attributed not to their merits but the grace of Christ."

If we accept Christ as the head, the life, and the unity of the Catholic Church, what difference does it make if we say that the Catholic Church represents the fullness of grace willed by Christ or to say that Christ is the criterion of unity? We were baptized not on the name of Peter or Paul but in the name of Christ. Was this not the ecumenical approach of Pope Paul at the opening of the second session when he said: "Let there be no other guiding light for this gathering but Christ the light of the world. Let the interest of our minds be turned to no other truth but the words of the Lord, our one master: let us be guided by no other desire but to be unconditionally

---

[3] Harold Schomer, "A Protestant Appraisal," in *The Catholic Reporter* (Kansas City, Missouri, January 24, 1964), p. 9.

loyal to Him. Let the only trust which sustains us come from those words of His which shore up our pitiful weakness, 'And behold I am with you forever, even to the end of the world' "?[4]

C. THE PRIMACY OF THE POPE

Pope Paul said that Christ should be the only guiding light for the Second Vatican Council. How is the primacy of Christ to be reconciled with the Roman Catholic doctrine of the primacy of the Pope?

Protestants and Orthodox find the Catholic doctrine of the papacy a major obstacle to Christian unity. To Catholics it seems paradoxical that the center of the Church's unity should be an obstacle to unity but that is the factual situation. Long centuries of emotional antagonism combined with theological objections have combined in the Protestant mind and heart to make the Catholic doctrine on the papacy a battleground. Luther himself called the Pope Anti-Christ and many a Protestant down the centuries has burned the Pope in effigy.

It is true that this Catholic teaching is less inflammable today but it would be wrong to imagine that Protestant objections to the papacy are blandly theological. They arise from a deep emotional commitment to primary Protestant principles and the sincere Protestant still considers the papacy a perverse attempt to divinize a human person. Pope Paul, in a talk to the Unity Secretariat on April 29, 1967 said: "The Pope, as we well know, is undoubtedly the gravest obstacle in the path of ecumenism!"

What are some of the main Protestant objections to the papacy? First, there are many Protestants who refuse to accept the papacy as a divine institution. Some say it emerged in the course of history as a product of the circumstances of the time, even that it served some good purposes, but that it was totally alien to the mind and

---

[4] *Council Speeches of Vatican II* (Glen Rock, New Jersey: Deus Books, Paulist Press, 1964), p. 20.

intention of Christ. These Protestants feel that Scripture texts adduced by Catholics to support the case for divine origin of the papacy fail to bear the weight that Catholics put upon them.

Certain Protestants admit that Peter, by divine appointment, was the leader of the Apostles but claim that there was among the Apostles a basic equality, hence that Peter was only in the position of an honorary leader without genuine supreme authority and jurisdiction over the other Apostles. Protestant scholars however are not unanimous in their interpretations of the Scripture texts relied on by Catholics. Oscar Cullmann, the noted Lutheran Scripture scholar, for instance, says that the famous "thou art Peter ..." text affirms the primacy of Peter but he claims that it was a trust given to Peter alone, not to his successors. Most Protestants, however, assert that nothing more than a primacy of honor was ever given to the Apostle Peter.

The Catholic response is contained in the Petrine text (Matthew 16:17–19). Christ was preparing to build His Church and He was anxious to build it solidly so that it would conserve His doctrine. The only type of solid foundation with which the Jews were familiar was a rock foundation for a house, so Christ called his chief Apostle by the Aramaic word *kepha,* which means rock. Previously the Apostle's name was Simon bar-Jona but after Jesus changed his name he was always called *kepha* which is translated into English as Peter.

In the famous Petrine text, Christ said that "the gates of hell" would not prevail against His Church, founded on a rock. That is, that the forces of Satan would never prevail against the Church. In that Church, moreover, Peter would be the bearer of the keys of the kingdom of heaven, the symbol of the control and authority of a master of the house. He would have the power of "binding and loosing," which signifies in Jewish lore the power to make and interpret laws.

Catholic theologians also see in Luke 22:31–32 a reference to the role of Peter. Here Christ indicated that all the Apostles would be tempted eventually but that Peter—after recovering his balance—should strengthen the others. "But I have prayed for thee, that thy faith may not

Obstacles to Unity

fail; and do thou, when once thou hast turned again, strengthen thy brethren." Again, on the shore of the Lake of Tiberias Christ twice addressed Peter, "Feed my lambs," and the third time, "Feed my sheep." Here the Catholic interpretation is that Christ as Good Shepherd was delegating to Peter the care of His flock, the Christian faithful.

Frederick Grant, the Anglican theologian, in his *Rome and Reunion* says that Matthew's Gospel was composed at a late date and reflects tradition that existed in Antioch in the first century or early in the second.[1] In general, Protestants do not accept the Petrine text in Matthew's Gospel as representing an authentic tradition or as referring to the continuing apostolic see. Dr. Grant himself accepts the papal primacy but as a historical development in the Church, not as a feature of the Church intended by Christ and built into the Church. He speaks of it as "a development that can be wholeheartedly regarded as divinely guided, without appeal to the New Testament or the early Fathers, or to their peculiar and fanciful exegesis" (p. 157). He sees the primacy as originating somewhere and growing steadily on the world scene but he claims that neither archaeology nor the citation of ancient texts lends support to the "legendary beginnings" of the papal primacy. Dr. Grant's position is that the early Christians did not look forward to later eras of Christianity but felt they were living in "the latter days"; therefore a permanent, continuing headship of the Church was the last thing that would occur to them.

Among the Orthodox generally the tendency is to admit the primacy of Peter but to claim that it was a primacy of honor and love, not a supreme power of jurisdiction over the other Apostles. Some say that the See of Rome enjoyed an eminence in the beginnings of Christianity but that its preeminence was based on fervor, orthodoxy, and charity and not on a divine grant of jurisdiction by Christ to Peter and his successors. The Orthodox theologian J. Meyendorff holds that the Greek Fathers

---

[1] Frederick C. Grant, *Rome and Reunion* (New York: Oxford University Press, 1965), p. 160.

supported the primacy of St. Peter but did not realize the implications of their policy. Another Orthodox scholar, Alexander Schmemann, says the Orthodox could accept the Pope as focus of unity but not as having supreme jurisdiction. The salient fact is that the Orthodox are ready to accept the Petrine text but not the Catholic interpretation of it.

When the First Vatican Council (1869–70) defined the primacy and infallibility of the Pope, there was dismay among many of the separated brethren. The impression spread abroad that the Roman Catholic Church was ruled by a monarch in lonely splendor who seemed like a reincarnation of the old pagan emperor, the imperial potentate. The Second Vatican Council was anxious to correct this image by formally proclaiming the doctrine that the bishops share in the universal government of the Church. The Council approved this doctrine of *collegiality*.

As Pope Paul said at the beginning of the second session, "You have resumed the interrupted course of the First Vatican Council. You have banished the uneasy assumption wrongly deduced from that Council..." [2] Now the old concept of the Pope as oriental potentate could give way to the concept of the apostolic college, a group of bishops caring for and supervising the flock of Christ as the small flock at Jerusalem was supervised by the college, with Peter as chief shepherd.

Under *collegiality* the Pope retains his power as chief bishop, but we do not get a true picture of his power except against the background of the power of the bishops. Said German Bishop Schwarzenberg at the First Vatican Council: "How is it possible to make a dogmatic statement about the center, the apex, the supreme and chief presiding authority without considering at the same time the other members of the apostolic body who also form part of the sacred authority?... If Peter is Pastor of both lambs and sheep, the bishops too are pastors. Peter both

---

[2] *Council Speeches of Vatican II* (Glen Rock, New Jersey, Deus Books, Paulist Press, 1964), p. 16.

Obstacles to Unity

binds and looses but both the one and the other are said too of the apostles..."[3]

Each Apostle originally founded a different local church with its own customs, history, and culture but each Apostle was to maintain his church in harmony with the other Apostles in the essentials of the faith, and in harmony with the chief of the Apostles, Peter. Thus the Church was to be one and at the same time universal with a solidarity centered in Peter as leader. So today the bishops, successors of the Apostles, work along with and under the Pope in the Synod of Bishops at Rome. His task is to make the Church relevant to the needs of each locality and yet to preserve whatever unity is necessary for the integrity of the faith.

The noted Swiss Catholic theologian Hans Küng has repeatedly made the point that the papacy's *manner* has been more of a stumbling-block to Protestants than the doctrine of papal primacy itself. Some Protestants have been so vehement in their criticism of the behavior of the popes that they have not taken the time to inquire carefully into the Christian origins of the papacy. At least in the earlier stages of the Reformation, the Reformers challenged the conduct of the popes rather than the doctrine of the papacy. The pomp and power, the magnificence and pageantry of the Vatican, the anathemas and interdicts seemed to them entirely out of line with evangelical simplicity. Today, also, much of the Protestant attitude is based on Vatican policy rather than on doctrinal objections. Some are, I believe, actually seeking a center of Christian unity that will be akin in spirit to the primacy of Peter among the fishermen Apostles of Galilee.

It is of great ecumenical importance to try to present the papacy to Protestants in the spirit of the New Testament. Peter was to have authority over his brethren but the authority described by Jesus in the New Testament was not the authority of a totalitarian dictator or Roman emperor. It was the authority of service: "You know that those who are regarded as rulers among the Gentiles lord

---

[3] Georges Dejaifve, S.J., "First Among the Bishops," in *Eastern Churches Quarterly*, XIV, No. 1, (1961), p. 10.

it over them, and their great men exercise authority over them. But it is not so among you. On the contrary, whoever wishes to become great shall be your servant; and whoever wishes to be first among you shall be the slave of all; for the Son of Man also has not come to be served but to serve, and to give his life as a ransom for many" (Mark 10:42–45).

This very text is used in Chapter III, Article 27, of the Constitution on the Church in describing the office of the bishop. The Council exhorts the bishops to keep before their eyes the example of the good shepherd, who came not to be ministered unto but to serve. What is said of all bishops applies with special appropriateness to the chief bishop. We are reminded again of Pope John who said at the time of his election that he would not be a great diplomat or administrator but simply a good shepherd.

Protestants generally assume our teaching makes the Pope an absolute monarch. Father Tavard in his *Holy Writ and Holy Church* quotes a Protestant as claiming that the Pope, like God himself, can say, "All power has been given to me in heaven and on earth." Consider the phrase in Chapter III, Article 22, of the Constitution on the Church: "In virtue of his office as Vicar of Christ and pastor of the whole Church, the Roman pontiff has full, supreme, and universal power over the Church and he is always free to exercise this power." The Protestant has no worries as long as a Pope John, a Pope Paul, or a Pius XII are in power, but he remembers all too well the bad popes of the past. What would happen if papal power got into the hands of a tyrant? Would the Church be powerless to defend itself? We cannot guarantee that evil will not enter into high places in the Church but we can at least explain that there are limitations on papal power.

Hans Küng in his *Structures of the Church* approaches the question of the Pope's absolute power from the angle of Church history. He cites the fact that popes have been deposed. In trials of the popes from the eighth century on, popes could be deposed for public lapse from the faith or for illegitimate acquisition of power through "invasion." The assumption was that a usurper of papal power was an intruder into the chair of Peter. "Invasion" was a technical term for an illegitimate pontificate. In these cases, the idea was that the intruder had never been truly Pope. The clergy and people of Rome, as well as the emperor, pronounced the verdict of deposition.[4]

According to the classical work on Catholic canon law by F. X. Wernz and P. Vidal, entitled *Ius Canonicum* (Vol. II, pp. 513-521), the Pope may lose his office or authority by (1) death, (2) resignation. If a Pope sees that he is no longer able to fulfill his office, he is morally obliged to surrender his office. He may lose office through mental illness, if the illness is certain and permanent. He may suffer the loss of his authority because of heresy. This must be notorious and publicly manifested. The verdict by a Council declares the Pope a heretic but by the very fact of heresy he retires from the papacy. The verdict simply makes public the fact that he is already condemned. A schismatic Pope is dealt with in the same way as a heretical Pope.

These points show how wrong they are who say that the Church cannot defend itself against the power of the Pope. In these cases the Pope is supposed to resign of his own free will and the Church is supposed to make him resign. The common teaching is that all the bishops of the Church must take action.

Sometimes it is said that the Pope alone, by divine law, has the right to convoke and preside over a council. The fact is that by canon law today only the Pope can convoke and preside over and close a Council but it is not asserted that he has the power by divine law. For the fact is that emperors in the early centuries did claim the right to open and close councils without the claim being disputed, and without any previous assent of the Pope.

At present we are far from any agreement among Christians on the role of the Pope in Christian life. There seems to be a trend toward recognition of the need of a central authority but at the same time a fear that this centralized authority might become too powerful. Time after time we hear Protestants express their yearnings for unity coupled with warnings against the rise of a super-

---

[4] Cited by Hans Küng in *Structures of the Church* (Camden, New Jersey: Thomas Nelson & Sons, 1964), p. 257 et seq.

church. It may well be then that the crucial question will be the manner in which the supreme authority in the Church is exercised. Will it be a ministry of power and domination or one of service?

George Lindbeck, a Lutheran observer at the Council, wrote an article entitled "The Future of Roman Catholic Theology in the Light of the First Session of the Second Vatican Council" in *Dialog* (Summer 1963). His conclusion is full of ecumenical implications: "Things are moving so fast in our world, such striking transformations have occurred, e.g. in the Roman Church in France, in a single generation, such remarkable changes are taking place among the younger men who will be the leaders of tomorrow even in places like South America, that there is a real possibility that within a few decades, within the lifetime of some of us, the old dream of an evangelical Pope may become a reality."

D. PAPAL INFALLIBILITY

Undoubtedly the Protestant image of the Pope is undergoing a change. A Calvinist creed, the Westminster Confession of 1647, said that the Pope is "that man of Anti-Christ, that man of sin, and son of perdition, that exalteth himself in the Church against Christ and all that is called God." In America, at least, this image of the Pope is being replaced by a milder concept but we have to remember that in the figure of the Anti-Christ the Reformers were usually attacking not an individual Pope but the papacy itself. Even today most Protestants, I believe, would regard the Anti-Christ as a caricature of the papacy but feel that in correcting a caricature, they are not yet ready to accept the presumptuousness that they claim to find in the doctrine of the infallibility of the Pope. It represents to them a pathetically human attempt to exalt the human.

Robert McAfee Brown, American theologian and Presbyterian observer at the Council, has described papal infallibility as a doctrine that Protestants simply cannot accept: "This is a part of Roman Catholic faith that will never

Obstacles to Unity

change. And it is no disservice to the Roman Catholic-Protestant dialogue to say forthrightly that it is a position the Protestant can never accept ... By the dogma of papal infallibility, Roman Catholicism has adopted a position incompatible with the notion that the Church is *semper reformanda,* always to be reformed. It has asserted not only that the Church need not be reformed but that it cannot be reformed, for in its highest reaches it is by definition 'irreformable.' The Protestant can only interpret this to mean that Roman Catholicism has become master of the Gospel rather than the servant." [1]

The author of these words has been outstanding for the genial irenicism of his ecumenical lectures and writings. At the second session of the Council he was official observer for the World Alliance of Reformed and Presbyterian Churches and was highly esteemed by American bishops as well as by *periti* (experts) of the Council. As a friendly critic, therefore, his comments are worthy of special attention.

To understand Protestant objections to papal infallibility, it is necessary to appreciate the Protestant viewpoint on the Word of God as the ultimate authority in religion. Catholics usually think of the Word of God as a general term applied to Bible texts and doctrines deduced from the Bible but the term means something far more than that to Protestants. The Methodist theologian Robert Nelson says: "Jesus Christ is the Word of God, and it is scarcely conceivable that in Christian theology the Word should be regarded as being in any way distinct from Him. To say that Jesus Christ in His earthly human life, in His death, and in His risen life is the Divine Word, above all other forms of it, is simply to restate the primary proposition of the Christian faith." [2]

Jesus as the Word communicates Himself to men as a person, not as a bundle of abstract ideas about divinity. When one grasps the life of Jesus from Bethlehem to

---

[1] Robert McAfee Brown, *The Spirit of Protestantism* (New York: Oxford University Press, 1961), p. 166.

[2] J. Robert Nelson, *The Realm of Redemption* (London: The Epworth Press, 1962), p. 106.

Pentecost, then he has heard the "good news." According to Nelson, the Protestant doctrine always implies the Gospel but the "good news" must be heard, felt, and experienced as a saving Presence: "God so loved the world that He gave His only begotten Son that whosoever believeth in Him should not perish but have everlasting life."

The practical question however is: "How do Christians come to know Jesus?" The Protestant view is that men come to know Jesus through preaching and the Scriptures. Through preaching God Himself speaks about Himself and if the preaching does not communicate Jesus then it is not the Word, no matter how eloquent it may be. No preaching about Jesus is the Word until the Holy Spirit actively interprets the message to the hearer.

Second, the Word may come to us through reading of the Scriptures. One gets the impression that Protestants consider the reading of Scripture as not quite the intimate form of communication that preaching is. (The early Christians believed on the oral word of the Apostles as well as on the oral word of Christ.) Nevertheless, Protestants hold all Scripture in great reverence for it bears witness to Jesus: ". . . what was from the beginning, what we have heard, what we have seen with our eyes, what we have looked upon and our hands have handled: of the Word of Life" (1 John 1:1).

How do we know what parts of the Bible are inspired? Protestants hold that it is not the Church that makes the decision. It is the Word of God that imposes itself authoritatively on the Church. W. L. Knox, a Protestant theologian, says that the canon of Scripture, to a large degree, was established on the basis of the proven ability of the sacred books to satisfy the religious experience of the believer.[3]

Protestants generally reject a "biblicism" that narrows the meaning of the Bible to the face value of the words. They feel that this is a form of idolatry of text that only serves to obscure the relevance of the Word to human experience. Both with preaching and the reading of Scripture, the visible or audible form is not of primary and

---

[3] Nelson, *op. cit.*, p. 111.

absolute importance. The Presbyterian "Confession of 1967" says that the Scriptures are given under the guidance of the Holy Spirit but are "nevertheless the words of men, conditioned by the language, thought forms and literary fashions of the places and times at which they were written."

What authority then does the Protestant recognize in his Church? There are Protestants who consider the literal words of the Gospel or of their Church creeds the primary authority. Most Protestants, however, affirm that documents such as the Presbyterian Westminster Confession or the Lutheran Augsburg Confession can be aids to belief but can never become the primary authority, which is the Word alone. Obviously they look with a cold eye on the Catholic teaching that the Church is the final authority in interpreting Scripture. They feel that papal utterances, encyclicals, dogmatic definitions, and Council declarations are pathetically human expressions of the Word. Older Protestants tended to consider papal pronouncements pompous and arrogant. Modern Protestants probably look on them in a softer light as pastoral directives containing many valid but purely human insights.

If the Word of God is the only final authority for the Protestant, how can he be sure, in reading Scripture or hearing a sermon, that he is grasping the true Word? How can he be sure that he will not misinterpret what he hears or reads? Protestants hold that the Holy Spirit helps us to discover the true Word, and that this belief, that the Holy Spirit enlightens the mind, is one of the bedrock teachings of Christianity. The Church and the members of the Church must learn Christ through the Spirit.

To a Catholic, this seems like a frightful responsibility, no matter how deep our devotion to the Spirit may be. We can rely on the Church for authoritative teaching but the Protestant has no such security. He admits that reliance on the indwelling Holy Spirit is a great responsibility but he sees the responsibility as the price of his glory and his freedom. Indeed, he feels that reliance on a human agency for authoritative teaching is a form of distrust of the Holy Spirit. This explains the Protestant hostility to any form of authoritarianism, for he feels that the Christian, as St. Paul said, is led by the Spirit and is free of bondage except to the Word.

Catholic devotion to the Holy Spirit is not as lively today as it should be. Our novenas to popular saints are well attended but our novenas to the Holy Spirit are far from popular, even though the latter is the only novena mentioned explicitly in the Code of Canon Law. Yet the Catholic does not deny the traditional teaching that the Holy Spirit enlightens the mind to see the truth. He is usually quite certain that the Spirit indwells in him to guide and help him but he is also realistic enough to know that what he considers to be an inspiration of the Holy Spirit may be a notion emerging from the depths of his subconscious. The Holy Spirit does not deceive but there are false inspirations that come out of nowhere that sometimes deceive even the elect. How many wise and holy men, Catholic and Protestant, have been the prey of subjective hallucinations and delusions!

In this matter of inspiration, Protestant teaching, which is usually more pessimistic than Catholic teaching on human nature, is here more optimistic. The Catholic teaching stresses the pitfalls and perils of human judgment; the Protestant teaching stresses personal freedom. Protestant theology presumes the Word of God can come safely through our private aberrations, and yet the Reformers constantly said that we must not put our trust in men. Calvin claimed that even ecumenical councils have erred, the Holy Spirit allowing them to suffer from human frailty so that we should not trust men. Protestants, therefore, will not accept the doctrine of papal infallibility simply because an Ecumenical Council approved it. Both Luther and Calvin said that councils can err. But Protestants object to the doctrine itself because they claim that it permits human tampering with the Word of God.

Does papal infallibility mean that a Pope can tamper with the Word of God? The doctrine as promulgated by Pope Pius IX at the First Vatican Council (1870) states: "We, with the approval of the sacred Council, teach and define that it is a divinely revealed dogma: that the Roman Pontiff, when he speaks *ex cathedra,* that is, when acting in the office of shepherd and teacher of all Christians, he defines, by virtue of his supreme apostolic authority, doctrine concerning faith or morals to be held by the universal Church, possesses through the divine assistance promised to him in the presence of St. Peter the infallibility with which the divine Redeemer willed His Church to be endowed in defining doctrine concerning faith or morals; and that such definitions of the Roman Pontiff are therefore irreformable because of their nature, but not because of the agreement of the Church." [4]

Hans Küng contends that this doctrine outlaws any possibility of human tampering with the revealed Word. It aims to preserve the word, relying on the divine promise that the Church would be prevented from introducing any human innovations.

We feel that some Protestants misunderstand the Catholic position. Karl Barth, for instance, says that Catholics do not draw a line of demarcation between the Church and the Word of God but regard them as identical. He claims that the Catholic effort has been to put tradition next to scripture and call it revelation, then demote Scripture to a level below tradition, then broaden the scope of tradition so as to almost stifle Scripture and declare that the whole complexus is divine revelation. Instead of obeying the Word, he says, the Church begins to think it possesses the Word, which it proceeds to control.

So, according to Barth, the Catholic Church first accepted the Scriptures, then the idea of tradition crept in, then finally it had the Scriptures, tradition, and the Church —and the greatest of these was the Church. Finally this aggrandizement by the Church, according to Barth, reached its apex when the First Vatican Council defined the infallibility of the Pope. Here, he claims, the Catholic notion of the Church as the prolongation of the Incarnation finally emerged in its inevitable form—the Pope as the infallible head of the Church—as infallible as the invisible head, Christ.

---

[4] Quoted in Hans Küng's *Structures of the Church* (Camden, New Jersey: Thomas Nelson & Sons, 1964), p. 352.

How can we respond to Barth's idea that the Catholic Church has been progressively identifying itself with divine revelation instead of merely guarding it? Küng points out that certain Catholic theologians do use terms which are misleading. In fact, Pope Pius XII in his encyclical on the Mystical Body noted that a false mysticism had entered into Catholic teaching on the Mystical Body, tending to eliminate the line of distinction between head and members, between Creator and creatures, thus perverting Holy Scripture. Küng says that the definition of Vatican I drew a sharp line of distinction between the Church and divine revelation. It established that the teaching office of the Church has the responsibility of communicating Christ's doctrine and preserving it in its integrity and purity. The Pope does not manufacture doctrine, he safeguards it. [5]

The Vatican I definition is very cautious. It does not say that the Pope receives inspiration or revelation. The spiritual gift received by the Pope does not help him to create new doctrines but to care for the old ones. He gets no special inner revelation but simply assistance in preserving the old revelation from intrusion of error. God protects the Pope from saying the wrong thing but does not inspire him to say the right thing. He simply keeps him from saying something wrong about a revealed doctrine.

Hans Küng feels that it would be desirable for the Catholic Church to make this distinction between Church and revelation still more obvious. The relationship of obedience to the Word must be presented as such, not as a relation of master to servant. The Church always stands under the judgment of the Word, it is pupil to Christ the master, earthly body to divine head. The teaching authority of the Church, then, is not a usurpation of the authority of the Word: it is obedience to the Word. The Church can never appropriate the authority of the Word. If it were to attempt to teach on its own authority, it would become like a tinkling cymbal.

The Second Vatican Council's Constitution on Divine Revelation explicitly acknowledges the Church's subjection

---

[5] Küng, *op. cit.,* p. 360.

Obstacles to Unity

to the Word of God. In Chapter II, Article 10, of that document we find the statement that the living teaching office of the Church is to authentically interpret the Word of God. "This teaching office is not above the Word of God but serves it, teaching only what has been handed on, listening to it devoutly, guarding it scrupulously and explaining it faithfully in accord with a divine commission and with the help of the Holy Spirit; it draws from this one deposit of faith everything which it presents for belief as divinely revealed."

Of course we must concede that although the distinction between the Church and the Word is clear in Catholic teaching, officials of the Church have at times acted in a self-glorifying manner that gave the impression of control over the Word. It would be dishonest to deny the Byzantine pomp of the papacy at times in the past, even its remnants in the present. Barth was simply reflecting the facts of history when he said, "I cannot hear the voice of the Good Shepherd from this Chair of Peter."

Protestants sometimes have a wrong notion of the extent of papal infallibility. We must remind them that it is severely limited. It is not an absolute privilege. Certain ultraconservative Catholics in the last century yearned for a wider scope of infallibility for the Pope but they were disappointed by the Vatican I declaration. One conservative editor of the last century wanted infallibility to cover all doctrinal instructions of all encylicals and papal allocutions and he even held that infallibility often amounts to inspiration. The Vatican I definition, however, states that the Pope is infallible only when he speaks as head of the Church intending to bind the whole Church in a matter of faith and morals. He is not infallible when he speaks as a private person or merely as Pope. Unless he expressly states that he intends to bind the whole Church on a matter of faith and morals, his statement is not infallible.

The Vatican I declaration says that infallible papal statements are "irreformable because of their nature but not because of the agreement of the Church." This may sound as though the Pope can speak infallibly even though his statement is entirely out of line with the traditional teaching of the Church. It does not mean that. As Küng points out, the infallible papal statement has not been divinely revealed or divinely inspired. The Pope must use reasonable means to discover the precise teaching held by the Church, especially by consulting with bishops and theologians. The phrase "irreformable because of their nature" means that the Pope's infallibility in this instance comes from the charism of infallibility and not from a fifty-one percent majority vote of the bishops. The Vatican I statement means that the Pope does not have to wait for a majority vote or even a consensus of the episcopate before he defines a doctrine. The Pope must make his decision on the basis of the teaching of the Church universal but his infallibility comes from a special privilege.

This special privilege is a reflection of the Church's own freedom from error. The Church is free from error permanently but the Pope only in extraordinary circumstances. The Pope, as a matter of fact, rarely uses the privilege. Between 1870 and 1950, for instance, no Pope spoke infallibly. However I doubt that the rarity of the use of the privilege makes much impression on Protestants. They insist that it is human to err and that anyone who claims to be infallible at any time is claiming a divine prerogative. Some will even say that the claim of human infallibility is really an expression of lack of trust in the Holy Spirit. A true believer does not demand a deus ex machina, an extraordinary intervention, but trusts in the Spirit who will somehow manage to work His purposes even though He works among frail and feeble human beings.

Küng admits that the Protestant objections admit of no easy answers. The First Vatican Council was chiefly concerned about exterminating Gallicanism and did not come to anticipate all the objections Protestants might offer against infallibility. Many questions are still unanswered. For instance, what can we learn from psychology, sociology, epistemology, etc., in arriving at a comprehensive concept of a dogmatic utterance? We can try to remove misunderstandings about papal infallibility but time is needed before theology can show how this dogma can be integrated into the structural framework of other Churches.

E. MARIOLOGY

If Protestants object to the Catholic dogma of papal infallibility on the grounds mentioned, it is to be expected that they will object to the specific doctrines that have been infallibly proclaimed by the popes. Notable among these of course are the doctrines pertaining to Mary, such as the Immaculate Conception (defined by Pope Pius IX in 1854) and the Assumption (defined by Pope Pius XII in 1950).

Among Protestants one will often find a distaste for certain Marian customs, practices, or popular beliefs, such as the devotions to Our Lady of Lourdes and Our Lady of Fatima or the legends connected with the Holy House of Loreto. Many Protestant theologians considered Pope Paul's visit to Fatima in May, 1967 a "setback to ecumenism."

Protestant rejection of Mariology, however, is far more than a rejection of what they judge to be excessive or eccentric practices and legends. They reject the official doctrines about Mary. They do not deny the Scriptural references to Mary but contend that Roman Catholic theologians and the popes have far exceeded the limited significance that should be attached to these references to her.

Thus, Protestant emotional reactions to Marian devotions, reinforcing Protestant theological objections, make Mariology a very difficult ecumenical area. "Both parties to the discussion," says the Lutheran theologian Warren Quanbeck, "must walk warily to avoid offending the other unnecessarily."

Mariology, therefore, seems like an unbridgeable chasm separating Catholics and Protestants. It is strange but all too true, that we and they are close in our beliefs regarding Jesus but far away from each other in our doctrines about His mother. The sharp, acid tone of earlier Protestant diatribes against Mary is missing today, yet we find outstanding theologians like Karl Barth, Reinhold Niebuhr and Paul Tillich inflexible in their criticism of Mariology. Many of them look upon Pope Pius XII's definition of the

Assumption, for instance, as a lamentable blunder that has done untold harm to the ecumenical movement.

Contemporary Protestant criticism of Mariology is directed, not against Mary herself, but against the Catholic Church for its permissiveness in allowing Mariology to develop to an excessive degree and in eccentric forms. For instance, many Protestants feel that the Church has permitted tradition to run away with Scripture, sanctioning Marian doctrines and devotions which are not only found in Scripture but which are in conflict with the fundamental attitude toward the eternal and infinite God that is demanded by the sacred writers of Scripture. In brief, Protestants tend to see in Mariology an usurpation of divinity. The exuberant praises of Mary, so dear to Catholics, Protestants regard as exaltation of a human person to a degree that approaches idolatry. Hence the epithet "Mariolatry" found in some Protestant writings. They view Catholic teaching on Mary as a pathetically human attempt to rob Christ of divine attributes in order to pay tribute to Mary. Fortunately, there are Catholic-Protestant dialogues in progress at present in the United States and these will help immeasurably to narrow the gap between our fundamental position in regard to the Blessed Virgin and that of our separated brethren. We do not want them to alter one iota their doctrine of "glory to God alone" but we do hope to show the affinity between this doctrine and our veneration of the mother of God.

What is the basis of the Catholic attitude toward Mary? Why these magnificent tributes in prose and song and stone? The simple answer is the Incarnation. Devotion to Mary is not meant to derogate from worship of Christ but to call attention to His mother's role in His birth and in His work of redemption. Underlying Mariology is the wonder of the Incarnation. Mary shines with a reflected glory, the radiance of her Son's redeeming death and glorious resurrection. From all eternity God planned to communicate Himself to men, to draw men into His world of life and light. They could not draw themselves into that world so God sent His Son to enter into their world, to become a man in order the more effectively to communicate God's life to man. This mysterious enterprise emerged in

Obstacles to Unity

visible form when the Child Jesus was born at Bethlehem. In communicating Himself, however, God did not want to coerce consciences. He wanted to be wanted, to come into men's hearts with their freely given welcome, not to impose Himself upon them like an oriental monarch on a nation of slaves but to offer Himself to their voluntary faith and affection.

The keystone of the whole divine plan was the *free* acceptance by a young Jewish girl of her destined role in the history of human salvation. She was the woman toward whom the entire Old Testament pointed, the virgin who was to bear a Redeemer. Her free consent was the pivotal point on which the origin of Christianity depended. God awaited her word that the Word might assume the human nature He needed for His work among men. It is for this reason that Catholics believe that no human words ever spoken in all history can compare in ultimate significance with Mary's "yes" to God's plan: "Be it done unto me according to Thy word."

To regard her role as merely a biological one would be totally out of line with the thinking of the early Christians. Mary was the mother of Jesus in the biological sense but far more importantly she was His mother by faith. She accepted her role unconditionally because her faith was free, unquestioning, absolute. Her consent to the divine plan, therefore, was a perfect act of faith in God. It can be said that the result of her act of faith was that the Word, the second person of the Trinity, became a member of our race through her and with her and in her.

I suppose that some Protestants are tempted to think of Mary as simply a good woman who fulfilled her function as mother in giving physical birth. Her motherhood, however, was not a private event. It had implications for all human history, casting its shadow backward to Abraham and forward to the second coming. Her "yes" was the key event in salvation history and we can say that she conceived our salvation. On the other hand, we have to remember not to go beyond the truth of Scripture. She was not the Redeemer. She was redeemed. She was the most perfectly redeemed of all mmbers of humanity but she was not the cause of our redemption. There was only one **Redeemer**, Jesus Christ.

It is true that there is little mention of Mary in Scripture but that does not exonerate us in disparaging her. After the nativity of her Son, she seems to retire into the shadows of her Son's greatness which is precisely what we would expect of Mary. Scripture from time to time gives us fleeting glimpses of her, at Cana, for instance, at the beginning of her Son's public career, and on Calvary at the bitter end of His life. Yet Scripture telescopes all her hidden life in a startling prophecy that no Christian can ignore: "... all generations shall call me blessed" (Luke 1:48).

The Catholic Church has not been reluctant to call her blessed. It has not restricted itself to a ritual repetition of a few Marian texts but it has meditated fruitfully and admiringly on scriptural passages pertaining to her, those passages applied to her directly as in the account of the nativity, or figuratively, as in the Canticle of Canticles. As a result of this meditation on Scripture, the Church has given her a type of veneration (hyperdulia) greater than any given to other saints precisely because Scripture reveals so clearly her role in the divine plan.

In the past, Protestants generally were hesitant to put very much trust in tradition, contending that the Catholic Church under the name of tradition had injected into Christianity elements that were foreign to it. Fortunately, as evidenced at the Faith and Order Conference at Montreal in 1963, Protestant theologians today show a greater readiness to admit tradition as a force in the development of Christian teaching. From our side, we readily admit that individual Catholics here and there have been guilty of abuses of the true Marian doctrine and devotion but we insist that our official Catholic teaching on Mary comes from Scripture, not necessarily full-blown from isolated texts, but as a logical result of the Church's meditation on all of Scripture. Deducing conclusions from primary principles, clarifying what is obscure, making explicit what is only implicitly contained in texts, the infallible Church has taught us about Mary, so we have devotion to her because we read Scripture along with the Church.

Obstacles to Unity

The Protestant has utmost respect for the Catholic conscience venerating Mary and may even admit that the Church is logical in her stand, yet he feels that it is a deceptive logic because it leads to an attitude of mind in which we exalt a human person, giving her homage that belongs to God "to whom be honor and glory forever." Is Christ not the source of all our life, the ineffable goodness and mercy? Why, then, honor someone who is less than God? We came from God's hand, we live by His life, we are destined to be happy with Him forever in the life to come. Why venerate a human person, even "our tainted nature's solitary boast," Mary, the mother of God?

In his *Mary, Mother of the Lord* Karl Rahner has a section in which he answers the question: Why a theology of man?[1] He points out that we must not exclude man from our theological considerations because God himself has become man. It is inconceivable that a Christian would discuss God at any length without inevitably mentioning the fact that God became man in Christ. And if we speak of Christ, is it irreverent that we speak of the pearl of humanity, of her in whose womb He became man?

Rahner contends that the fundamental idea of Mariology is that Mary is the most perfect expression of Christianity. We praise her because she is the most perfect Christian. What is perfect Christianity? Rahner summarizes perfect Christianity as the receiving of God in grace-given freedom with heart and soul, mind and body, and in serving the salvation of others, devoting oneself not to this or that person but serving all. Mary is then the perfect realization of Christianity because she represents the pure, free acceptance of salvation. "Mary is the perfect Christian, the Christian human being exemplified as such, because in the faith of her spirit, and in her blessed womb, with body and soul, then, and all the powers of her being, she received the eternal Word of the Father."[2]

Again, if perfect Christianity means the radiation of one's grace in unselfish service of others, she is the most

---

[1] Karl Rahner, *Mary, Mother of the Lord; Theological Meditations* (New York: Herder & Herder, 1963), p. 36–37.
[2] Rahner, *op. cit.,* p. 36.

perfect because she conceived the salvation of us all by her consent in faith to the divine plan and by her physical motherhood.

The Council Fathers voted in favor of discussing Marian doctrine within the text of the Constitution on the Church rather than in a separate document devoted exclusively to Mary. The eighth chapter of the Constitution, therefore, deals with the Blessed Virgin. The reasoning of the Council Fathers apparently was that the preparation of a separate Marian document would tend to confirm the false impression among certain Christians that Catholics regard Mary as a sort of goddess in her own right, independent of Christ. So we find Mary discussed in the Constitution as a member of the Church, the most perfect member.

But we do not expect that this procedure will be a final answer to all Protestant objections to Mary. For Protestants criticize the Catholic Church itself in much the same way as they criticize Mariology. They feel that the Catholic Church's concept of itself does not give sufficient attention to God. "Glory to God alone" is the theme of many of their objections to the Catholic concept of the Church.

The charge is made that the Catholic concept attributes special divine prerogatives to the Church, thus divinizing the Church which is only a human institution. They see the infallibility of the Pope as a supreme example of this tendency to divinize the human. In short, they feel that the Catholic Church, in its theology of the Church, as in its Mariology, attempts to usurp the glory that should be given to God alone. This surprises the Catholic who is familiar with the Catholic teaching that God in His grace is at the beginning and end of every good act, every good thought. Without Him we can do nothing but with Him as partner, we can move mountains.

Most Protestants, however, hold that the entire work of redemption is a divine work and no human person can enter into it in any way. They do not admit human cooperation. It is all God's work. Karl Barth says that Catholic devotion to Mary is the heresy which enables Protestants to understand the fundamental fallacy of Catholicism. She is the example par excellence of the notion that the human person can cooperate in his or her own salvation. And Mary is, according to Barth, a summary of the Church as Catholics understand it, a Church of men cooperating with grace.

We admit there is a close parallel between Mary and the Church. In Catholic tradition she is a type of the Church. As the most perfect member, she can be taken as a symbol of the Church. Many figures of speech, such as Ark of the Covenant, or Gate of Heaven, are applied equally to Mary and to the Church. Both are mothers who bring forth Christ. In the baptistery of the Church of St. John Lateran in Rome there in an inscription which says that ". . . at this spring the Church our mother bears in her virginal womb the sons whom she has conceived under the breath of God."[3] The allusion to Mary is unmistakeable.

Henri de Lubac, the noted French Jesuit scholar, also quotes in this connection a writer who says that Mary offering her Child is the Church delivering the Word. It is true that the Theological Commission at the Second Vatican Council did not want to use the term "Mary, Mother of the Church" but Pope Paul did use it and the idea, though not the term itself, is contained in the eighth chapter of the Constitution. Mary is mother of the new People of God not merely because she is the most perfect member but also because she was given by Christ to the Church as mother on Calvary when He said to St. John, "Son behold thy mother." John is taken by Catholic writers to symbolize the Church.

Sometimes it is said that Catholics give Mary undue praise by calling her "mediatrix of all graces." The Council Fathers refrained from using the term because they felt it had some dubious overtones in popular piety. They did refer to her as "mediatrix" and that she is a mediatrix is a doctrine we commonly hold. However, we should be ready to explain it.

In the sense in which we refer to Christ as "the only mediator," He is truly the only mediator between God and

---

[3] Henri de Lubac, S.J., *The Splendour of the Church* (New York: Sheed & Ward, 1956), p. 245.

man. He alone is God and man, the bridge between eternity and time. He alone is the efficient cause of our salvation. But if we use the term "mediator" in speaking of Mary, we are using it in an entirely different sense and we are constrained to use it simply because we have no fitting substitute in English. Here we are using it in the sense in which each Christian is a mediator to the other. For after all, how do we come to acquire salvation? Is it not through priests, teachers, parents, friends? They minister the Word to us. [4] They do not create grace—nor does Mary—but they help others with the grace they possess. Since there are human mediators here on earth, it is to be expected there will be human mediators in heaven. To deny it is to deny the doctrine of the communion of saints. Mary still gives her assent to the divine plan as she did centuries ago. She has not retracted it and when Christ dispenses His grace, He does so in awareness of her consent. He knows that she had a beginning role in the divine plan and that she still prays for us sinners now and at the hour of our death.

In 1950 Pope Pius XII proclaimed the doctrine of the Assumption, stating that Mary was assumed body as well as soul into heaven. This of course is no new truth. It has been taught and believed by Catholics for centuries.

The Assumption is, nevertheless, a doctrine that is particularly difficult for a Protestant to accept. Like several other Marian doctrines, it is the fruit of the Church's prolonged meditation on Scripture and is not to be found explicitly stated in individual Scripture texts. The Church, guided by the Holy Spirit, realizes that Scripture, like the kingdom of heaven, is a seed that must grow.

How has the Church deduced this doctrine? Knowing that Mary was perfectly redeemed, the Church has attributed to her the fruits of perfect redemption. We ordinary Christians hope for the fruits of redemption, knowing them to be a sharing—body and soul—in the glory of heaven. There will come a time when we too, like Christ, will enter into His glory by rising bodily at the last day.

---

[4] Rahner, *op. cit.*, p. 95.

Obstacles to Unity

But we also know that we have not been perfectly redeemed and that we will have to wait before we share in the full rewards of redemption. But there was no need for Mary to wait. Her body could share in the glory as soon as she died because she was perfectly redeemed. Is this impossible for humanity? Christ Himself, a member of our human race, has risen from the dead. If He rose from the dead in His humanity, why should Mary, who had achieved beatitude, have to wait for the general judgment?

Behind the Protestant concept of Mariology there are noble intentions and objections based on fundamental Christian principles such as "glory to God alone." In God's good time, Catholic and Protestant theologians will study the Scriptures on Our Lady together and, God willing, come to a common agreement. The journey ahead may be a long one but we will have the best of guides, the Holy Spirit of God.

XIII
The Future

This is a great time to be alive. One can almost feel the presence of the Holy Spirit working through the vast renewal of the Roman Catholic Church. In this new springtime, the winter of a four-centuries-old hostility has begun to disappear and we find ourselves living in a very different climate from that of the Catholic-Protestant cold war. We realize now that the men and women we had thought of as enemies, or at least as competitors, are in reality our own brethren. The time has come for us to gather together, forgetting the polemics and bitterness of the past and meeting as members of one great Christian family.

This, however, will be a task of monumental proportions, no matter how bright the future. Christian unity is the work of the Holy Spirit and it will be achieved at the moment and in the manner in which He desires it. But He is calling every Christian, not only the professional theologian but every member of the People of God, to cooperate with Him.

This means that every Catholic should collaborate with Protestants, according to the scope of his talents and the circumstances of his life, in some form of dialogue or community cooperation that can further the advance of the ecumenical movement. What an amazing profusion of ecumenical activities is beginning to open up on the American scene! The National Council of Churches, with combined Church constituencies of more than forty million Protestants, brings the ecumenical movement to local communities all over America, initiating and maintaining dialogue with Roman Catholics as well as with Churches

The Future

not members of the National Council. On the Catholic side, the Bishops' Committee for Ecumenical and Interreligious Affairs directs organized ecumenical activities by Catholics. Its secretariat for Christian Unity has seven subcommissions appointed to engage in dialogue with representatives of seven other religious groups: the Orthodox, the National and World Councils, the Protestant Episcopal Church, the Lutherans, the Presbyterians and Reformed, the Methodists, and other Christian Churches. (There is also a secretariat for Catholic-Jewish relations, one for relations with non-Christian religions and one for secular humanists.)

Living Room Dialogues co-published by the National Council of Churches and the Paulist Press, has had major impact. This book, with its planned program of ecumenical activities, has brought the ecumenical movement into the American home. The Committee for Ecumenism in Education, a special subcommission of the central Bishops' Committee, advises Catholic colleges, primary and high schools, Newman Centers and adult education groups on the integration of ecumenism into Catholic education. Then too there are the innumerable diocesan ecumenical commissions all over the country, each conducting its own ecumenical program. Certainly there is no ecumenical ennui in the United States. Some of these ecumenical projects may be overlapping in certain sections of the country, some will meet with hostility or calculated indifference, but the ecumenical movement generally is off to a good start in America.

Enthusiasm of course is not enough. For fruitful ecumenical activity, information is necessary. The Catholic ecumenist must acquire correct information about Protestants and Protestant teaching in order to dissipate the caricatures, stereotypes, and lying fables that have caused such scandalous quarrels in the past. Second, he must be loyal to the eternal Gospel. There will be days of anguish in the immediate future when certain exuberant Catholics may want to jump ahead of the ecumenical movement by engaging in highly dubious ecumenical experiments or by playing down truth in a misguided eagerness to achieve unity. For the ecumenist cannot hope to piece together the broken parts of Christendom overnight. Loyalty to the Gospel means love of the brethren and one of the finest expressions of this love is mutual forgiveness for the sins of the past. Pope John expressed it in unforgettable words: "We do not intend to conduct a trial of the past; we do not want to prove who was right or who was wrong. All we want to say is, 'Let us come together. Let us make an end of our divisions.' "

XIV
Secular Ecumenism

A new type of ecumenism, called *secular ecumenism,* has now come to the fore. It is the cooperation in social affairs mentioned in Chapter Eight. The secular ecumenist fixes his attention not so much on the unification of the churches or on theology as on the work that the Church should be doing in the world. Early ecumenists often stressed personal piety, regarding it as the invisible bond that might unite members of all churches into a unity. Later ecumenists began to distrust feelings of personal piety and private religious experience and they looked forward to a unity of churches. In fact, they came to view divisions among the Christian churches as a sin and scandal. The World Council of Churches, as its name implies, is based on the hope of a unity of churches, not of individual Christians.

The institutional Church, however, has been under a barrage of criticism in recent years and a new ecumenism has made its appearance. Says Albert van den Heuvel: "There is a growing feeling among many Christians who are engaged in the ecumenical movement that something new is trying to break through; a new understanding of the ecumenical movement that is the product of all these types mentioned above but at the same time different from them all." [1]

Secular ecumenism then speaks about the relation of the Church to the world rather than the relations among the churches. This emphasis on the world derives from

---

[1] Albert van den Heuvel, *The Humiliation of the Church* (Westminster, 1966), p. 104.

new thinking on the mission of the Church. Contemporary missiologists point out that the Church addresses the world not only because it was established for the salvation of the world but also because Christ is at work in the world. Christ is the light of the world even in those parts of the world that do not know Him: the Christian's task is to call attention to Him as the true light. Van den Heuvel says that Christians are "scouts for the footprints of the Master in the world", alert to signs of His presence and ready to celebrate them.[2]

Secular ecumenists believe firmly that "we must do all things together except those things conscience requires us to do separately" and they believe we must do them together in the world. They do not disparage theology or Scripture but are interested in them insofar as they have something to offer toward the solution of secular problems such as peace, poverty and racial injustice. For them, renewal means renewal of the Church's mission to the world. Obviously, they totally reject the conservative thesis that "The Church should be the Church and stop meddling with the affairs of the world."

This ecumenical orientation toward the world was reflected in the discussions at the World Conference on Church and Society held at Geneva, Switzerland, July 12-26, 1966. The report of the Working Group on Theology and Social Ethics at this meeting pointed out that the Christian must take part in the struggle to achieve a responsible society of justice and peace since the world is the place of his calling and witness: "The task of bringing about effective social change and of discerning in the protest of the poor and the oppressed the relative historical justice at work, is especially his."[3]

In the vast social revolutions under way at the present time at home and abroad, the secular ecumenist tries to discern signs of Christ's presence: he consults Scripture and the mind of the Church throughout history to discover what is just and unjust, what is human and inhuman,

---

[2] van den Heuvel, *op. cit.*, p. 108.

[3] *Christians in the Technical and Social Revolutions of Our Time* (Forward Movement Publications, 1966), p. 38.

Secular Ecumenism

but he also uses the best insights of social scientific analysis. This is imperative if he is to distinguish the spurious from the authentic in these revolutions. The devil may be at work in the winds of change sweeping over the world just as he may be at work in the status quo. Secular ecumenism therefore is a Christian response to those who claim that God is dead or that religion is an anachronism irrelevant to the modern world.

Secular ecumenism seems to have a special attraction for American Christians. Other types of ecumenical activity are still in evidence in the United States: we hear about mergers of churches, top-level theological conversations and ecumenical retreats but secular ecumenism has the headlines. Why is this? Is it because of the dramatic impact of the march on Selma in which priests, nuns, ministers and rabbis linked arm in arm to protest against racial injustice?

Possibly the explanation is that its popularity in the United States derives from the fact that Americans are temperamentally a practical-minded, down-to-earth people who like "to give a helping hand to the neighbor." We have been dismissed as a nation of "do-gooders" and "bleeding hearts." We like to be where the action is and we would rather run the risk of doing the wrong thing than engage in barren study that produces no concrete results. In his *Reflections on America,* Jacques Maritain lamented the anti-intellectualism he found in places in America but he pointed out (perhaps too eulogistically) that in the American set of values, goodness takes precedence over intelligence with the result that neighborliness and sociability are the top values.[4]

Perhaps, too, the American ecumenists feel a sense of impatience with certain theological controversies which they regard as ancient quarrels inherited from their forebears but irrelevant to our time. Rather than haggle over controversies that spawn friction they would prefer to spend their time in civic and social action. (This of course could lead to false irenicism.) But we do hear repeatedly

---

[4] Jacques Maritain, *Reflections on America* (Doubleday Image Books, 1964), pp. 38–47.

the theme that ecumenism really begins in earnest only when Catholics, Protestants and Orthodox get together to do the work of the Church in the world. And in many cases, Christians are collaborating with Jews and even with secularists to combat evils and help improve conditions in the local community.

Since Vatican II, the Catholic Church has given special attention to its mission to the world. Whereas it formerly tended to remain aloof from the secular world, now we find it entering into the world's agonies and heartaches with a resolve to play the role of good Samaritan to all in need. As Pope Paul phrased it at the second session of the Council, "Let the world know this: the Church looks at the world with profound understanding, with sincere admiration and with the sincere intention not of conquering it but of serving it; not of despising it but of appreciating it; not of condemning it but of strengthening it and saving it." His talk at the United Nations, pleading for peace, was a supreme example of the Church's mission to the world.

This mission to the world derives not only from the command to teach all nations but also from the command to engage in social action that is so obvious on page after page of the Gospel, as well as of the Old Testament. In St. Matthew's Gospel, (Ch. 25, v. 31-46), for instance, we find the unforgettable call to Christian social action. The Son of Man, according to St. Matthew, will invite the just into the Kingdom prepared for them, saying "I was hungry and you gave me to eat; I was thirsty and you gave me to drink . . . sick and you visited me; I was in prison and you came to me." And when the just ask when it was that they fed the Son of Man, he will respond: "As long as you did it for one of these the least of my brethren, you did it for me." The amazing charitable work of the early Christian era was sometimes forgotten in later ages as Christians put an almost exclusive emphasis on the preservation of the purity of doctrine or the cultivation of personal holiness with the result that in recent centuries, the Church relaxed its social concern. It did little to promote reform legislation and inaugurate social and economic changes that would help the poor and the oppressed.

Secular Ecumenism

Instead it seemed to content itself with alleviating the miseries caused by social evils rather than attacking them at the source. During nineteenth-century social revolutions in Europe, Catholicism ceased to be a major force for social reform while secular humanists, separating religion from society, built impressive records of achievement in improving the structures of society.

Even in the twentieth century we did very little in supporting civil liberties. (Consider the Catholic attitude to the American Civil Liberties Union). But now the Second Vatican Council has spoken vigorously in support of civil liberties: "Therefore, by virtue of the Gospel committed to her, the Church proclaims the rights of man. She acknowledges and greatly esteems the dynamic movements of today by which these rights are everywhere fostered." The editorial footnote to this text in *The Documents of Vatican II* (Herder and Herder and Association Press: 1966) says very aptly (p. 241): "Whatever the regrettable misunderstandings that turned the 'rights of man' into a rallying cry of the Church's bitter foes in the 18th and 19th centuries and entrenched the Church in a role of intransigent resistance to the movements for social revolution in many parts of the world, the Council now makes it unequivocally plain that the Church intends to play its true historic role as a champion of human rights and to align itself with those who fight for these rights."

The Council, however, went further, pointing out that although it has no explicitly political, economic or social mission, yet out of its religious mission comes a light and energy which can serve to structure and consolidate the human community. "The Church further recognizes that worthy elements are found in today's social movements, especially an evolution toward unity, a process of wholesome socialization and of association in civic and economic realms." (No. 42). Other Christian churches are also laying a heavy emphasis on the need for social concern, notably "The Confession of 1967" approved by the United Presbyterian Church in the U.S.A. It makes social action officially a part of basic Presbyterian doctrine and places upon its members an obligation to work for racial integration, peace and the elimination of poverty.

How do we go about an ecumenical discussion of these issues of social concern? It seems to me that Christians should first deal with conscience, with the Christian's obligation to face up to these problems. This should precede any discussion of the substantive issues themselves. This handling of the question of conscience will come to grips with the Christian conservative's protest that all Christian Churches should stick to their business and stay out of politics and the affairs of the world in general. In dealing with conscience, it is best to deal with it not only as private conscience but also as the conscience of the Church expressed in official statements. (I speak figuratively of course: there is only one conscience, the private conscience; there is no such thing as collective conscience, any more than there is collective guilt. God judges *my* conscience.)

At Boston, May 7-8, 1967, the Bishops' Ecumenical Commission, the National Council of Churches and the Synagogue Council of America held an ecumenical conference on "The Role of Conscience." The main speakers, Rev. Bernard Haring, C.SS.R., Dr. E. Clinton Gardner and Rabbi Eugene Borowitz treated of conscience in general as studied in their respective theologies: Dr. Philip Rieff, a professor of Sociology, acted as a sort of *advocatus diaboli*. The delegates then dispersed into 5 workshops on peace and war, poverty, racial justice, state aid to religious schools, and the binding force of civil laws in conscience. The delegates were asked to examine their particular topic from these angles: how does your religious community go about formulating its position on the particular issue that is your topic for discussion? What in your religious tradition contributes to this official formulation? What is it in your church or synagogue that facilitates or blocks the implementation of your Church's position on this issue? How does your religious community establish its authority to speak on this issue? What are the challenges from the members of your faith who question your community's authority to deal with this issue? What do you say to those members who want to do more than your community in this problem area? For Catholics, for instance, these questions applied to peace and war might

Secular Ecumenism 179

have these implications: Was Pope Paul expressing a private or official opinion in his speech at the U.N. on war? Do Catholics have to agree with him? Who are the Catholics who are questioning his right to speak on war and peace and what are they saying?

Logically and chronologically, this question of conscience and its binding force has priority in any ecumenical program of study and action. One might get from a computer reams of information about the social plight of cities and the social, economic and political arguments supporting or opposing American involvement in a particular war, but after telling us the what and the how of a problem, the computer cannot tell us why we should act. In all these matters of social concern, the big question is: Why should we be concerned? This is the conscience factor. The human tendency is to evade the unpleasant obligation of getting involved in a messy situation. More importantly, *I* must make the decision in conscience. My church or my friends can help me to make the decision but ultimately I have to make the decision—no one can make it for me. Pope Paul undoubtedly had this in mind when he said in talking about war and peace to officials of *Pax Christi:* "For certain people, the temptation is great to ask you to make for them decisions which they would content themselves to make known around them. You must, on the contrary, awaken their initiative and their generosity so that they may know how to engage themselves..." (C.A.I.P. News, January 1967).

The American bishops, in their statement on Peace (November 21, 1966), also emphasized this duty to form one's conscience on this great secular issue, peace. They said that although they could not resolve all the issues involved in the Vietnam conflict, "it is clearly our duty to insist that they be kept under constant moral scrutiny." They went on to reiterate the warning of Vatican II that no man is free to evade personal responsibility by leaving it to others to make moral judgments. They cited especially the words of the Council to the effect that "men should take heed not to entrust themselves only to the efforts of others while remaining careless about their own attitudes. For government officials, who must simultaneously guarantee the good of their own people and promote the universal good, depend on public opinion and feeling to the greatest possible extent."[5]

PEACE

In ecumenical discussions of current secular issues, participants are naturally interested in finding out if there is any ecumenical consensus on the issues. Do the Christian Churches agree on the question of peace, for instance? In this connection, I might mention an interesting talk given by Dr. O. Frederick Nolde, Director of the Commission on the Churches (World Council of Churches) at Buck Hill Falls, Pennsylvania, April 26, 1963. His topic was "Unity for Peace in Diversity of Faith." Dr. Nolde drew up a list of parallel statements that can be found in Pope John's *Pacem in Terris* and in declarations of the World Council of Churches. This method of comparative sampling took its inspiration, said Dr. Nolde, from a remark made by President John F. Kennedy. The former President said that *Pacem in Terris* taken along with notable expressions from other faiths, especially from the World Council of Churches, shows that we are learning to talk the language of progress and peace across the barriers of sect and creed.

In his "sampling comparison", Dr. Nolde did not attempt to make any detailed study of the similarities and differences but expressed the hope that there would be later discussion of these similarities and differences. The "twin" quotations from the encyclical and the World Council documents pertained to: the concept of a well-ordered society, human rights, religious liberty, the dignity of man, race, colonial independence, refugees, foreign domination, economic assistance, disarmament, cessation of testing, peaceful adjustment, the United Nations.

In the second part of his talk, Nolde took up the

---

[5] *Pastoral Constitution on the Church in the Modern World,* Part II, Ch. 5, Sec. 1, *Documents of Vatican II* (Gould Press), p. 296.

question of obstacles to the effective release of spiritual resources for peace. They are: the complexity of international problems, the irrepressible emergence of ever new problems of war and peace, the danger of thinking that a solution that works in one case will inevitably succeed in another case, the suspicion and misunderstanding that divide peoples as in the case of cessation of testing, the awful reality of uninformed and indifferent public opinion. He concluded by enumerating five factors that contribute to effective release of spiritual resources and eight conditions that are favorable to cooperation. An ecumenical study group taking this approach would find their work productive, as Nolde contends, provided they are serious, not superficial but penetrating, courageous and idealistically pragmatic.

Another example of a somewhat similar approach that might be used by a dialogue group is the method used by Dr. Eugene Carson Blake, General Secretary of the World Council of Churches, in a talk on "Ecumenism and Peace" (Norwalk, Connecticut, April 26, 1967). Dr. Blake listed six points concerning peace on which the Christian Churches generally share the same convictions. All agree, for instance, that permanent peace must be based on justice and freedom. These six points show that a common conscience on peace and war is developing throughout the whole ecumenical movement.

POVERTY

Modern communications and transportation have made us aware of the frightful truth about the millions on our planet who are living in poverty and hunger. For long centuries, Christians had no contact with the terrible realities in far-away countries but are now painfully conscious of the plight of the underdeveloped countries and anxious to afford some help. The World Council of Church has its Division of Inter-Church Aid, Refugee and World Services to help the needy. Pope Paul VI established the Pontifical Commission for Justice and Peace and the American Bishops have followed suit by establishing the

U.S. Bishops' World Justice and Peace Secretariat. Both bodies will cooperate to the fullest possible extent with other churches in alleviating poverty, as well as with Jewish and secular agencies. (Long Island Catholic, May 18, 1967; p. 1)

Here at home the poverty problem looms large in our big cities. The conscience of Christians is disturbed by the fact that wealthy Christians tend to reside in the suburbs and the poor in the center of the city, sometimes called the inner city. Precisely because of this fact, the tendency in the past has been for Christian Churches to look with a cold eye on forward-looking social improvements. Seeing no poverty about them in the suburbs, Churchmen saw no reason for many proposals for social reform. This attitude of mind has been responsible for the foot-dragging of many Churches in the field of social action and so we have what has been called "the suburban captivity of the Churches." Now, however, we find many clergy reacting against this and focusing their conscientious attention on the inner city and on the social evils bred by poverty. Fortunately, this uneasiness of conscience has developed at a time when the Churches are emphasizing the concept of the Church as servant of the world rather than as the spearhead of anti-Communism or God's agency for peace of mind.

The Christian Churches are beginning to fight poverty together, cooperating in inter-church, inter-denominational and inter-faith alliances. The National Council of Churches especially has done good work in this field, acting as a clearing house for information and as a goad to the Christian Churches.

The American Government, in its Economic Opportunity Act (1964), launched its all-out war on poverty and sought the help of all possible allies such as voluntary welfare agencies, labor unions and the Churches. Many Churches gladly accepted the federal funds given them for the war on poverty and the association with other Churches brought them closer to each other but, at the same time, some Churches found themselves involved in alliances that made them uneasy. For instance, the Government in the Head Start program has allowed the use of church facilities for anti-poverty work, provided all religious symbols have been removed. It is easy to see what complications can arise for Churches who have hitherto looked askance at any kind of federal aid to religious schools as a violation of the First Amendment. Again, in the Elementary and Secondary Education Act of 1965, the Government used the child-benefit theory in allocating federal funds for aid to children in religious schools. The Act assumed the funds would be given to the children as citizens, not to the religious schools for purposes of sectarian education. Some Churches receiving funds under the Act began to wonder if they were part and parcel of a conspiracy to break down the wall of separation erected by the First Amendment.

There is no lack of subject matter for discussion of joint ecumenical action in the war against poverty. One of the main questions, however, is: Can this involvement of the Church in such a secular problem be considered an authentic role for the Church? The conservative Christian will insist that the Church is meddling in the business of Government. Again, much study should be given to the question of the relation of the Churches toward the secular agencies with whom they are cooperating, especially the federal government. Is it wise for Church and State to work together so closely? What is the difference between the concern of the Churches and the concern of labor unions and charitable agencies in this activity? If the Church is worried as to the propriety of its involvement, can it do a good job on the problem itself?

The ecumenist, convinced that the Church is servant, knows that aid to the poor is a tradition that comes down from the Prophets, from Christ and from the early Fathers of the Church, but he is also quite sure that the Church has a special contribution to make: It can do something that secular agencies cannot do. As Lyle E. Schaller says: "The call is to be present as a watchdog, as a critic, as a supporter and as enabler." One of the finest things the Church can do is to further "maximum feasible participation" of the poor themselves in the poverty project in order to give them a handup rather than a handout, and in this way make them aware of their personal dignity, of their personal talents and responsibility. Of course, clergy anxious for recognition and advancement in the Church can easily mess up a good anti-poverty project by striving for publicity or by trying to build up the prestige of their Church. The important thing is to try to alleviate the causes as well as the effects of poverty, and to treat the poor as subjects, not objects, striving to help them develop a sense of dignity and self-esteem so they can become the persons God intended them to be.[6]

RACIAL JUSTICE

The most dramatic example of interreligious cooperation in the field of racial justice was the National Conference on Religion and Race held at Chicago, January 14-17, 1963. It was the first time in history that the National Council of Churches, the Social Action Department of the National Catholic Welfare Conference and the Synagogue Council of America had convened to promote racial justice. It brought together groups as diverse as the Southern Baptists, the Greek Orthodox and the National Council of Catholic Men. As for actual results, *The Christian Century* wisely said: "Such conferences do not solve problems. They discover problems, they lift up unresolved issues, identify the unused talent and resources, dramatize the unfinished business, renew the faltering commitments. In these respects, the National Conference on Religion and Race was successful, not only in the interfaith but also in the interracial quest. Two, three, five years from now will be soon enough to ask what good came of it." (*The Christian Century,* January 30, 1963, p. 134)

Some of the problems touched upon were: the elimination of racial barriers in church-related schools and institutions, projects under religious auspices to help Negro families find homes in restricted white neighborhoods, interreligious task forces in inner-city and suburban areas

---

[6] Cf. Lyle E. Schaller, *The Churches' War on Poverty* (Abingdon Press, 1967), p. 99.

Secular Ecumenism

to bring about freedom of residence, more religious participation in urban planning, the development of community organizations to help improve social conditions. Cardinal Meyer, in his address, claimed that the central issues of city race relations were the expansion of employment training and job opportunities, and the elimination of housing discrimination practices.

At the present time, ecumenical activity connected with civil rights seems to have bogged down somewhat because the pace of the civil rights movement itself has slowed down. Churches are finding a great amount of apathy among members in the implementation of official church statements on racial justice. At the General Assembly of the United Presbyterians (May 23, 1967), it was said that progress in civil rights has been "painfully slow" and that there is a big gap between "proclamation and performance." The reasons for this general slow-down probably are the white backlash to boasts of "black power" by civil rights leaders like Stokely Carmichael, the loss of white support due to attempts to link civil rights with anti-Vietnam war agitation, the riots in places like Watts, the behavior of men like Cassius Clay in attempting to evade the draft.

The painful fact, however, is that there is probably more need than ever of support for the civil rights movement. The plight of the Negro today is described by many experts as worse than it was ten years ago. The gap between the income of whites and that of Negroes widens year after year. Precisely because the civil rights movement is losing popularity the participation of dedicated white Christians is needed more than ever. Civil rights is a vast challenge to Christian ecumenists. There is so much to be done: job training, counselling programs for youth, improved education, better housing, administration of equal justice, the protection of Negroes from intimidation, improvement of police-community relations and better health services for the poor. The task is of colossal proportions but there is one encouraging fact that will make ecumenical work lighter—all faiths agree in their teachings on racial justice and they agree also on the fact of injustice inflicted on the Negro who, as a child of God, has been assigned to a sub-human existence in the ghettos of the Northern cities or in the sharecroppers' hovels on Southern farms.

STATE AID TO RELIGIOUS SCHOOLS

The question of federal or state aid to religious schools has been a source of constant interfaith friction for the last quarter century. The core of the problem is a legal one: does the First Amendment of the Constitution permit the use of tax funds in any shape or form for the support of children attending Church-controlled schools? Because of the size of the Roman Catholic school system this is a problem that relates specially to Catholic schools.

For years the question has been discussed from a legal viewpoint. What does the First Amendment ban on "an establishment of religion" mean? What does the Amendment mean when it says that Congress shall not restrict the free exercise of religion? The Catholic parent who sends his child to a Catholic school exercises his right to religious freedom: does the Federal Government or the State penalize him for exercising the right by refusing to help pay for the child's education but yet demand of him payment of taxes for the public schools? If Catholic school children may borrow books from the public library, may they not ask to borrow school books for use in class?

Recently, the controversy has expanded. Many Americans have said that the issues should be judged against the background of national welfare. It is in the national interest that all children in America should receive a good education. Therefore, certain legislators feel that aid should be given to children at religious schools in order that they might receive as good an education as that given at public schools. This seems to have been the motivation behind the 1965 Elementary and Secondary Education Act. The Act bases certain forms of aid on the child-benefit theory, that is, that certain services such as training of the handicapped are aid to the children, even though given on Church-controlled property. Critics of the Act say this amounts to indirect aid to the sectarian school and that it is an indirect way of circumventing the First Amendment ban on aid to religion.

Obviously, ecumenically-minded Christians will discuss the issues from a legal as well as national welfare angle but they ought to keep in mind their duty to discuss these issues irenically for heated debate can quickly stir up sectarian hostility. Yet this reminder to discuss the question in irenic fashion is sometimes rejected as a trick to gag non-Catholic critics of aid to Catholic schools. There is in Protestantism a hard core of anti-ecumenical church members who suspect the whole ecumenical movement of being a hoax to induce in Protestants an euphoria that will desensitize them to Catholic skullduggery. Among them there is still a fear of the Catholic hierarchy and a suspicion that the Catholic parishioners are led sheep-like hither and yon by their leaders. They do not fear the Catholic neighbor next door but fear that his Church will pressure him into voting the Catholic party line at the next elections.

In ecumenical discussions on state aid to religious schools, we often find Orthodox Jews aligned with Roman Catholics in favor of state aid, while conservative Protestants and Reformed and Conservative Jews are on the other side. The former usually ask for State aid to support the teaching not of religious subject matter but of secular subjects at Church-controlled schools. The latter feel that the public school is a democratizing and integrating force in American society and that State aid to religious schools will only weaken the public schools and encourage separation along religious and social lines.

The ecumenist should be alert to the ever-changing nuances of the controversy. In earlier years, Catholic Churchmen generally opposed any aid to Catholic schools on the ground that "he who pays the piper calls the tune." A few years ago, many Catholics deplored the "secularism" and "godlessness" of public schools. Now that the Second Vatican Council has extolled the validity of the secular, we seldom hear about "godless schools" and the Catholic case for State aid takes a more positive form, such as the parents' right to exercise of religious freedom and their right to a fair share of public tax funds. At any rate, the ecumenist can play an invaluable role in the discussion by helping to dissipate the fear and suspicion that befog so much of the controversy.

CIVIL LAW AND CONSCIENCE

Concerned about the welfare of society, the secular ecumenist is also very much concerned about the observance of civil law. For civil law is the great agency for peace in the community, preventing those invasions of personal and property rights that cause outbursts of violence. Special problems of lawlessness have made their appearance in recent years: all those instances of draft card burning, draft evasion, sit-ins, illegal demonstrations and in general, civil disobedience. What is new about many of these violations of law is that the lawbreakers claim they are following conscience in breaking the law.

Every Christian must foster respect for civil law but he must also show due respect for the rights of conscience. Traditionally American law has shown a somewhat guarded and gingerly respect for conscience. Chief Justice Hughes reflected the traditional position when he said: "When one's belief collides with the power of the state, the latter is supreme within its sphere and submission or punishment follows. But in the forum of conscience, duty to a moral power higher than the state has always been maintained." (328 US 61 [1946]). The American courts have permitted exemption from military service for conscientious objectors who refuse to serve because their religious belief condemns war as immoral. Lately some clergy and legislators have asked for expansion of the exemption to include even those who are not pacifists but who have religious objections to a particular war. The Second Vatican Council supported the rights of conscientious objectors: "It seems right that laws make humane provisions for the case of those who for reasons of conscience refuse to bear arms, provided, however, that they accept some other form of service to the human community."

This is a real problem that will engage the attention of Christians as long as war exists. Some Christians feel

Secular Ecumenism

so deeply on this question that they appeal to schools to inform youths about the right of conscientious objection, they send out caravans called "end-the-draft caravans" to high schools and colleges and they urge adults not to pay taxes for the support of "immoral wars".

All Christian faiths hold for the moral obligation to obey civil laws but of course, the assumption is that the laws be just. They also hold that there is no obligation to obey an unjust civil law—but are reluctant to allow the individual citizen to decide what is a just or unjust civil law. Yet if the issue involved is a major one and a Christian honestly and conscientiously deems a law immoral, he must follow his conscience rather than the law. "We must obey God rather than men" said St. Peter and the Apostles. St. Thomas More is admired by Catholics precisely because he followed his conscience rather than the law in refusing to sign the oath approved by his King, the Parliament and the majority of bishops of England.

At any rate, this whole question of civil disobedience is one that will loom ever larger in our society as American law continues to show a greater respect for the rights and dignity of the human person. Previously our Courts have shown a somewhat grudging recognition of the rights of conscientious objectors whenever the national security or the welfare of society were at stake, but there are signs of a change for a future. The Christian ecumenist needs to give this question a great amount of study for it does present a dilemma. Violation of law leads to violence and anarchy but violation of one's own conscience strikes at the heart of responsible society. How to reconcile the claims of society with the claims of conscience—that is the problem.

Appendix One

PAUL, BISHOP
SERVANT OF THE SERVANTS OF GOD
TOGETHER WITH THE FATHERS OF THE SACRED COUNCIL
FOR EVERLASTING MEMORY

DECREE ON ECUMENISM

INTRODUCTION[1]

1. The RESTORATION OF UNITY among all Christians is one of the principal concerns of the Second Vatican Council. Christ the Lord founded one Church and one Church only. However, many Christian Communions [2] present themselves to men as the true inheritors of Jesus Christ; all indeed profess to be followers of the Lord but they differ in mind [3] and go their different ways, as if Christ Himself were divided (Cf. 1 Cor. 1, 13). [4] Cer-

---

[1] The 1963 text had no introduction. It was added to place the theme in its historical setting and to show the purpose and opportuneness of the Decree.

[2] "Communions" is used in the Decree when it speaks without judgment or distinction between Orthodox, Anglican, Protestant, and Catholic.

[3] Before the papal change: "...; the followers of the Lord differ in mind..."

[4] In the official final text of a conciliar document references can only be made to Holy Scripture, the Fathers of the Church, and former Ecumenical Councils. All other references in the notes of the working drafts drop out (*e.g.,* papal encyclicals, works of outstanding theologians).

Appendix One

tainly, such division openly contradicts the will of Christ, scandalizes the world, and damages that most holy cause, the preaching of the Gospel to every creature.

The Lord of Ages nevertheless wisely and patiently follows out the plan of His grace on our behalf, sinners that we are. In recent times He has begun to bestow more generously upon divided Christians remorse over their divisions and longing for unity.

Everywhere large numbers have felt the impulse of this grace, and among our separated brethren also there increases from day to day a movement, fostered by the grace of the Holy Spirit, for the restoration of unity among all Christians. Taking part in this movement, which is called ecumenical, are those who invoke the Triune God and confess Jesus as Lord and Savior. [5] They do this not merely as individuals but also as members of the corporate groups in which they have heard the Gospel, and which each regards as his Church and indeed, God's. And yet, almost everyone, [6] though in different ways, longs for the one visible Church of God, a Church truly universal and sent forth to the whole world that the world may be converted to the Gospel and so be saved, to the glory of God.

The sacred Council gladly notes all this. It has already declared its teaching on the Church, and now, moved by a desire for the restoration of unity among all the followers of Christ, it wishes to set before all Catholics guidelines, helps and methods, by which they too can respond to the grace of this divine call.

---

[5] In the working draft, explicit reference was made in the notes to the "Basis" formula of the World Council of Churches, as adopted by the Third World Assembly in New Delhi (1961). The Basis reads: "The World Council of Churches is a fellowship of churches which confess the Lord Jesus Christ as God and Savior according to the Scriptures and therefore seek to fulfill together their common calling to the glory of the one God, Father, Son and Holy Spirit" (*The New Delhi Report,* London, 1962, p. 152). This Basis is also implied in the first sentence of n. 20 below.

[6] The Holy Father added "almost". It is true that some Protestant Communities deny the necessity of a *visible* Church.

Chapter I

CATHOLIC PRINCIPLES ON ECUMENISM

2. What has revealed the love of God among us is that the only-begotten Son of God has been sent by the Father into the world, so that, being made man, He might by His redemption of the entire human race give new life to it and unify it (Cf. 1 Jn. 4, 9; Col. 1, 18-20; Jn. 11, 52). Before offering Himself up as a spotless victim upon the altar of the cross, He prayed to His Father for those who believe: "that they all may be one; even as thou, Father, art in me, and I in thee, that they also may be one in us, so that the world may believe that thou hast sent me" (Jn. 17, 21). In His Church He instituted the wonderful sacrament of the Eucharist by which the unity of the Church is both signified and brought about. He gave His followers a new commandment to love one another (Cf. Jn. 13, 34), and promised the Spirit, their Advocate (Cf. Jn. 16, 7), who, as Lord and life-giver, should remain with them forever.

After being lifted up on the cross and glorified, the Lord Jesus poured forth the Spirit whom He had promised, and through whom He has called and gathered together the people of the New Covenant, which is the Church, into a unity of faith, hope and charity, as the Apostle teaches us: "There is one body and one Spirit, just as you were called to the one hope of your calling; one Lord, one faith, one baptism" (Eph. 4, 4-5). For "all you who have been baptized into Christ have put on Christ... for you are all one in Christ Jesus" (Gal. 3, 27-28). It is the Holy Spirit, dwelling in those who believe [7] and pervading and ruling over the entire Church, who brings about that wonderful communion of the faithful and joins them together

---

[7] Some Fathers had objected to this, claiming that the Holy Spirit dwells only in the soul quickened by charity. The response was Ephesians 3, 17, "to have Christ dwelling through faith in your hearts". Where Christ is, there is also the Spirit. The Spirit is present even in the believing sinner, though not in the same way as in the just.

Appendix One

so intimately in Christ that He is the principle of the Church's unity. By distributing various kinds of spiritual gifts and ministries (Cf. 1 Cor. 12, 4-11), He enriches the Church of Jesus Christ with different functions "in order to equip the saints for the work of service, so as to build up the Body of Christ" (Eph. 4, 12).

In order to establish this His holy Church everywhere in the world till the end of time, Christ entrusted to the College of the Twelve the task of teaching, ruling and sanctifying (Cf. Mt. 28, 18-20, in conjunction with Jn. 20, 21-23). Among their number He chose Peter. And after his confession of faith, He determined that on him He would build His Church; to him He promised the keys of the kingdom of heaven (Cf. Mt. 16, 19, in conjunction with Mt. 18, 18), and after his profession of love, entrusted all His sheep to him to be confirmed in faith (Cf. Lk. 22, 32) and shepherded in perfect unity (Cf. Jn. 21, 15-18), with Himself, Christ Jesus, forever remaining the chief cornerstone (Cf. Eph. 2, 20) and shepherd of our souls (Cf. 1 Pet. 2, 25; I Vatican Council, Sess. IV [1870], The Constitution *Pastor Aeternus:* Coll. Lac. 7, 482 a).

It is through the faithful preaching of the Gospel by the Apostles and their successors—the bishops with Peter's successor at their head, through their administering the sacraments, and through their governing in love, that Jesus Christ wishes His people to increase, under the action of the Holy Spirit; and He perfects its fellowship in unity: in the confession of one faith, in the common celebration of divine worship, and in the fraternal harmony of the family of God.

The Church, then, God's only flock, like a standard high lifted for the nations to see it (Cf. Is. 11, 10-12), ministers the Gospel of peace to all mankind (Cf. Eph. 2, 17-18, in conjunction with Mk. 16, 15), as it makes its pilgrim way in hope toward its goal, the fatherland above (Cf. 1 Pet. 1, 3-9).

This is the sacred mystery of the unity of the Church, in Christ and through Christ, with the Holy Spirit energizing its various functions. The highest exemplar and source of this mystery is the unity, in the Trinity of Persons, of one God, the Father and the Son in the Holy Spirit.[8]

3. In this one and only Church of God from its very beginnings there arose certain rifts (Cf. 1 Cor. 11, 18-19; Gal. 1, 6-9; 1 Jn. 2, 18-19), which the Apostle strongly censures as damnable (Cf. 1 Cor. 1, 11ff.; 11, 22). But in subsequent centuries much more serious dissensions appeared and quite large Communities became separated from full communion with the Catholic Church—for which, often enough, men of both sides were to blame. However, one cannot charge with the sin of the separation those who at present are born into these Communities and in them are brought up in the faith of Christ, and the Catholic Church accepts them with respect and affection as brothers. For men who believe in Christ and have been properly baptized[9] are brought into certain, though imperfect, communion with the Catholic Church. Without doubt, the differences that exist in varying degrees between them and the Catholic Church—whether in doctrine and sometimes in discipline, or concerning the structure of the Church—do indeed create many obstacles, sometimes serious ones, to full ecclesiastical communion. The ecumenical movement is striving to overcome these obstacles. But even in spite of them it remains true that all who have been justified by faith in baptism are incorporated into Christ (Cf. Council of Florence, Sess. VIII [1439], The Decree *Exultate Deo:* Mansi 31, 1055 A); they therefore have a right to be called Christians, and with good reason

---

[8] *"In* the Holy Spirit" rather than *"and* the Holy Spirit" emphasizes that the Spirit is the bond of charity between the Father and the Son. Compare this sentence with the opening sentence of the World Council of Churches' *Statement on Unity:* "The love of the Father and the Son in the unity of the Holy Spirit is the source and goal of the unity which the Triune God wills for all men and creation. We believe that we share in this unity in the Church of Jesus Christ.. " *The New Delhi Report* (London, 1962), p. 116.

[9] "Properly" (*rite*) is used to allay fears that the Council may not be aware that the baptismal practices in some dissident Communions are not in accord with the Catholic understanding of the necessary conditions for valid baptism.

Appendix One

are accepted as brothers by the children of the Catholic Church (Cf. St. Augustine, *In Ps. 32, Enarr. II, 29: PL* 36, 299).

Moreover, some, even very many of the most significant elements and endowments, which together go to build up and give life to the Church itself, can exist [10] outside the visible boundaries of the Catholic Church: the written Word of God; the life of grace; faith, hope and charity, with the other interior gifts of the Holy Spirit, as well as visible elements. All of these, which come from Christ and lead back to Him, belong by right [11] to the one Church of Christ.

The brethren divided from us [12] also carry out many liturgical actions of the Christian religion. In ways that vary according to the condition of each Church or Community, these most certainly can truly engender a life of grace, and, one must say, can aptly give access to the communion of salvation.

It follows that the separated Churches (Cf. IV Lateran Council [1215], Constitution IV: Mansi 22, 990; II Council of Lyons [1274], Profession of faith of Michael Palaeologos: Mansi 24, 71 E; Council of Florence, Sess. VI [1439], Definition *Laetentur caeli:* Mansi 31, 1026 E) and Communities as such, though we believe they suffer from defects already mentioned, have been by no means deprived of significance and importance in the mystery of salvation. For the Spirit of Christ has not refrained from using them as means of salvation which derive their efficacy from the very fullness of grace and truth entrusted to the Catholic Church. [13]

Nevertheless, our separated brethren, whether considered as individuals or as Communities and Churches,

---

[10] *De Ecclesia* is stronger: elements of sanctification and truth *do* exist outside of the visible boundaries of the Catholic Church (n. 8).

[11] "By right" is a papal addition.

[12] *"Fratres a nobis seiuncti."* This is the most exact expression to use. Even though the Decree often uses only "separated brethren", the expression means "separated from us", not from Christ or from each other.

[13] "Catholic" is a papal addition.

are not blessed with that unity which Jesus Christ wished to bestow on all those to whom He has given new birth into one body, and whom He has quickened to newness of life—that unity which the Holy Scriptures and the ancient Tradition of the Church proclaim. For it is through Christ's Catholic Church alone, which is the all-embracing means of salvation,[14] that the fullness of the means of salvation can be obtained. It was to the apostolic college alone, of which Peter is the head, that we believe that our Lord entrusted all the blessings of the New Covenant, in order to establish on earth the one Body of Christ into which all those should be fully incorporated who belong in any way to the people of God. During its pilgrimage on earth, this people, though still in its members liable to sin,[15] is growing in Christ and is guided by God's gentle wisdom, according to His hidden designs, until it shall happily arrive at the fullness of eternal glory in the heavenly Jerusalem.

4. Today, in many parts of the world, under the inspiring grace of the Holy Spirit,[16] many efforts are being made in prayer, word and action to attain that fullness of unity which Jesus Christ desires. The sacred Council exhorts, therefore, all the Catholic faithful to recognize the signs of the times and to take an active and intelligent part in the work of ecumenism.

The term "ecumenical movement" indicates the initiatives and activities encouraged and organized, according to the various needs of the Church and as opportunities

---

[14] *"Generale auxilium salutis."* The Decree takes over the expression used in the Letter of the Holy Office to Cardinal R. J. Cushing of Boston concerning the "Feeney Case" (August 8, 1949). Cf. *The American Ecclesiastical Review,* Oct. 1952, p. 308.

[15] The papal addition "in its members" avoids the theological issue of whether the Church as such is liable to sin.

[16] Another precision by a papal change. The earlier text read "under the inspiration of the Holy Spirit (*Spiritu Sancto afflante*)", an expression that has commonly been used since Pope Pius XII's encyclical on Biblical Studies, *Divino Afflante Spiritu* (1943) to signify the specific inspiration of the Sacred Writers of the Bible.

Appendix One

offer, to promote Christian unity. These are: first, every effort to avoid expressions, judgments and actions which do not represent the condition of our separated brethren with truth and fairness and so make mutual relations with them more difficult. Then, "dialogue" between competent experts from different Churches and Communities; in their meetings, which are organized in a religious spirit, each explains the teaching of his Communion in greater depth and brings out clearly its distinctive features. Through such dialogue everyone gains a truer knowledge and more just appreciation of the teaching and religious life of both Communions. In addition, these Communions engage in that more intensive cooperation in carrying out any duties for the common good of humanity which are demanded by every Christian conscience. They also come together for common prayer, where this is permitted. Finally, all are led to examine their own faithfulness to Christ's will for the Church and, wherever necessary, undertake with vigor the task of renewal and reform. [17]

Such actions, when they are carried out by the Catholic faithful with prudent patience and under the attentive guidance of their bishops, promote justice and truth, concord and collaboration, as well as the spirit of brotherly love and unity. The result will be that, little by little, as the obstacles to perfect ecclesiastical communion are overcome, all Christians will be gathered, in a common celebration of the Eucharist, into the unity of the one and only

---

[17] Although "renewal" and "reform" are often used interchangeably, their use in church documents often shows a distinction: (1) to *renew* is to adopt new attitudes, new liturgical and pastoral structures, because the old ones, good in themselves, are no longer very apt in carrying out the mission of the Church. Such renewal is a normal evolution owing to the Church's limitation by space and time (*e.g.,* with the growth of a more united and mature, easily communicating world-wide episcopacy should come less centralization around the Roman Curia); (2) to *reform* is to restore to pristine vigor what has been *de*formed owing to weakness and sin (*e.g.,* from any authoritarian or merely juridical exercise of authority to its evangelical exercise in the spirit of Christian service).

Church, which Christ bestowed on His Church from the beginning. This unity, we believe, subsists in the Catholic Church as something she can never lose, and we hope that it will continue to increase until the end of time.

However, it is evident that the work of preparing and reconciling those individuals who wish for full Catholic communion is of its nature distinct from ecumenical action. But there is no opposition between the two, since both proceed from the marvelous ways of God. [18]

In ecumenical work, Catholics must assuredly be concerned for their separated brethren, praying for them, keeping them informed about the Church, making the first approaches toward them. But their primary duty is to make a careful and honest appraisal of whatever needs to be renewed and done in the Catholic household itself, in order that its life may bear witness more clearly and faithfully to the teachings and institutions which have been handed down from Christ through the Apostles.

For although the Catholic Church has been endowed with all divinely revealed truth and with all means of grace, yet its members fail to live by them with all the fervor that they should. As a result the radiance of the Church's face shines less brightly in the eyes of our separated brethren and of the world at large, and the growth of God's kingdom is retarded. Every Catholic must therefore aim at Christian perfection (Cf. James 1, 4; Rom. 12, 1-2) and, each according to his station, play his part that the Church, which bears in her own body the humility and dying of Jesus (Cf. 2 Cor. 4, 10; Phil. 2, 5-8), may daily be more purified and renewed, against the day when Christ will present her to Himself in all her glory without spot or wrinkle (Cf. Eph. 5, 27).

While preserving unity in essentials, let everyone in the Church, according to the office entrusted to him, preserve a proper freedom in the various forms of spiritual life and discipline, in the variety of liturgical rites, and even in the theological elaborations of revealed truth. In all things let

---

[18] The text prior to the papal change read: "since both are a work inspired (*inspiratum*) by the Holy Spirit". Cf. footnote 16.

Appendix One

charity prevail. If they are true to this course of action, they will be giving ever richer expression to the authentic catholicity and apostolicity of the Church.

On the other hand, Catholics must gladly acknowledge and esteem the truly Christian endowments from our common heritage which are to be found among our separated brethren. It is right and salutary to recognize the riches of Christ and virtuous works [19] in the lives of others who are bearing witness to Christ, sometimes even to the shedding of their blood. For God is always wonderful in His works and worthy of all praise.

Nor should we forget that anything wrought by the grace of the Holy Spirit [20] in the hearts of our separated brethren can contribute to our own edification. Whatever is truly Christian is never contrary to what genuinely belongs to the faith; indeed, it can always bring a more perfect realization of the very mystery of Christ and the Church.

Nevertheless, the divisions among Christians prevent the Church from realizing the fullness of catholicity proper to her in those of her sons who, though joined to her by baptism, are yet separated from full communion with her. Furthermore, the Church herself finds it more difficult to express in actual life her full catholicity in all its aspects.

This sacred Council is gratified to note that the participation by the Catholic faithful in ecumenical work is growing daily. It commends this work to the bishops everywhere in the world for their diligent promotion and prudent guidance. [21]

---

[19] The Pope changed from "and the gifts of the Holy Spirit". The gifts are not always visible in any Christian. The "interior gifts of the Holy Spirit" outside the visible limits of the Catholic Church are recognized in n. 3, para. 2.

[20] The Pope's change from "by the Holy Spirit".

[21] In suggested amendments (*modi*) for many passages in the Decree, bishops were requesting the addition of clauses that would state the necessity of episcopal supervision. The reason presented by the Secretariat why these amendments were not accepted was that this concluding sentence of n. 4 covered the anxiety.

Appendix One

Chapter II

THE PRACTICE OF ECUMENISM

5. The concern for restoring unity involves the whole Church, faithful and clergy alike. It extends to everyone, according to the talent of each, whether it be exercised in daily Christian living or in theological and historical studies. This concern itself already reveals to some extent the bond of brotherhood existing among all Christians and it leads toward full and perfect unity, in accordance with what God in His kindness wills.

6. Every renewal of the Church (Cf. V Lateran Council, Sess. XII [1517], Constitution *Constituti:* Mansi 32, 988 B-C) essentially consists in an increase of fidelity to her own calling. Undoubtedly this explains the dynamism of the movement toward unity.

Christ summons the Church, as she goes her pilgrim way, to that continual reformation of which she always has need, insofar as she is an institution of men here on earth. [22] Consequently, if, in various times and circumstances, there have been deficiencies in moral conduct or in church discipline, or even in the way that church teaching has been formulated—to be carefully distinguished from the deposit of faith itself [23]—these should be set right at the opportune moment and in the proper way.

---

[22] The Decree takes over the expression used by Pope Paul VI in his Allocution to the Roman Curia, September 21, 1963: "...this unceasing reform of which the Church herself, insofar as she is a human institution belongs to this world, has constant need". *A.A.S.* 55 (1963), p. 797.

[23] The drafting Commission had considered the importance of theological renewal in the sense here expressed, but it anticipated severe opposition and thus omitted it from the first session draft. But the idea was added because of the support given to it by Pope John XXIII in his opening address to the first session: "The deposit of faith is one thing, the way that it is presented is another; for the truths preserved in our sacred doctrine can retain the same substance and meaning under different forms of expression". *A.A.S.* 54 (1962), p. 792.

Appendix One

Church renewal therefore has notable encumenical importance. Already this renewal is taking place in various spheres of the Church's life: the biblical and liturgical movements, the preaching of the Word of God and catechetics, the apostolate of the laity, new forms of religious life and the spirituality of married life, and the Church's social teaching and activity. All these should be considered as promises and guarantees for the future progress of ecumenism.

7. There can be no ecumenism worthy of the name without interior conversion. For it is from newness of attitudes of mind (Cf. Eph. 4, 23), from self-denial and unstinted love, that desires of unity take their rise and develop in a mature way. We should therefore pray to the Holy Spirit for the grace to be genuinely self-denying, humble, gentle in the service of others and to have an attitude of brotherly generosity toward them. The Apostle of the Gentiles says: "I, therefore a prisoner for the Lord, beg you to lead a life worthy of the calling to which you have been called, with all humility and meekness, with patience, forebearing one another in love, eager to maintain the unity of the spirit in the bond of peace" (Eph. 4, 1-3). This exhortation is directed especially to those raised to sacred orders in order that the mission of Christ may be continued. He came among us "not to be served but to serve" (Mt. 20, 28).

St. John has testified: "If we say we have not sinned, we make Him a liar, and His word is not in us" (1 Jn. 1, 10). This holds good for sins against unity. Thus, in humble prayer we beg pardon of God and of our separated brethren, just as we forgive them that trespass against us. [24]

---

[24] Pope Paul's opening address to the second session helped greatly to support the demands of many Fathers that a simple confession of guilt should be added to the prior text: "If we are in any way to blame for that separation", the Holy Father said in speaking directly to the Observers, "we humbly beg God's forgiveness. And we ask pardon too of our brethren who feel themselves to have been injured by us. For our part, we willingly forgive the injuries which the Catholic Church has suffered, and forget the grief during the long series of dissensions and separations. May the heavenly

The faithful should remember that they are better promoting union among Christians, indeed living it better, the more they strive to live holier lives according to the Gospel. For the closer their union with the Father, the Word, and the Spirit, the more deeply and easily will they be able to grow in mutual brotherly love.

8. This change of heart and holiness of life, along with public and private prayer for the unity of Christians, should be regarded as the soul of the whole ecumenical movement, and merits the name, "spiritual ecumenism". [25]

It is a recognized custom for Catholics to meet for frequent recourse to that prayer for the unity of the Church with which the Savior Himself on the eve of His death so fervently appealed to His Father: "That they may all be one" (Jn. 17, 20).

In certain special circumstances, such as in prayer services "for unity" and during ecumenical gatherings, it is allowable, indeed desirable that Catholics should join in prayer with their separated brethren. Such prayers in common are certainly a very effective means of petitioning for the grace of unity, and they are a genuine expression of ties which still bind Catholics to their separated brethren. "For where two or three are gathered together in my name, there am I in the midst of them" (Mt. 18, 20).

Yet worship in common (*communicatio in sacris*) is not to be considered as a means to be used indiscriminately for the restoration of unity among Christians. There are two main principles upon which the practice of such common worship depends: first, that of the unity of the Church which ought to be expressed; and second, that of the sharing in means of grace. The expression of unity very generally forbids common worship. Grace to be obtained sometimes commends it. The concrete course to be

---

Father deign to hear our prayers and grant us true brotherly peace." The Decree added both the admission (cf. n. 3, para. 1) and the simple confession here, simple because there can be triumphalism even in the beating of breasts.

[25] The expression is new to Anglo-Saxon tradition, but has been a favorite among French ecumenists, especially the pioneer, Abbé Couturier.

Appendix One

adopted, when due regard has been given to all the circumstances of time, place and persons, is left to the prudent decision of the local episcopal authority, unless the Bishops' Conference according to its own statutes, or the Holy See, has determined otherwise. [26]

9. We must get to know the outlook of our separated brethren. Study is absolutely required for this, and it should be pursued in fidelity to truth and with a spirit of good will. Catholics, who already have a proper grounding, need to acquire a more adequate understanding of the respective doctrines of our separated brethren, their history, their spiritual and liturgical life, their religious psychology and cultural background. Most valuable for this purpose are meetings of the two sides—especially for discussion of theological problems—where each can treat with the other on an equal footing, [27] provided that those who take part in them under the guidance of the authorities are truly competent. [28] From such dialogue will emerge still more clearly what the situation of the Catholic Church really is. In this way, too, we will better understand the outlook of our separated brethren and more aptly present our own belief.

10. Sacred theology and other branches of knowledge, especially those of an historical nature, [29] must be taught with due regard also for the ecumenical point of view, so that they may correspond as exactly as possible with the facts.

It is important that future pastors and priests should have mastered a theology that has been carefully worked

---

[26] The 1963 text was more general: the decision is left to "episcopal authority". 212 Council Fathers objected in their *modi:* some wanted only the local bishop, some only Episcopal Conferences, others only the Holy See. Thus, the change in the re-submitted Decree.

[27] *"Par cum pari"*. The Decree takes over the expression used in the Instruction of the Holy Office on the Ecumenical Movement. *A.A.S.* 42 (1950), p.145.

[28] The competency is somewhat relative, depending on the subject discussed, the composition of the group, its supervision, etc.

[29] The 1963 text mentioned only sacred theology.

out in this way and not polemically, especially with regard to those aspects which concern the relations of separated brethren with the Catholic Church. For it is the formation which priests receive upon which so largely depends the necessary instruction and spiritual formation of the faithful and of religious.

Moreover, Catholics engaged in missionary work in the same territories as other Christians ought to know, particularly in these times, the problems and the benefits which affect their apostolate because of the ecumenical movement.

11. The manner and order in which Catholic belief is expressed should in no way become an obstacle to dialogue with our brethren. It is, of course, essential that the doctrine be clearly presented in its entirety. Nothing is so foreign to the spirit of ecumenism as a false irenicism which harms the purity of Catholic doctrine and obscures its assured genuine meaning.

At the same time, Catholic belief must be explained more profoundly and precisely, in such a way and in such terms as our separated brethren can also really understand it.

Furthermore, in ecumenical dialogue, Catholic theologians, standing fast by the teaching of the Church yet searching together with separated brethren into the divine mysteries, should do so with love for the truth, with charity, and with humility. When comparing doctrines with one another, they should remember that in Catholic doctrine there exists an order or "hierarchy" of truths, since they vary in their relation to the foundation of the Christian faith. [30] Thus the way will be opened whereby this kind of "fraternal rivalry" will incite all to a deeper realization and a clearer expression of the unfathomable riches of Christ (Cf. Eph. 3, 8).

12. Before the whole world let all Christians confess their faith in God, one and three, in the incarnate Son of God, our Redeemer and Lord. United in their efforts, and with mutual respect, let them bear witness to our com-

---

[30] This sentence was added as a result of the *modi*. It may be the most important change made during the fourth session development of the text.

Appendix One

mon hope which does not play us false. Since cooperation in social matters is so widespread today, all men without exception are called to work together; with much greater reason are all those who believe in God, but most of all, all Christians in that they bear the seal of Christ's name. Cooperation among Christians vividly expresses that bond which already unites them, and it sets in clearer relief the features of Christ the Servant. Such cooperation, which has already begun in many countries, should be developed more and more, particularly in regions where a social and technical evolution is taking place. It should contribute to a just appreciation of the dignity of the human person, to the promotion of the blessings of peace, the application of Gospel principles to social life, and the advancement of the arts and sciences in a truly Christian spirit. It should also be intensified in the use of every possible means to relieve the afflictions of our times, such as famine and natural disasters, illiteracy and poverty, lack of housing, and the unequal distribution of wealth. Through such cooperation, all believers in Christ are able to learn easily how they can understand each other better and esteem each other more, and how the road to the unity of Christians may be made smooth.

Appendix One

Chapter III

CHURCHES AND ECCLESIAL COMMUNITIES
SEPARATED FROM THE ROMAN APOSTOLIC SEE [31]

13. We now turn our attention to the two principal types of division which affect the seamless robe of Christ.

The first divisions occurred in the East, either because of the dispute over the dogmatic formulae of the Councils of Ephesus and Chalcedon, [32] or later by the dissolving [33] of ecclesiastical communion between the Eastern Patriarchates and the Roman See.

---

[31] The title of the 1963 draft read "Christians separated from the Catholic Church". The improved version shows that the chapter treats not of individual Christians as such but Churches and Communities as Communions and that there is not complete separation from the Catholic Church as such.

The Decree is the first church document to use the expression "ecclesial community". *Ecclesialis* was coined in preference to a more exact Latin *ecclesiastica* lest the latter, especially in translations, smack too much of a juridical, external label. *De Ecclesia,* however, uses *"communitates ecclesiasticae"* (n. 15).

[32] The Council of Ephesus (431) defined that there is one person in Jesus Christ, the divine, and that the Blessed Virgin Mary is rightly called "Theotokos"—Mother of God. Those who did not accept this decision later formed the Church to which the name Nestorian is sometimes given. Today its members are found mostly in Iraq, Persia and Syria. The Council of Chalcedon (451) defined the two natures in one person of Our Lord Jesus Christ. Those who did not accept the decision of the Council have organized Churches along national lines—the Coptic, Ethiopian, Syrian, Armenian Churches as well as the Syrian Church of South India.

[33] *"Per solutionem"*. The word was chosen to indicate the gradual estrangement which took place over the centuries between East and West. It is difficult to indicate the exact point at which the separation actually was hardened but historians cite such events as the conflict between Patriarch Michael Cerularius and Cardinal Humbert (11th century), the sack of Constantinople by the Crusaders (13th century) and the rejection of the Council of Florence (15th century).

Appendix One

Still other divisions arose in the West [34] more than four centuries later. These stemmed from the events which are commonly referred to as the Reformation. As a result, many Communions, national or confessional, were separated from the Roman See. Among those in which Catholic traditions and institutions in part continue to exist, the Anglican Communion occupies a special place.

These various divisions, however, differ greatly from one another not only by reason of their origin, place and time, but still more by reason of the nature and seriousness of questions concerning faith and church order. Therefore, without minimizing the differences between the various Christian bodies, and without overlooking the bonds which continue to exist among them in spite of the division, the Council has decided to propose the following considerations for prudent ecumenical action.

I

THE SPECIAL POSITION OF THE EASTERN CHURCHES

14. For many centuries the Churches of the East and of the West went their own ways, though a brotherly communion of faith and sacramental life bound them together. If disagreements in faith and discipline arose among them, the Roman See acted by common consent as moderator. [35]

This Council gladly reminds everyone of one highly significant fact among others: in the East there flourish many particular or local Churches; among them the

---

Here the text refers primarily to the Patriarchate of Constantinople and the other ancient Eastern Patriarchates (Alexandria, Antioch and Jerusalem), all of the Byzantine (Orthodox) tradition.

[34] The papal change was from "in the Western Church itself".
[35] Examples may be found in the appeal to Rome of St. John Chrysostom, in the initiatives taken by the See of Rome and the appeals made to it during the Monophysite controversies of the 5th and 6th centuries. Frequent appeals to Rome were made during the Iconoclast controversy and St. Theodore Studite wrote quite explicitly of the role of the Church of Rome in giving authoritative decisions about disputed points.

Patriarchal Churches hold first place, [36] and of them many glory in taking their origins from the Apostles themselves. [37] Hence, of primary concern and care among the Orientals has been, and still is, the preservation in a communion of faith and charity of those family ties which ought to exist between local Churches, as between sisters.

From their very origins the Church of the East have had a treasury from which the Church of the West has drawn largely for its liturgy, [38] spiritual tradition and jurisprudence. Nor must we underestimate the fact that the basic dogmas of the Christian faith concerning the Trinity and the Word of God made flesh from the Virgin Mary [39] were defined in Ecumenical Councils held in the East. [40] To preserve this faith, these Churches have suffered, and still suffer much.

---

[36] Constantinople, Antioch, Alexandria and Jerusalem are Patriarchal Churches of the *Greek* tradition; joined to this tradition are the autocephalous Churches of Greece and Cyprus. In the *Slavic* tradition are the Patriarchates of Moscow, Serbia (Belgrade) and Bulgaria (Sophia), as well as the autocephalous Churches of Poland, Czechoslovakia and Finland. The Patriarchate of Rumania (Bucharest) and the Church of Georgia are related to both traditions.

[37] Before the papal change the text read: "... many took their origin from. ..." *E.g.,* the Churches of Jerusalem (St. James the Less, cf. Gal. 1, 18-19); Antioch (St. Peter, cf. Gal. 2, 11-14); Cyprus and Athens (St. Paul, cf. Acts 13, 4-12; 17, 16-34). Tradition ascribes Alexandria to St. Mark. Such episcopal sees as Thessalonica and Corinth also trace their origins to St. Paul.

[38] *E.g.,* the Gloria in Excelsis, and Agnus Dei of the Mass of the Roman rite, the observance of certain liturgical feasts such as the Presentation of Our Lord (February 2) and the Birth of Our Lady (Sept. 8) etc.

[39] Before the papal change the text read: "from the Virgin Mother of God."

[40] The first seven Ecumenical Councils were held in the vicinity of Constantinople, with the majority of the participants coming from the surrounding areas: Nicea (325); First Constantinople (381); Ephesus (431); Chalcedon (451); Second Constantinople (553); Third Constantinople (680), and Nicea (787). Delegates of the Bishop of Rome attended all

Appendix One

However, the heritage handed down by the Apostles was received in different forms and ways, so that from the very beginnings of the Church it had a varied development here and there, owing also to diverse mentalities and conditions of life. These reasons, plus external causes as well [41] as the lack of charity and mutual understanding, lay the way open to divisions.

For this reason the Council urges all, but especially those who commit themselves to the work for the restoration of the full communion that is desired [42] between the Eastern Churches and the Catholic Church, to give due consideration to this special feature of the origin and growth of the Churches of the East, [43] and to the character of the relations which obtained between them and the Roman See before the separation, and to form for themselves a correct evaluation of these facts. The careful observation of this will greatly contribute to the dialogue in view.

15. Everyone knows with what love the Eastern Christians celebrate the Sacred Liturgy, especially the eucharistic mystery, source of the Church's life and pledge of future glory. In this mystery the faithful, united with their bishop, have access to God the Father through the Son, the Word made flesh who suffered and was glorified, in the outpouring of the Holy Spirit. And so, made "sharers of the divine nature" (2 Pet. 1, 4), they enter into communion with the most holy Trinity. Hence, through the celebration of the Eucharist of the Lord in each of these Churches, the Church of God is built up and grows in stature (Cf. St. John Chrysostom, *In Ioannem Homelia*

---

the Eastern Councils except First Constantinople, and Pope Vigilius was present for part of Third Constantinople.

[41] *"Etiam"*, a papal change from "... external causes *and* the lack ..."

[42] "That is desired" is a papal addition.

[43] In the text of this Decree, the designation "Churches of the East" (*Ecclesiae Orientis*) refers to all the local Churches, without distinction between those separated from, or united to the Roman Apostolic See. "Eastern Churches" (*Ecclesiae Orientales*), on the other hand, refers only to the separated Churches.

XLVI, PG 59, 260-262), and through concelebration, [44] their communion with one another is made manifest.

In this liturgical worship, the Eastern Christians pay high tribute, in beautiful hymns of praise, to Mary ever Virgin, whom the ecumenical Synod of Ephesus solemnly proclaimed to be the holy Mother of God in order that Christ might be truly and properly acknowledged as Son of God and Son of Man, according to the Scriptures. [45] They also give homage to the saints, among them Fathers of the universal Church. [46]

These Churches, although separated from us, yet possess true sacraments, above all—by apostolic succession —the priesthood and the Eucharist, whereby they are still joined to us in closest intimacy. Therefore some worship in common (*communicatio in sacris*), given suitable circumstances and the approval of church authority, is not merely possible but is encouraged.

Moreover, in the East are to be found the riches of those spiritual traditions which are given expression especially in monastic life. From the glorious times of the holy Fathers, that monastic spirituality flourished in the East which later flowed over into the Western world, and there provided a source from which Latin monastic life took its rise and has often drawn fresh vigor ever since. [47]

---

[44] Concelebration of the Liturgy was common in both the Eastern and Western Churches in the early centuries. It still remains a common practice in the East. Until the promulgation of the Constitution on the Sacred Liturgy (nn. 57-58), its use in the Church of the West was restricted to ordinations to the priesthood and to episcopal consecrations.

[45] In addition to many feast days and special devotions to the Blessed Virgin Mary, every liturgical celebration in the Eastern Churches of the East has joined to it a special commemoration of Our Lady.

[46] *E.g.*, Basil of Cappadocia, Gregory of Nyssa, Gregory of Nazienzus, John Chrysostom, Athanasius of Alexandria and Ephrem, the Syrian.

[47] Both the solitary life of the hermit and the communal monastic life began in the East. St. Pachomius (+348) was the first to lay down regulations for a cenobitic, organized life with a hierarchical structure centered on a liturgical

Appendix One 211

Therefore, it is earnestly recommended that Catholics avail themselves more often [48] of the spiritual riches of the Eastern Fathers which lift up the whole man to the contemplation of divine mysteries.

Everyone should realize that it is of supreme importance to understand, venerate, preserve and foster the rich liturgical and spiritual heritage of the Eastern Churches in order faithfully to preserve the fullness of Christian tradition, and to bring about reconciliation between Eastern and Western Christians.

16. From the earliest times the Churches of the East followed their own disciplines, sanctioned by the holy Fathers, by Synods, and even by Ecumenical Councils. Far from being an obstacle to the Church's unity, such diversity of customs and observances only adds to her comeliness, and contributes greatly to carrying out her mission, as has already been stated. To remove all shadows of doubt, then, this holy Synod solemnly declares that the Churches of the East, while keeping in mind the necessary unity of the whole Church, have the power [49] to govern

---

prayer life. St. Basil (+379) codified Pachomius' rules. The monastic life spread gradually to the West reaching its full development as an organized communal life under St. Benedict (+543), who warmly recognized in his Rule Eastern monastic sources and expressly mentions the Lives of the Fathers and the Rule of St. Basil.

[48] Pope Paul added "more often". Without the change, the text could imply that Catholics have not tapped the Eastern spiritual riches up to now.

[49] The Holy Father changed the phrase from "right and duty" (*ius et officium*) to "power" (*facultatem*). The change weakens the text, even though in Canon Law *facultas* means *ius et officium*. In an almost identical declaration in the approved *Decree on the Catholic Churches of the Eastern Rite,* we find: "(The sacred Council) solemnly declares that the Churches of the East, as much as those of the West, *have a full right and are in duty bound (iure pollere et officio teneri)* to rule themselves, each in accordance with its own established disciplines, since these are all praiseworthy by reason of their venerable antiquity, more harmonious with the character of the faithful and more suited to the promotion of the good of souls" (n. 5).

themselves according to their own disciplines, since these are better suited to the character of their faithful and better adapted to foster the good souls. The perfect observance of this traditional principle—which indeed has not always been observed [50]—is a prerequisite for any restoration of union.

17. What has already been said about legitimate variety we are pleased to apply to differences in theological expressions of doctrine. In the study of revealed truth East and West have used different methods and approaches in understanding and confessing divine things. It is hardly surprising, then, if sometimes one tradition has come nearer to a full appreciation of some aspects of a mystery of revelation than the other, or has expressed them in a better manner. In such cases, these various theological formulations are to be considered often as complementary rather than conflicting. [51] With regard to the authentic theological traditions of the Orientals, we must recognize that they are rooted in an admirable way in Holy Scripture, fostered and given expression in liturgical life, and nourished by the living tradition of the Apostles and by

---

[50] *E.g.*, in formulating disciplinary measures for the Italo-Greeks, for the Ukrainians at the Synod of Zamosch (1720), and for the Syrian Malabarese Christians of India at the Synod of Diamper (1599). This last Synod placed the Malabarese Catholics under the Archbishop of Goa, a Latin. It stripped their Liturgy of much of its Syrian character by imposing Roman discipline: the Roman Rituals and Pontificals in a poor Syrian translation, communion under only one species, Roman vestments; clerical celibacy was also imposed.

[51] "Often" (*non raro*) is a papal change from: "considered *more* as..." *E.g.* the classical misunderstanding between the East and the West in the *Filioque* clause of the Creed. This clause concerns the relation of the Holy Spirit to the other two Persons of the Trinity. The Council of Florence has already declared that the Western position—the Holy Spirit proceeds from the Father "and the Son"—does not conflict with the Eastern position—the Holy Spirit proceeds "through the Son." Theologians maintain that these two explanations complement each other in trying to give further insight into the mystery of the holy Trinity.

Appendix One

the works of the Fathers and spiritual writers of the East; they are directed toward a right ordering of life, indeed, toward a full contemplation of Christian truth.

This sacred Council, while thanking God that many Eastern children of the Catholic Church, who are preserving this heritage and wish to express it more faithfully and completely in their lives, are already living in full communion with their brethren who follow the tradition of the West, [52] declares that this entire heritage of spirituality and liturgy, of discipline and theology, in their various traditions, belongs to the full catholic apostolic character of the Church.

18. After taking all these factors into consideration, this sacred Council confirms what previous Councils and Roman Pontiffs have proclaimed: in order to restore communion and unity or preserve them, one must "impose no burden beyond what is indispensable" (Acts 15, 28). It is the Council's urgent desire that every effort should be made toward the gradual realization of this unity in the various organizations and living activities of the Church, especially by prayer and by fraternal dialogue on points of doctrine and the more pressing pastoral problems of our time. Similarly, to the pastors and faithful of the Catholic

---

[52] The Pope inverted the paragraph structure. The prior text began with the last part, "declares that this entire heritage ... of the Church." In the course of history certain groups from within the separated Eastern Churches resumed ecclesiastical communion with Rome, while retaining their own hierarchical organizations and liturgical traditions: *e.g.,* the Armenian, Chaldean, Coptic, Ethiopian, Melchite, Syrian, Rumanian and Ukrainian Churches. There have also been other groups of Ruthenians, Russians and Greeks. These Churches are widely known as "Uniates", originally a derogative term (Polish) first used in the 16th century by the Orthodox with reference to the Ukrainians who had entered into communion with Rome. The polemical use given to this term makes it advisable not to use it but to refer simply to the Armenian Catholics, Ukrainian Catholics, etc. Of all the Oriental Catholic Churches the Maronite Church in Lebanon, which considers that it never broke full communion with Rome, is the only one which does not have a non-Catholic Community corresponding to it.

Church, it commends close relations with those no longer living in the East but far from their homeland, so that friendly collaboration with them may increase in a spirit of love, without bickering or rivalry.[53] If this task is carried on wholeheartedly, the Council hopes that with the removal of the wall dividing the Eastern and Western Church at last there may be but the one dwelling, firmly established on the cornerstone, Christ Jesus who will make both one (Cf. Council of Florence, Sess. VI [1439], Definition *Laetentur caeli:* Mansi 31, 1026 E).

II

THE SEPARATED CHURCHES AND
ECCLESIAL COMMUNITIES IN THE WEST

19. The Churches and ecclesial Communities which were separated from the Apostolic See of Rome during the grave crisis that began in the West at the end of the Middle Ages [54] or in later times, are bound to the Catholic Church by a specially close relationship as a result of the long span of earlier centuries when the Christian people had lived in ecclesiastical communion.

But since these Churches and ecclesial Communities differ considerably not only from us, but also among themselves, due to their different origins and convictions in doctrine and spiritual life, the task of describing them adequately is extremely difficult; we do not propose to do it here.

Although the ecumenical movement and the desire for peace with the Catholic Church have not yet taken hold

---

[53] This commendation refers especially to the immigrants who for economic and political reasons in the upheavals of Eastern Europe and the Near East, form large communities in Western Europe, and in North and South America. Frequently, these groups face difficulties in church organization, especially the lack of adequate clergy, and experience more than their brethren in the homeland the need of necessary adaptation and *aggiornamento*.

[54] *E.g.,* the Waldensians in the latter half of the 12th century.

Appendix One

everywhere, it is nevertheless our hope that the ecumenical spirit and mutual esteem will gradually increase among all men. [55]

At the same time, however, one should recognize that between these Churches and ecclesial Communities on the one hand, and the Catholic Church on the other, there are very weighty differences not only of an historical, sociological, psychological and cultural character, but especially in the interpretation of revealed truth. To facilitate entering into the ecumenical dialogue in spite of those differences, we wish to set down in what follows some considerations which can, and indeed should serve as a basis and encouragement for such dialogue.

20. Our thoughts are concerned first of all with those Christians who openly confess Jesus Christ as God [56] and Lord and as the only mediator between God and man for the glory of the one God, the Father, the Son and the Holy Spirit. We are indeed aware that there exist considerable differences from the doctrine of the Catholic Church even concerning Christ the Word of God made flesh and the work of redemption, and thus concerning the mystery and ministry of the Church and the role of Mary in the work of salvation. But we rejoice that our separated brethren look to Christ as the source and center of ecclesiastical communion. Their longing for union with Christ impels them ever more to seek unity, and also to bear witness to their faith among the peoples of the earth.

21. A love and reverence—almost a cult—of Holy Scripture leads our brethren to a constant and diligent study of the sacred text. For the Gospel "is the power of God for salvation to everyone who has faith, to the Jew first and then to the Greek" (Rom. 1, 16).

While invoking the Holy Spirit, they seek in these very

---

[55] This short paragraph was not in the 1963 text, but was added to eliminate any naive impression that all non-Catholic Christian Communions are committed to the ecumenical movement.

[56] The addition of "as God" was an accepted *modus* in order to imply that those who deny the divinity of Christ are only Christians in an analogous way.

Scriptures God as He speaks to them in Christ, the One whom the prophets foretold, the Word of God made flesh for us. [57] In the Scriptures they contemplate the life of Christ, as well as the teachings and the actions of the Divine Master for the salvation of men, in particular the mysteries of His death and resurrection.

But when Christians separated from us affirm the divine

---

[57] The final draft submitted to the Council Fathers read: "As the Holy Spirit moves them, they *find* in these very Scriptures God speaking to them in Christ ... (*Spiritu Sancto movente, in ipsis Sacris Scripturis Deum* inveniunt *sibi loquentem in Christo* ...)". But the Holy Father's suggestion was incorporated into the text approved by the Council on November 21: "*Spiritu Sancto invocantes, in ipsis Sacris Scripturis Deum* inquirunt quasi *sibi loquentem in Christo* ..."

The change was made, it seems, in order to avoid a possible implication that the Decree approves of the *direct* individual inspiration of the Holy Spirit (*S. Sancto* movente) in the *private* and *infallible* interpretation of Scriptures (inveniunt). Such a theory would make the teaching authority or magisterium of the Church objectively superfluous. According to Catholic belief, as is stated below in the same n. 21, the Church's "authentic teaching office (*magisterium*) has a special place in expounding and preaching the written Word of God."

The changed text, then, does not mean that when one reads the Bible he in no way finds God therein and is in no way assisted by the Holy Spirit. In the final, approved schema *On Divine Revelation,* we read that "in the Holy Scriptures the heavenly Father lovingly encounters his own sons and converses with them" (Chap. 6).

Furthermore, the original text, in the mind of the Holy Father, could convey a sterile rest with what one has found. But, as he told the official Observers at the second session: "Divine truth, whose depths we must never cease trying to plumb, so as to have a better grasp of it, and to live by it more fully. 'To seek in order to find, and to find in order to seek again'—that saying of St. Augustine concerns *us all;* a true Christian does not know immobilism" (*L'Osservatore Romano,* Oct. 19, 1963). N. 11 of the Decree asks Catholic theologians to search together with separated brethren into the divine mysteries with a "fraternal rivalry" which will "incite all to a deeper realization and a clearer expression of the infathomable riches of Christ."

Appendix One

authority of the Sacred Books, they think differently from us—different ones in different ways—about the relationship between the Scriptures and the Church. For in the Church, according to Catholic belief, its authentic teaching office has a special place in expounding and preaching the written Word of God.

Nevertheless, in the dialogue itself, the Sacred Word is a precious instrument in the mighty hand of God for attaining to that unity which the Savior holds out to all men. [58]

22. By the sacrament of baptism, whenever it is properly conferred in the way the Lord determined and received with the proper dispositions of soul, man becomes truly incorporated into the crucified and glorified Christ and is reborn to a sharing of the divine life, as the Apostle says: "For you were buried together with Him in baptism, and in Him also rose again through faith in the working of God who raised Him from the dead" (Col. 2, 12; cf. Rom. 6, 4).

Baptism, therefore, constitutes the sacramental bond of unity existing among all who through it [59] are reborn. But baptism, of itself, is only a beginning, a point of departure, for it is wholly directed toward the acquiring of fullness of life in Christ. Baptism is thus ordained toward a complete profession of faith, a complete incorporation into the system of salvation such as Christ Himself willed it to be, and finally, toward a complete integration into eucharistic communion.

Although the ecclesial Communities separated from us lack the fullness of unity with us which flows from baptism, and although we believe they have not preserved the proper reality of the eucharistic mystery in its fullness, [60]

---

[58] The schema *On Divine Revelation* commends to Christian scholars collaboration wherever possible in a common translation of the Bible.

[59] *I.e.*, through the sacramental bond.

[60] The nineteenth and last of the papal changes. Formerly: "the reality of the eucharistic Mystery in its fullness". The change is in the Latin rather than the meaning. Formerly: *"plenam realitatem* Mysterii eucharistici"; the final text: *"genuinam atque integram substantiam* Mysterii eucharistici".

especially because of the absence of the sacrament of Orders, nevertheless when they commemorate the Lord's death and resurrection in the Holy Supper, they profess that it signifies life in communion with Christ, and await His coming in glory. For these reasons, the doctrine about the Lord's Supper, about the other sacraments, worship, and ministry in the Church, should form subjects of dialogue.

23. The Christian way of life of these brethren is nourished by faith in Christ. It is strengthened by the grace of baptism and the hearing of the Word of God. This way of life expresses itself in private prayer, in meditation of the Scriptures, in the life of a Christian family, and in the worship of the community gathered together to praise God. Furthermore, their worship sometimes displays notable features of a liturgy once shared in common.

The faith by which they believe in Christ bears fruit in praise and thanksgiving for the benefits received from the hands of God. Joined to it is a lively sense of justice and a true charity toward others. This active faith has been responsible for many organizations for the relief of spiritual and material distress, the furtherance of education of youth, the improvement of social conditions of life, and the promotion of peace throughout the world.

And if in moral matters there are many Christians who do not always understand the Gospel in the same way as Catholics, and do not admit the same solutions for the more difficult problems of modern society, they nevertheless want to cling to Christ's word as the source of Christian virtue and to obey the command of the Apostle: "Whatever you do in word or in work, do all in the name of the Lord Jesus, giving thanks to God the Father through Him" (Col. 3, 17). Hence, the ecumenical dialogue could start with the moral application of the Gospel.

24. Now, after this brief exposition of the conditions under which ecumenical activity may be practiced, and of the principles by which it is to be guided, we confidently look to the future. This sacred Council urges the faithful to abstain from any frivolousness or imprudent zeal, for these can cause harm to true progress toward unity. Their ecumenical activity cannot be other than fully and

sincerely catholic, that is, loyal to the truth we have received from the Apostles and the Fathers, and in harmony with the faith which the Catholic Church has always professed, and at the same time tending toward that fullness in which Our Lord wants His Body to grow in the course of time.

This sacred Council firmly hopes that the initiatives of the sons of the Catholic Church joined with those of the separated brethren will go forward, without obstructing the ways of divine Providence, and without prejudging the future inspirations of the Holy Spirit. Further, this Council declares that it realizes that this holy objective—the reconciliation of all Christians in the unity of the one and only Church of Christ—transcends human powers and gifts. It therefore places its hope entirely in the prayer of Christ for the Church, in the love of the Father for us, and in the power of the Holy Spirit. "And hope does not disappoint, because God's love has been poured forth in our hearts through the Holy Spirit who has been given to us" (Rom. 5, 5).

The entire text and all the individual elements which have been set forth in this Decree have pleased the Fathers. And by the Apostolic power conferred on Us by Christ, We, together with the Venerable Fathers, in the Holy Spirit, approve, decree and enact them; and We order that what has been thus enacted in Council be promulgated, to the glory of God.

Rome, at St. Peter's, November 21, 1964.

I, PAUL, Bishop of the Catholic Church

There follow the signatures of the Fathers.

Appendix Two

BISHOPS' COMMISSION FOR ECUMENICAL AFFAIRS

**Interim Guidelines
for Prayer in Common
and Communicatio
in Sacris**

The Decree of Ecumenism of the Second Vatican Council speaks of change of heart, holiness of life, and prayer for unity as the "soul" of the ecumenical movement (Ch. II, 8). The Bishops' Commission for Ecumenical Affairs, while taking steps to engage in dialogue and common action with the representatives of other Churches, realizes that the question of prayer in common and *communicatio in sacris* is the most pressing of its tasks.

In presenting recommendations for common worship and prayer the Bishops' Commission recognizes that it is the local bishop who has the authority to make dispositions in this matter. The Secretariat for the Promotion of Christian Unity will, in time, present a directory for the practice of ecumenism which will be applicable throughout the universal Church. In the absence of such a directory and in the absence of legislation enacted by the Episcopal Conference of the United States, the Bishops' Commission for Ecumenical Affairs offers the following recommendations for the interim to the bishops of the United States.

I. *Diocesan Ecumenical Commissions*
   In guiding the course of ecumenism within their own

dioceses, especially in presenting guidelines for prayer and *communicatio in sacris,* it is highly recommended that local bishops establish diocesan ecumenical commissions. Among the members of these commissions it would be desirable to include priests, religious and members of the laity who, by reason of their expert knowledge, can contribute to the work of the commissions, and who are also representative of the local churches. As the involvement of Catholics in dialogue, in joint action, and in prayer with other Christians increases such commissions could be of inestimable value to the local bishops.

II. *Prayer in Common between Catholics and Christians of Other Churches*
Principles governing prayer in common, drawn from the Decree on Ecumenism, Chapter II, 8:

"This change of heart and holiness of life, along with public and private prayer for the unity of Christians, should be regarded as the soul of the whole ecumenical movement, and merits the name, 'spiritual ecumenism.'

"It is a recognized custom for Catholics to meet for frequent recourse to that prayer for the unity of the Church with which the Saviour Himself on the eve of His death so fervently appealed to His Father: 'That they may all be one.' (Jn. 17, 20)

"In certain circumstances, such as in prayer services 'for unity' and during ecumenical gatherings, it is allowable, indeed desirable that Catholics should join in prayer with their separated brethren. Such prayers in common are certainly a very effective means of petitioning for the grace of unity, and they are a genuine expression of the ties which still bind Catholics to their separated brethren. 'For where two or three are gathered together in my name, there am I in the midst of them.' " (Mt. 18, 20)

In accordance with Section 8 of the Decree on Ecumenism the participation of Catholics with other Christians in services which are not part of the official liturgies of any communion, if these services are devoted to the cause of Christian unity, is highly desirable. Such services could fittingly be called "Ecumenical Services." Participation of Catholics in such services, whether they are held for the sake of promoting Christian unity in accordance with the Decree or, in the spirit of the Decree, for some other purpose, e.g., for peace, in time of public need, mourning, thanksgiving, etc., remains under the guidance of the local bishop.

The place chosen for the conduct of these ecumenical services should provide a worthy setting which is acceptable to all the participants and which, according to the prudent decision of the local bishop, is considered suitable.

With the approval of the local bishop, priests are to be encouraged to take an active part in the conduct of services, e.g. by reading Scripture lessons, preaching homilies, offering prayers and giving blessings.

The vesture to be worn at such services is also to be determined by the local bishop. In some circumstances ordinary civil attire may be the only appropriate form of dress for the participating priest. In other circumstances, since it is in accordance with Catholic usage even in the conduct of non-liturgical services, the use of the cassock and surplice may be considered. Another form of dress which is neither liturgical nor merely civil, namely, the use of the ferraiuola, may also be desirable on certain occasions. The value of some kind of "sacred" vesture is not to be underestimated in creating the right atmosphere for prayer in common. In reaching decisions concerning ecclesiastical vesture on these occasions it is highly recommended that there be consultation with the clergy of the other church bodies which are to participate in such services.

On occasion members of the Catholic laity may also be invited to take an active part in ecumenical services. They may, for example, be called upon to read the Scripture lessons. Under the guidance of the local bishop, who may well wish to consult his ecumenical commission regarding the qualifications of the laity invited to take these leading roles, such participation on the part of laymen has much to recommend it. The acceptance of such a policy could become one more manifestation of the Church's doctrine on the laity as found in the Constitution on the Church.

In preparing for and conducting these ecumenical serv-

Appendix Two

ices the principle of "reciprocity" should be kept in mind: to accept an invitation may often seem to entail an obligation to extend a similar invitation and to proffer an invitation may imply a readiness to receive one; one should not, therefore, accept an invitation if, according to Catholic norms, one cannot proffer a similar invitation.

All such joint services of prayer should be carefully prepared in accordance with the principle of "collaboration." The leaders of the participating groups should, after careful consideration, agree on the format of the services and on the choice of themes, Scripture readings and hymns. Prayers and hymns and homilies which may be unacceptable either to Catholics or to other Christians are to be avoided.

These ecumenical services, it is hoped, will complement the programs of prayer for unity which continue in our churches.

III. *Communicatio in Sacris*
Principles governing communicatio in sacris:

"Yet worship in common (*communicatio in sacris*) is not to be considered as a means to be used indiscriminately for the restoration of unity among Christians. There are two main principles upon which the practice of such common worship depends: first, that of the unity of the Church which ought to be expressed; and second, that of the sharing in means of grace. The expression of unity for the most part forbids common worship. Grace to be obtained sometimes commends it. The concrete course to be adopted, when due regard has been given to all the circumstances of time, place and persons, is left to the prudent decision of the local episcopal authority, unless the Bishops' Conference according to its own statutes, or the Holy See, has determined otherwise." — *The Decree on Ecumenism,* Chapter II, 8.

1) *Participation of Christians of Other Churches in the Liturgy of the Catholic Church*

Christians of other communions should be made welcome in attending Catholic liturgical celebrations. It is recommended, however, that great care be taken in issuing general invitations. The sensibilities of other ecclesial Communities on proselytizing should also be respected in extending such invitations. It would be well to consult with leaders of other churches in formulating them. It is also worthy of note that general invitations may evoke invitations of a similar nature from other church bodies.

Baptism and Confirmation: From the nature of the office of sponsor, Christians of other communions may not be invited to act as sponsors at baptism and confirmation. The sponsor does not act only as a friend of the family nor only as one who promises to provide for the Christian education of the person to be baptized or confirmed, but also as a representative of the community of the Catholic faithful. As a representative of the community the sponsor stands as guarantor of the faith of the candidate he presents. A Christian not of our communion cannot be asked to assume this role.

Holy Eucharist: The Eucharist is the sign and at the same time is the cause of the unity of the Church. The restoration of Eucharistic Communion is the goal of our ecumenical effort. At the present time, however, except in particular cases of members of the Eastern Orthodox Church intercommunion with Christians of other denominations should not be permitted (cf. *Decree on the Catholic Churches of the Eastern Rite,* 26-29; *Decree on Ecumenism,* Ch. III, 15). Our separation is most keenly felt at the Table of the Lord, and the sense of sorrow awakened by a deepening realization of the meaning of this tragic separation should in itself provide a powerful stimulus to ecumenical concern among our people.

When, however, Christians of other communions are present at the Sacrifice of the Mass in our churches they may be invited to join, if they so desire, in the dialogue, in the recitation of prayers and in the singing of hymns. Christians of other Churches may not, however, be invited to assume roles of leadership within the assembly, e.g., that of lector.

One of the great achievements of the Second Vatican Council is the Constitution on the Sacred Liturgy, and one of the most important emphases found in this document is that concerning the homily of the Mass (cf. Article 52).

Appendix Two

The homily is an integral part of the liturgy and normally will be given by the celebrating bishop or priest. In breaking the bread of doctrine the homilist speaks on behalf of the local bishop and, in a sense, on behalf of the entire episcopal college. A clergyman of another communion cannot be asked to accept such a role.

Following the example of the liturgy of Good Friday it is recommended that public prayers for Christians of other communions be admitted within the liturgical celebrations. It is recommended, for example, that, when the presiding priest judges it appropriate, the names and intentions of Christians of other communions be included within the *Prayer of the Faithful*.

Holy Orders: In the conferral of Holy Orders Christians of other communions must not be invited to take active roles. For reasons of friendship or courtesy, however, they may be invited to be present.

Matrimony: Christians of other Churches may be admitted as witnesses and attendants at the celebration of matrimony within the Catholic Church.

For the celebration of marriage between Catholics and Christians of other communions it is highly recommended that sacred rites be used according to the *Collectio Rituum* of 1964 and that the officiating priest be vested in cassock, surplice and stole.

Clergymen of other communions should not be invited to take an active role in the ceremony.

Funerals: It is recommended that, when requested by the family of the deceased, priests be permitted to conduct funeral services and to lead prayers at wakes for those not of our Church. It is for the local bishop to determine what rites are to be used on these occasions. In such circumstances burial in Catholic cemeteries may be permitted to those not of our communion, especially to spouses and relatives of Catholics. On the occasion of burials in Catholic cemeteries of those who were not Catholics it is also recommended that clergymen of other Churches be permitted to conduct graveside services.

Sacramentals: The sacramentals of the Church may be given to those not of our communion who desire to receive them.

2) *Participation of Catholics in the Official Worship of Other Churches*

The Decree on Ecumenism does envisage *communicatio in sacris,* i.e., the participation of Catholics, under the supervision of the local bishop, in the liturgy of other communions (cf. Chapter II, 8). Catholics may attend official services of other Churches which have special civic or social significance especially weddings and funerals. It should be remembered, however, that the Decree on Ecumenism makes repeated recommendations for caution and states that "worship in common (*communicatio in sacris*) is not to be considered as a means to be used indiscriminately to restore unity among Christians."

Baptism and Confirmation: Catholics may not act as sponsors at the conferral of baptism or confirmation in Churches not of our communion; for reasons of friendship or courtesy, however, they may be present at these ceremonies.

Holy Eucharist: Catholics, accepting Eucharistic separation from their brothers of other Churches in a penitential spirit and bearing in mind the principles mentioned above concerning the restoration of Eucharistic Communion, may not participate in the Eucharistic celebrations of other Churches. For reasons of friendship or courtesy, however, they may be present at these services.

Catholic priests, remembering the Church's view regarding the homily at Holy Mass, may not accept invitations to preach during the Eucharistic celebrations of other Churches.

Holy Orders: Catholics may not take an active role in the ordination ceremonies of other Churches. Invitations to be present for these ceremonies, with the approval of the local bishop, may be accepted for reasons of friendship or courtesy.

Matrimony: Catholics, under the guidance of the local bishop, may be permitted to serve as witnesses at marriages which are celebrated in churches of other communions.

Catholics should be mindful that attendance at services in other churches is not a substitution for, nor fulfillment of, their obligation to participate in the celebration of Holy Mass on Sundays, and days of precept.

Appendix Two

IV. *Communicatio in Sacris and Relations with the Eastern Orthodox Church*

With regard to *communicatio in sacris* with the Eastern Orthodox Church, the Decree on Ecumenism, Ch. III, 15, reads: "These Churches, although separated from us, yet possess true sacraments, above all—by apostolic succession—the priesthood and the Eucharist, whereby they are still joined to us in closest intimacy. Therefore some worship in common (*communicatio in sacris*), given suitable circumstances and the approval of church authority, is not merely possible but is encouraged."

The Decree on the Catholic Churches of the Eastern Rite (cf. articles 26-27) established a new "conciliatory policy with regard to *communicatio in sacris* with the brethren of the separated Eastern Churches." Article 29 places the supervision of this policy in the care and control of local bishops. It encourages combined consultation on the part of these bishops and, if need be, consultation with the bishops of the Orthodox Churches.

The fulfillment of these articles is a matter of the utmost delicacy and the members of the Bishops' Commission for Ecumenical Affairs agree that there should be consultation concerning this matter with the ecclesiastical authorities of the Orthodox Churches. A subcommission has been established by the Bishops' Commission under the chairmanship of the Most Reverend Bernard J. Flanagan, Bishop of Worcester, and it will be among the tasks of this subcommission to explore, together with representatives appointed by the bishops of the Orthodox Church, this difficult question of *communicatio in sacris*.

V. Throughout this statement of recommendations, it should be noted, frequent reference has been made to the role of the local bishop in guiding the practice of ecumenism within his diocese. This emphasis is, the members of the Bishops' Commission for Ecumenical Affairs are convinced, in accord not only with the Decree on Ecumenism but also with the spirit of the Constitution on the Church (Chapter III, 25-27) and the Constitution on the Sacred Liturgy. (Chapter I, 22, 41-42)

The unity of the Church is a "sacred mystery" and

"the highest exemplar and source of this mystery is the unity, in the Trinity of Persons, of one God, the Father and the Son in the Holy Spirit." (*Decree on Ecumenism,* Ch. I, 2). In offering these recommendations the members of the Bishops' Commission for Ecumenical Affairs are guided by this vision of unity as a "mystery" and consequently share a conviction that Catholic participation in ecumenism must move beyond dialogue, programs of education, and cooperation in social matters to "spiritual ecumenism."

The renewal of the Church, and especially of the sacred liturgy, which is the concern of the Second Vatican Council, will, it is hoped, prepare our people for participation in the ecumenical movement and for prayer in common with other Christians. It is confidently expected that the annual observance of the Week of Prayer for Christian Unity, together with other programs of prayer, following the spirit of the renewed liturgy, will be extended and intensified in our churches. Our confidence in the efficacy of such prayer is based on the words of Our Lord, "For where two or three are gathered together in my name, there am I in the midst of them." (Mt. 18, 20)

At the first Eucharist, in the moments which preceded His passion and death, the Lord addressed Himself to His Father in His priestly prayer for unity. This prayer of Christ has become the prayer of the Church not only when these words are read and listened to, but above all, when the Church celebrates the Eucharist. While the Pilgrim Church awaits the return of the risen Christ and the final consummation of all things in Him, the Eucharist remains the great sign and cause of the mysterious unity of the Church, and it is hoped that the Holy Sacrifice will be offered frequently for the cause of Christian unity.

In all of these endeavors which we describe as ecumenical—in dialogue, in giving common witness to the world, and in common prayer—we find the assurance we seek and require in the words of Christ's prayer: "that they all may be one; even as thou, Father, art in me, and I in thee, that they also may be one in us, so that the world may believe that thou hast sent me." (Jn. 17, 21)

Appendix Three

DIRECTORY FOR THE APPLICATION OF THE DECISIONS OF THE SECOND ECUMENICAL COUNCIL OF THE VATICAN CONCERNING ECUMENICAL MATTERS
PART ONE

Introduction

1. "The concern for restoring unity involves the whole Church, faithful and clergy alike. It extends to everyone, according to the talent of each...." (Decree on Ecumenism *Restoration of Unity* n. 5) The Ecumenical Directory is being published to encourage and guide this concern for unity, so that what was promulgated in this field by the decrees of the Second Vatican Council may be better put into practice throughout the Catholic Church. This must be done in a manner faithful to the mind of the Church. "Ecumenical activity cannot be other than fully and sincerely Catholic, that is, loyal to the truth we have received from the Apostles and the Fathers, and in harmony with the faith which the Catholic Church has always professed, and at the same time tending towards that fullness in which Our Lord wants His Body to grow in the course of time." (Decree on Ecumenism n. 24)
2. The Decree on Ecumenism insists in a number of places that it is the business of the Apostolic See and the bishops, with due regard for the rights of Patriarchs and their synods, to decide ecumenical policy after taking all circumstances into account (cf. n. 4, n. 8, n. 9). Proper care must be taken in these matters so that the ecumenical movement itself is not impeded and the faithful do not suffer harm due to the danger of false irenicism or indifferentism. This is a pastoral care, which will be the

more effective as the faithful become more solidly and fully instructed in the teaching and authentic tradition both of the Catholic Church and of the Churches and communities separated from her. Against the dangers and harm that may arise, this accurate knowledge of teachings and traditions will be a better safeguard than the kind of ignorance which is often reinforced by false fear: fear of those adjustments which, in accordance with the spirit and decisions of the Second Vatican Council, are necessary to any genuine renewal of the Church.

Ecumenical movement begins with the renewal by which the Church expresses more fully and perfectly the truth and holiness which comes from Christ Our Lord. Everyone of the faithful, as a member of the Church, should share in this renewal in truth and charity so as to grow in faith, hope and charity and bear witness in the Church to God and our Saviour, Jesus Christ, by his own Christian life.

Since this movement has been set on foot by the Holy Spirit, what follows here is put forward with the intention and in a manner to be of service to the bishops in putting into effect the Decree on Ecumenism, "without obstructing the ways of divine Providence, and without prejudging the future inspirations of the Holy Spirit". (Decree on Ecumenism n. 24)

I. THE SETTING UP OF ECUMENICAL COMMISSIONS

(A) *The Diocesan Commission*

3. It seems very suitable to set up a council, commission or secretariat, either for several dioceses grouped together or, where circumstances call for it, in each diocese, charged to promote ecumenical activity by the Episcopal Conference or of the local Ordinary. In those dioceses which cannot have their own commission there should at least be one person delegated by the bishop for these duties.

4. This commission should cooperate with such ecu-

Appendix Three

menical institutions or enterprises as already exist or may be launched, making use of their help where occasion offers. It should also be prompt to help other diocesan work and individual initiative, by exchanging information and ideas with those concerned, to mutual advantage. This should all be done in harmony with the principles and general norms already existing in this matter.

5. To make clearer and foster better the concern for unity which belongs to the Church as a whole, where possible the commission should include among its members not only diocesan clergy but also religious of both sexes and suitable laymen and women.

6. Besides the other functions assigned to it, the commission should:
   (a) put into practice, according to local situations, the decisions of Vatican II on ecumenical affairs;
   (b) foster spiritual ecumenism according to the principles laid down in the Decree on Ecumenism (see especially n. 8) about public and private prayer for the unity of Christians;
   (c) promote friendliness, cooperation and charity between Catholics and their brothers who are not in their communion;
   (d) initiate and guide dialogue with them, bearing in mind the adaptation to be made to the types of participants according to nn. 9 and 11 of the Decree on Ecumenism;
   (e) promote in common with our separated brethren joint witness to the Christian faith as well as cooperation in such areas as, e.g., in education, morality, social and cultural matters, learning and the arts (cf. Decree on Ecumenism n. 12, also the Decree *Ad Gentes* n. 12);
   (f) appoint experts to undertake discussions and consultations with the other Churches and communities in the diocese;
   (g) offer help and encouragement for the instruction and education to be given to clergy and laity and for conducting one's life in an ecumenical spirit, with special emphasis being given to preparing seminary students, to preaching, catechetics and

other kinds of teaching dealt with in the Decree on Ecumenism n. 10;
- (h) maintain relations with the territorial ecumenical commission, (see below) adapting the latter's advice and recommendations to local diocesan conditions, and, in addition, when circumstances suggest, useful information should be sent to the Secretariat for Promoting Christian Unity in Rome, which can help the latter in carrying on its own work.

(B) *The Territorial Commission*

7. Each National Episcopal Conference* and also those which according to circumstances, include more than one nation should establish in accordance with their own statutes a commission of bishops for ecumenical affairs assisted by experts. This commission should have a mandate from the Episcopal Conference of the territory to give guidance in ecumenical affairs and determine concrete ways of acting in accordance with the Decree on Ecumenism and with other ordinances and legitimate customs, taking account of the time, place and persons they are concerned with but also of the good of the universal Church. If possible, this commission should be assisted by a permanent secretariat.

8. The functions of this commission will include all those listed under n. 6 insofar as they enter into the competence of a territorial Episcopal Conference. In addition let it carry out other tasks, of which some examples are given here:
- (a) putting into practice the rules and instructions issued by the Apostolic See in these matters;
- (b) giving advice and assistance to the bishops who are setting up an ecumenical commission in their own dioceses;

---

* References in this directory to "Episcopal Conference" also apply, *servatis de jure servandis* with due consideration for the requirements of law, to the patriarchal synods and synods of major archbishops in the Catholic Eastern Churches.

Appendix Three

- (c) giving spiritual and material help where possible to both existing ecumenical institutions and to ecumenical enterprises to be promoted either in the field of instruction and research or in that of pastoral care and the promotion of Christian life according to the principles set out in the Decree on Ecumenism nn. 9 to 11;
- (d) establishing dialogue and consultation with the leaders and with ecumenical councils of the other Churches and communities which exist on a national or territorial (as distinct from diocesan) scale;
- (e) appointing of those experts who, by a public mandate of the Church are designated for the conversations and consultations with experts of the communities referred to under (d) above;
- (f) setting up, if need be, a special subcommission for ecumenical relations with the Easterns;
- (g) maintaining relations between the territorial hierarchy and the Holy See.

II. THE VALIDITY OF BAPTISM CONFERRED BY MINISTERS OF CHURCHES AND ECCLESIAL COMMUNITIES SEPARATED FROM US

9. The Church's practice in this matter is governed by two principles: that baptism is necessary for salvation, and that it can be conferred only once.

10. The ecumenical importance of baptism is clear from documents of the Second Vatican Council: "He Himself (Jesus Christ) in explicit terms affirmed the necessity of faith and baptism (cf. Mk. 16:16, Jn. 3:5), and thereby affirmed also the necessity of the Church, for through baptism as through a door men enter the Church." (Dogm. Const. on the Church n. 14)

"The Church recognizes that in many ways she is linked with those who, being baptised, are honoured with the name of Christian, though they do not profess the faith in its entirety or do not preserve unity of communion with the successor of Peter." (Ibid. n. 15)

"For men who believe in Christ and have been properly baptised are brought into a certain, though imperfect, communion with the Catholic Church... all who have been justified by faith in baptism are incorporated into Christ; they therefore have a right to be called Christians, and with good reason are accepted as brothers by the children of the Catholic Church." (Decree on Ecumenism n. 3)

"On the other hand, Catholics must gladly acknowledge and esteem the truly Christian endowments from our common heritage which are to be found among our separated brethren." (Ibid. n. 4)

11. Baptism is, then, the sacramental bond of unity, indeed the foundation of communion among all Christians. Hence its dignity and the manner of administering it are matters of great importance to all Christ's disciples. Yet a just evaluation of the sacrament and the mutual recognition of each other's baptisms by different communities is sometimes hindered because of a reasonable doubt about the baptism conferred in some particular case. To avoid difficulties which may arise when some Christian separated from us, led by the grace of the Holy Spirit and by his conscience, seeks full communion with the Catholic Church, the following guiding principles are put forward.

12. There can be no doubt cast upon the validity of baptism as conferred among separated Eastern Christians.* It is enough therefore to establish the fact that baptism was administered. Since in the Eastern Churches the sacrament of confirmation (chrism) is always lawfully administered by the priest at the same time as baptism, it often happens that no mention is made of the confirmation in the canonical testimony of baptism. This does not give grounds for doubting that the sacrament was conferred.

13. In respect of other Christians a doubt can sometimes arise:

(a) Concerning *matter and form*. Baptism by immer-

---

* With regard to all Christians, consideration should be given to the danger of invalidity when baptism is administered by sprinkling, especially of several people at once.

Appendix Three

sion, pouring or sprinkling, together with the Trinitarian formula is of itself valid. (Cf. CIC canon 758) Therefore if the rituals and liturgical books or established customs of a Church or community prescribe one of these ways of baptising, doubt can only arise if it happens that the minister does not observe the regulations of his own community or Church. What is necessary and sufficient, therefore, is evidence that the minister of baptism was faithful to the norms of his own community or Church.

For this purpose generally one should obtain a written baptismal certificate with the name of the minister. In many cases the other community may be asked to cooperate in establishing whether or not, in general or in a particular case, a minister is to be considered as having baptised according to the approved ritual.

(b) Concerning *faith and intention*. Because some consider that insufficiency of faith or intention in the minister can create a doubt about baptism, these points should be noted:
—The minister's insufficient faith never of itself makes baptism invalid.
—Sufficient intention in a baptising minister is to be presumed unless there is serious ground for doubting that he intends to do what Christians do. (Cf. Response of the Holy Office, Jan. 30, 1833: "It is sufficient to do what Christians do"; Sacred Congregation of the Council. Decrees approved by Pius V, June 19, 1570, cited by the Provincial Council of Evreux, France, 1576.)

(c) Concerning the *application of the matter*. Where doubt arises about the application of the matter, both reverence for the sacrament and respect for the ecclesial nature of the other communities demand that a serious investigation of the community's practice and of the circumstances of the particular baptism be made before any judgement is passed on the validity of a baptism by reason of its manner of administration (cf. CIC canon 73781).

14. Indiscriminate conditional baptism of all who desire full communion with the Catholic Church cannot be approved. The sacrament of baptism cannot be repeated (cf. Code of Canon Law, can. 732,1) and therefore to baptise again conditionally is not allowed unless there is prudent doubt of the fact, or of the validity, of a baptism already administered. (Cf. Council of Trent, S.VII, can. 4; Code of Canon Law, can. 732,2.)

15. If after serious investigation as to whether the baptism was properly administered, a reasonable doubt persists, and it is necessary to baptise conditionally, the minister should maintain proper regard for the doctrine that baptism is unique by (a) suitably explaining both why he is in this case baptising conditionally and what is the significance of the rite of conditional baptism; (b) carrying out the rite according to the private form (cf. CIC can. 737,52).

16. The whole question of the theology and practice of baptism should be brought up in dialogue between the Catholic Church and the other separated Churches or communities. It is recommended that ecumenical commissions should hold such discussions with Churches or Councils of Churches in various regions and, where convenient, come to a common agreement in this matter.

17. Out of reverence for the sacrament of initiation which the Lord instituted for the New Covenant, and in order to clarify what is necessary for its proper administration, it is most desirable that dialogue with our separated brethren be not restricted to the sole question of what elements are absolutely necessary for valid baptism. Attention should also be given to the fullness of the sacramental sign and of the reality signified (or *"res sacramenti"*), as these emerge from the New Testament; this will make it easier for Churches to reach an agreement on mutual recognition of baptism.

18. Placing a proper value on the baptism conferred by ministers of the Churches and ecclesial communities separated from us has ecumenical importance; baptism is thereby really revealed as the "sacramental bond of unity

binding all who are regenerated by it". (Decree on Ecumenism n. 22; Dogm. Const. on the Church n. 15.)*
Therefore it is to be hoped that all Christians will grow continually more reverent and faithful in their regard for what the Lord instituted concerning its celebration.

19. The Decree on Ecumenism makes clear that the brethren born and baptised outside the visible communion of the Catholic Church should be carefully distinguished from those who, though baptised in the Catholic Church, have knowingly and publicly abjured her faith. According to the Decree (n. 3) "one cannot charge with the sin of separation those who at present are born into these communities and in them are brought up in the faith of Christ." Hence, in the absence of such blame, if they freely wish to embrace the Catholic faith, they have no need to be absolved from excommunication, but after making profession of their faith according to the regulations set down by the Ordinary of the place they should be admitted to the full communion of the Catholic Church. What canon 2314 prescribes is only applicable to those who, after culpably giving up the Catholic faith or communion, repent and ask to be reconciled with mother Church.

20. What has just been said of absolution from censures obviously applies for the same reason to the abjuring of heresy.

III. FOSTERING SPIRITUAL ECUMENISM IN THE CATHOLIC CHURCH

21. "This change of heart and holiness of life, along with public and private prayer for the unity of Christians, should be regarded as the soul of the whole ecumenical movement, and merits the name, 'spiritual ecumenism'." (Decree on Ecumenism n. 8)

---

* Cf. also the Report of the Mixed Commission between the Roman Catholic Church and the World Council of Churches (Oss. Rom. Feb. 20, 1966, p. 7); The Report of the Fourth International Conference on "Faith and Order", Montreal 1963 nn. 111, 113, and 154.

In these few words the Decree defines spiritual ecumenism and stresses its importance in order that Christians may, both in prayer and in the celebration of the Eucharist and indeed in their entire daily life, carefully keep in view the aim of unity. Every Christian, even though he does not live among separated brethren, always and everywhere has his part in this ecumenical movement, through restoring the whole Christian life according to the spirit of the Gospel, as has been taught by the Second Vatican Council—leaving out nothing of the common Christian heritage. (Cf. Decree on Ecumenism n. 6; Decree on the Church's Missionary Activity, n. 36)

22. It is fitting that prayers for unity be offered regularly at fixed times, v.g.:

   (a) the week from January 18-25, called the Week of Prayer for Christian Unity, in which often many Churches and communities join in praying to God for unity;
   (b) the days from the Ascension to Pentecost, which commemorate the community at Jerusalem waiting and praying for the coming of the Holy Spirit to confirm them in unity and universal mission.

Additional examples are:

   (a) the days about the Epiphany, when we commemorate the manifestation of Christ in the world and the link connecting the Church's function with unity;
   (b) Maundy Thursday, when we commemorate the institution of the Eucharist, the sacrament of unity, and Christ our Saviour's prayer in the supper room for the Church and for her unity;
   (c) Good Friday, or the Feast of the Exaltation of the Holy Cross, when we commemorate the mystery of the Holy Cross—by which the scattered sons of God are reunited;
   (d) Easter, when all Christians share with one another the joy of Our Lord's Resurrection;
   (e) on the occasion of meetings or other important events of ecumenical origin or specially likely to serve ecumenical purposes.

23. "It is a recognized custom for Catholics to meet for

Appendix Three

frequent recourse to prayer for the unity of the Church with which the Saviour Himself on the eve of His death so fervently appealed to His Father 'That they may all be one'." (Decree on Ecumenism n. 8) Therefore, let all pray for unity in a way consonant with Christ's prayer at the Last Supper: that all Christians may achieve "that fullness of unity which Jesus Christ wishes". (Ibid. n. 4)

24. Pastors should see to it that, as circumstances of places and persons suggest, gatherings of Catholic faithful are arranged to pray for unity; and since the Holy Eucharist is that marvellous sacrament "by which the unity of the Church is signified and brought about", (Decree on Ecumenism n. 2) it is very valuable to remind the faithful of its importance; public prayers for Christian unity should be encouraged at Mass (v.g. during the Prayer of the Faithful or in the litanies called "Ecteniae") as well as the celebration of votive masses for Christian unity. Further those Rites which have special liturgical prayers of petition, like the "Litia" and "Moleben" and similar supplications can properly use them to pray for unity.

IV. SHARING OF SPIRITUAL ACTIVITY AND RESOURCES WITH OUR SEPARATED BRETHREN

A. *Introduction*

25. "Fraternal charity in the relations of daily life is not enough to foster the restoration of unity among all Christians. It is right and proper that there should also be allowed a certain *'communicatio in spiritualibus'*—i.e., that Christians should be able to share that spiritual heritage they have in common, in a manner and to a degree permissible and appropriate in their present divided state. From those elements and endowments which together go to build up and give life to the Church herself, some, even very many, can exist outside the visible boundaries of the Catholic Church" (Decree on Ecumenism n. 3). These elements "which come from Christ and lead to Him rightly belong to the one Church of Christ" (Ibid.); they can contribute appropriately to our petitioning for the

grace of unity; they can manifest and strengthen the bonds which still bind Catholics to their separated brethren.

26. But these spiritual endowments are found in different ways in the several Christian communities, and sharing in spiritual activity and resources cannot be independent of this diversity; its treatment must vary according to the conditions of the people, Churches and communities involved. For present conditions the following guiding principles are offered.

27. There should be regard for a certain give-and-take ("reciprocity") if sharing in spiritual activity and resources, even within defined limits, is to contribute, in a spirit of mutual goodwill and charity, to the growth of harmony among Christians. Dialogues and consultations on the subject between Catholic local or territorial authorities and those of other communions are strongly recommended.

28. In some places and with some communities, sects and persons, the ecumenical movement and the wish for peace with the Catholic Church have not yet grown strong (cf. Decree on Ecumenism n. 19), and so this reciprocity and mutual understanding are more difficult; the local Ordinary or, if need be, the Episcopal Conference may indicate suitable measures for preventing the dangers of indifferentism and proselytism* among their faithful in these circumstances. It is to be hoped, however, that through the grace of the Holy Spirit and the prudent pastoral care of the bishops, ecumenical feeling and mutual regard will so increase both among Catholics and among their separated brethren that the need for these special measures will gradually vanish.

29. The term, sharing of spiritual activity and resources (*communicatio in spiritualibus*) is used to cover all prayer offered in common, common use of sacred places and objects, as well as all sharing in liturgical worship (*communicatio in sacris*) in the strict sense.

---

* The word "proselytism" is here used to mean a manner of behaving, contrary to the spirit of the Gospel, which makes use of dishonest methods to attract men to a community—v.g. by exploiting their ignorance or poverty. (Cf. Declaration on Religious Liberty n. 4)

Appendix Three

30. There is *"communicatio in sacris"* when anyone takes part in the liturgical worship or in the sacraments of another Church or ecclesial community.

31. By "liturgical worship" is meant worship carried out according to the books, prescriptions or customs of a Church or community, celebrated by a minister or delegate of such Church or community, in his capacity as minister of that community.

B. *Prayer in Common*

32. "In certain special circumstances, such as prayer services 'for unity' and during ecumenical gatherings, it is allowable, indeed desirable that Catholics should join in prayer with their separated brethren. Such prayers in common are certainly a very effective means of petitioning for the grace of unity, and they are a genuine expression of the ties which still bind Catholics to their separated brethren." (Decree on Ecumenism n. 8) The Decree is dealing with prayers in which members and even ministers of different communities take an "active" part. Where Catholics are concerned, this kind of participation is committed to the guidance and encouragement of local Ordinaries. The following points should be noted.

33. It is to be hoped that Catholics and their other brethren will join in prayer for any common concern in which they can and should cooperate—e.g. peace, social justice, mutual charity among men, the dignity of the family and so on. The same may be said of occasions when according to circumstances a nation or community wishes to make a common act of thanksgiving or petition to God, as on a national feast-day, at a time of public disaster or mourning, on a day set aside for remembrance of those who have died for their country. This kind of prayer is also recommended so far as is possible at times when Christians hold meetings for study or common action.

34. However, common prayer should particularly be concerned with the restoration of Christian unity. It can center on, e.g., the mystery of the Church and her unity, baptism as a sacramental bond of unity however incom-

plete, the renewal of personal and social life as a necessary way to achieving unity and the other themes set out under n. 22.

35. The form of the Service.
    (a) Representatives of the Churches or communities concerned should agree and cooperate in arranging such prayer—in deciding who should take part, what themes, hymns, Scripture readings, prayers and the like should be used.
    (b) In such a service there is room for any reading, prayer and hymn which manifests the faith or spiritual life shared by all Christians. There is a place for an exhortation, address or biblical meditation drawing on the common Christian inheritance which may lead to mutual goodwill and promote unity among Christians.
    (c) It is desirable that the structure of services of this kind, whether confined to Catholics, or held in common with our separated brethren, should conform to the pattern of community prayer recommended by the liturgical revival. (Cf. Constitution on the Sacred Liturgy, v.g. nn. 30, 34, 35.)
    (d) When services are arranged to take place in an Eastern Church, it should be borne in mind that an official liturgical form is considered among Orientals as particularly well adapted to prayer of petition; particular consideration should therefore be given to the liturgical order of this Church.

36. The Place.
    (a) A place should be chosen which is acceptable to all those taking part. Care should be taken that everything is properly prepared and conducive to devotion.
    (b) Although a church building is the place in which a community is normally accustomed to celebrating its own liturgy, there is nothing which in itself prevents holding the common services mentioned in nn. 32-35, in the church of one or other of the communities concerned if there is

need for this and the local Ordinary approves. In fact the situation may make this the suitable thing.
(c) It should be remembered, when arranging prayer services with the Eastern Orthodox brethren, that all Eastern Christians regard the church as far and away the most suitable place for public prayer.

37. Dress. There is nothing against the use of choir dress, where circumstances may indicate this and there is common agreement among the participants.

C. *Sharing in Liturgical Worship*

38. "Yet sharing in liturgical worship (*communicatio in sacris*) is not to be considered as a means to be used indiscriminately for the restoration of unity among Christians. There are two main principles upon which the practice of such common worship depends: first, that of the unity of the Church which ought to be expressed; and second, that of the sharing in means of grace. The expression of unity very generally forbids common worship. Grace to be obtained sometimes commends it." (Decree on Ecumenism n. 8)

(1) *Sharing in Liturgical Worship with Our Separated Eastern Brothers*

39. "Although these (Eastern) Churches are separated from us, yet they possess true sacraments, above all—by apostolic succession—the priesthood and the Eucharist, whereby they are still joined to us in closest intimacy. Therefore some sharing in liturgical worship (*communicatio in sacris*), given suitable circumstances and the approval of church authority, is not merely possible but is encouraged. (Ibid. n. 15; cf. also the Decree on the Eastern Catholic Churches, nn. 24-29.)

40. Between the Catholic Church and the Eastern Churches separated from us there is still a very close communion in matters of faith (cf. Decree on Ecumenism n. 44); moreover, "through the celebration of the Eucharist of the Lord in each of these Churches, the Church of God is built up and grows in stature" and "although

separated from us, yet these Churches possess true sacraments, above all—by apostolic succession—the priesthood and the Eucharist . . ." (Ibid. n. 15)

This offers ecclesiological and sacramental grounds for allowing and even encouraging some sharing in liturgical worship—even eucharistic—with these Churches "given suitable circumstances and the approval of church authority". (Decree on Ecumenism n. 15)

Pastors should carefully instruct the faithful so that they will be clearly aware of the proper reasons for this kind of sharing in liturgical worship.

41. The principles governing this sharing set out in the Decree on Eastern Churches (cf. nn. 26-29) should be observed with the prudence that the Decree recommends; the norms which apply to Oriental Catholics apply equally to the faithful of any rite, including the Latin.

42. It is particularly opportune that the Catholic authority, whether the local one, the synod or the Episcopal Conference, does not extend permission for sharing in the reception or administration of the sacraments of penance, Holy Eucharist or anointing the sick except after satisfactory consultations with the competent authorities (at least local ones) of the separated Oriental Church.

43. In granting permission for sharing in the sacraments it is fitting that the greatest possible attention be given to "reciprocity".

44. Besides cases of necessity, there would be reasonable ground for encouraging sacramental sharing if special circumstances make it materially or morally impossible over a long period for one of the faithful to receive the sacraments in his own Church, so that in effect he would be deprived without legitimate reason, of the spiritual fruit of the sacraments.

45. Since practice differs between Catholics and other Eastern Christians in the matter of frequent communion, confession before communion and the eucharistic fast, care must be taken to avoid scandal and suspicion among the Orthodox, created by Catholics not following the Orthodox usage. A Catholic who legitimately communicates with the Orthodox in the cases envisaged here must observe the Orthodox discipline as much as he can.

Appendix Three

46. Those Eastern Christians who, in the absence of sufficient confessors of their own Church, spontaneously desire to do so may go to a Catholic confessor. In similar circumstances a Catholic may approach a confessor of an Eastern Church which is separated from the Apostolic Roman See. Reciprocity should be maintained here too. Both sides should of course take care to arouse no suspicion of proselytising.*

47. A Catholic who occasionally, for reasons set out below (cf. n. 50) attends the Holy Liturgy (Mass) on a Sunday or holiday of obligation in an Orthodox church is not then bound to assist at Mass in a Catholic church. It is likewise a good thing if on such days Catholics, who for just reasons cannot go to Mass in their own Church, attend the Holy Liturgy of their separated Oriental brethren, if this is possible.

48. Because of the close communion between the Catholic Church and the separated Eastern Churches, as described above (n. 40), it is permissible for a member of one of the latter to act as godparent, together with a Catholic godparent, at the baptism of a Catholic infant or adult so long as there is provision for the Catholic education of the person being baptised, and it is clear that the godparent is a suitable one. A Catholic is not forbidden to stand as godparent in an Orthodox church, if he is so invited. In this case, the duty of providing for the Christian education of the baptised person binds in the first place the godparent who belongs to the Church in which the child is baptised.

49. Brethren of other Churches may act as bridesmaid or best man at a wedding in a Catholic church. A Catholic too can be best man or bridesmaid at a marriage properly celebrated among separated brethren.

50. Catholics may be allowed to attend Orthodox liturgical services if they have reasonable grounds, e.g. arising out of a public office or function, blood relationships, friendships, desire to be better informed, etc. In such cases there is nothing against their taking part in the common responses, hymns, and actions of the Church in which they

---

* Cf. Note on n. 28.

are guests. Receiving Holy Communion however, will be governed by what is laid down above, nn. 42 & 44. Because of the close communion referred to earlier (n. 40) local Ordinaries can give permission for a Catholic to read lessons at a liturgical service, if he is invited. These same principles govern the manner in which an Orthodox may assist at services in Catholic churches.

51. Regarding participation in ceremonies which do not call for sacramental sharing the following should be observed:

(a) In ceremonies carried out by Catholics, an Oriental clergyman who is representing his Church should have the place and the liturgical honours which Catholics of equal rank and dignity have.

(b) A Catholic clergyman present in an official capacity at an Orthodox service can, if it is acceptable to his hosts, wear choir dress or the insignia of his ecclesiastical rank.

(c) There should be meticulous regard for the outlook of the clergy and faithful of the Eastern Churches, as well as for their customs which may vary according to time, place, persons and circumstances.

52. Because sharing in sacred functions, objects and places with all the separated Eastern brethren is allowed for a reasonable cause (cf. Decree on Eastern Catholic Churches n. 28), it is recommended that with the approval of the local Ordinary separated Eastern priests and communities be allowed the use of Catholic churches, buildings and cemeteries and other things necessary for their religious rites, if they ask for this and have no place in which they can celebrate sacred functions properly and with dignity.

53. The authorities of Catholic schools and institutions should take care to offer Orthodox clergy every facility for giving spiritual and sacramental ministration to their own faithful who attend such schools and institutions. As far as circumstances allow, and with the local Ordinary's permission, these facilities can be offered on the Catholic premises, including the church.

54. In hospitals and similar institutions conducted by

Appendix Three

Catholics, the authorities should promptly advise the Orthodox priest of the presence of his faithful, and give him facilities to visit the sick and administer the sacraments to them in dignified and reverent conditions.

(2) *Sharing in Liturgical Worship with Other Separated Brethren*

55. Celebration of the sacraments is an action of the celebrating community, carried out within the community, signifying the oneness in faith, worship and life of the community. Where this unity of sacramental faith is deficient, the participation of the separated brethren with Catholics, especially in the sacraments of the Eucharist, penance and anointing of the sick, is forbidden. Nevertheless, since the sacraments are both signs of unity and sources of grace (cf. Decree on Ecumenism n. 8) the Church can for adequate reasons, allow access to those sacraments to a separated brother. This may be permitted in danger of death or in urgent need (during persecution, in prisons) if the separated brother has no access to a minister of his own communion, and spontaneously asks a Catholic priest for the sacraments—so long as he declares a faith in these sacraments in harmony with that of the Church, and is rightly disposed. In other cases the judge of this urgent necessity must be the diocesan bishop or the Episcopal Conference. A Catholic in similar circumstances may not ask for these sacraments except from a minister who has been validly ordained.

56. A separated brother is not to act as a Scripture reader or to preach during the celebration of the Eucharist. The same is to be said of a Catholic at the celebration of the Lord's Supper or at the principal liturgical service of the Word held by the Christians who are separated from us. At other services, even liturgical ones, it is allowable to exercise some functions, with the previous permission of the local Ordinary and the consent of the authorities of the community concerned.

57. With the exception already dealt with above (n. 48) it is not permissible for a member of a separated community to act as godparent in the liturgical and canonical sense at baptism or confirmation. The reason is that a godparent is not merely undertaking his responsibility for

the Christian education of the person baptised or confirmed as a relation or friend—he is also, as a representative of a community of faith, standing as sponsor for the faith of the candidate. Equally a Catholic cannot fulfill this function for a member of a separated community. However, because of ties of blood or friendship, a Christian of another communion, since he has faith in Christ, can be admitted with a Catholic godparent as a Christian witness of the baptism. In comparable circumstances a Catholic can do the same for a member of a separated community. In these cases the responsibility for the Christian education of the candidate belongs of itself to the godparent who is a member of the Church in which the candidate is baptised. Pastors should carefully explain to the faithful the evangelical and ecumenical reasons for this regulation, so that all misunderstanding of it may be prevented.

58. The separated brethren may act as "official" witnesses (bridesmaid or best man) at a Catholic marriage, and Catholics at a marriage which is properly celebrated between our separated brethren.

59. Catholics may be allowed to attend occasionally the liturgical services of other brethren if they have reasonable ground, e.g. arising out of a public office or function, blood relationship or friendship, desire to be better informed, an ecumenical gathering, etc. In these cases, with due regard to what has been said above—there is nothing against Catholics taking some part in the common responses, hymns and actions of the community of which they are guests—so long as they are not at varience with Catholic faith. The same principles govern the manner in which our separated brethren may assist at services in Catholic churches. This participation, from which reception of the Eucharist is always excluded, should lead the participants to esteem the spiritual riches we have in common and at the same time make them more aware of the gravity of our separations.

60. When taking part in services which do not call for sacramental sharing, ministers of other communions may, by mutual consent, take a place suitable to their dignity. So too Catholic ministers who are present at ceremonies

celebrated by other communions, may, with due regard for local customs, wear choir dress.

61. If the separated brethren have no place in which to carry out their religious rites properly and with dignity, the local Ordinary may allow them the use of a Catholic building, cemetery or church.

62. The authorities of Catholic schools and institutions should take care to offer to ministers of other communions every facility for giving spiritual and sacramental ministration to their own communicants who attend Catholic institutions. These ministrations may be given in Catholic buildings, in accordance with the above, n. 61.

63. In hospitals and similar institutions conducted by Catholics, the authorities in charge should promptly advise ministers of other communions of the presence of their communicants and afford them every facility for visiting the sick and giving them spiritual and sacramental ministrations.

* * * *

In an audience granted to the Secretariat for Promoting Christian Unity, April 28, 1967, the Sovereign Pontiff, Paul VI, approved this Directory, confirmed it by his authority and ordered that it be published. Anything to the contrary notwithstanding.

Rome, May 14, 1967, Pentecost Sunday.

Augustin Cardinal Bea
President of the Secretariat
for Promoting Christian Unity

✟ John Willebrands
Tit. Bishop of Mauriana
Secretary

Index

A.A.S., 200n, 203n
Acton, Lord John, 37
Acts, Book of, 213
Adam, Karl, 46
Adsumus (prayer), 81
Alexandria, 207n, 208n
Alfrink, Cardinal, 47
Amay, Belgium, 44, 47
American Ecclesiastical Review, 196n
"Americanism," 51
Amsterdam, Holland, 51
Anglican Church, 125-27; attempts at reconciliation with, 43-49, 53; collegiality of bishops, 63-64; Decree on Ecumenism, 207; ecumenical movement, 49-50, 144; joint prayer with, 94-95
Antioch, 97, 147, 207n, 208n
Apostles (*see also* specific Apostles), Decree on Ecumenism and, 68, 100, 192, 196, 208; and papal primacy, 146-49
Appeal to the Nobility of the German Nation, An (Luther), 25
Armenian Church, 207n, 213n
Assumption, 90, 140; defined by Pius XII, 161-62, 168
Athanasius of Alexandria, 210n
Athenagoras, Patriarch, 20-21, 97
Athens, 208n
Atonement Friars, 51
Aubert, Roger, 38
Augsburg Confession, 107, 155
Augsburg, Peace of, 25
Augustine, St., 29, 128, 195, 216n

Baptism, 58-59, 223-24, 226; Anglicans on, 126; conditional, 109-11; conservatives on, 124; Decree on Ecumenism on, 69, 109-11, 192, 194-95, 216-18; rebaptism, 109-11
Baptists, 73-74, 113-14, 120
Barth, Karl, 60-61, 74-75, 127-28; influence of his commentary on St. Paul's Epistle to the Romans on neo-orthodoxy, 123-24; on Mariology, 162, 166-67; on papal infallibility, 157, 159
Barnes, Roswell P., 112-13
Basil of Cappadocia, St., 210n
Baum, Gregory, 86-87
Bea, Augustin Cardinal, 11-12, 46-47, 54; clarifies "heresy" and "heretics," 11-12, 70; heads Secretariat for Promoting Christian Unity, 53-54
Beauduin, Dom Lambert, 46-47
Beaupère, Père, 48-49
Belfast, Ireland, 43
Belgium, 44-46

250

Index

Bellarmine, Cardinal, 61-62
Benedict, St., 210n
Benedict XV, Pope, 43-44
Bible (Scriptures) (*see also* Word of God, specific Books), American Protestantism centered on, 127; Luther on, 28-30; and Mary, 163-65; neo-orthodoxy and, 123; and papal infallibility, 153-60; and papal primacy, 146; Protestant modernists, conservatists, and liberals and, 120-24, 126; Protestant reverence for, 106-09, 111, 113-14, 116-17, 120ff, 215-16; Scots' love of as bridge to unity, 43-44; service for Christian unity, 93-95
"Biblical criticism," 50-51, 120-21, 122-24, 126. *See also* "Higher criticism"; Modernism
Biel, Gabriel, 31
Birth control, 92-93
Blake, Dr. Eugene Carson, 51-52; Blake-Pike plan for merger, 128-29
Boniface VIII, Pope, 79
Bossuet, Jacques, 6; and reconciliation, 42
Brent, Bishop, 8
Brown, Robert McAfee, 81-82, 88-89; on papal infallibility, 152-53
Bulgaria, Patriarchate of, 208n
Brunner, Emil, 124
Bryan, William Jennings, 122
Bultmann, Rudolf, 124
Byzantine Empire, 15ff, 97
Byzantium, 15

Cadorna, General Luigi, 36
Cajetan, Cardinal, 24
Calvin, John, and Calvinism, 30-33, 80-81, 112; and Bible as source of living faith, 107; and capitalism, 112; neo-orthodoxy a return to, 123; and papal infallibility, 156
Canon law, 100-01, 151
Capitalism, 112
Carberry, Bishop John, 54, 171
Carter, Bishop G. Emmett, 13
Cary-Elwes, Dom Columba, 49-50
Casserly (Anglican theologian), 124
Casti Connubii (encyclical), 113
Catholic Conference for Ecumenical Questions, 46-47
Catholic World, 38-39, 50
Celibacy, clerical, 136-38, 212n
Centralization, 9-11, 124-25
Chalcedon, Council of, 16, 97, 206, 208n
Chaldean Church, 213n
Charity, Protestant, 111, 127-28
Charlemagne, 16
Charles V, Holy Roman Emperor, 25, 137
Chevetogne, Belgium, 46
Chicago, Ill., 50
Christian Scholar in the Age of the Reformation, The (Harbison), 31-32
Christianity and Crisis, 53-54
Church Unity Octave, 46-48
Civil law, and ecumenism, 188-89
Civil rights, 92-94, 113
Civil Rights Act, 113
Civiltà Cattolica, 11-12, 70
Clancy, William, 53
Clergy, 20-21, 117, 127 (*see*

also Orders, religious); celibacy of, 136-37, 212n; clericalism, 34-37, 79-80, 85-86; Decree on Ecumenism on, 78-80; Orthodox, 20-21; and prayer in common, 221-23; workers, 113-14; Protestant, 117, 127-28; Protestant concept of Catholic, 63-64; vesture for, 221-23, 225

Clericalism, 34-37, 79-80, 85-86

Cochlaeus, John, 132

Collectio Rituum, 225

College of Bishops, collegiality, 18-19, 62-65, 148, 192; Convocation of Bishops, (1563), 125; Orthodox position on supreme authority of, 98-99; and papal primacy, 148-49

Colossians, Epistle to the, 192, 218-19

Committee on Catholic Education and Ecumenism, 171

Common life, the, 117

Communicatio in Sacris (worship in common), 76, 82, 84, 202-03, 210, 220-28; interim guidelines for, 220-28; text of service, 93-95

Communion. *See* Eucharist

Communism, 112

Confession, 20-21, 87-88

Confirmation, 226, 252-54

Congar, Yves, 11-12, 48-49; on importance of personal contact, 84-86; on Luther, 131-32

Conscience, 107; and ecumenism, 188-89

Conservatives (evangelicals), 10, 108-09, 113-15, 119-27; fundamentalism as an antidote to secularism, 128-29

Constantine, 15, 61

Constantinople, 15-18, 21, 119, 206n; first seven Ecumenical Councils at, 208n

Constitution, Irish, 43

Constitution, United States, 9

Constitution on the Church (*De Ecclesia*), 12-13, 56-68, 127, 139, 144, 195n, 227; and bishops, 19, 62-65, 150; and Mary, 165-66

Constitution on Divine Revelation, 158, 216n

Constitution on the Sacred Liturgy, 210, 224, 227

Conversions, 71-72, 142

Convocation of Bishops (1563), 125

Coptic Church, 206n, 213n

Corinth, 208n

Corinthians, Epistles to the, 190, 192-93

Counter-Reformation, 24, 61, 71, 77, 79; polemics on Luther, 131-33, 135

Couturier, Paul, 46-47, 81-82, 202n

Crusades, crusaders, 17, 98-99, 206n

Cullmann, Oscar, 146

Cushing, Richard Cardinal, 24, 196n

Cyprus, Church of, 208n

Czechoslovakia, Church of, 208n

d'Ailly, Pierre, 30

Dante Alighieri, 77

Death (*see also* Funerals), giving sacraments to the dying, 83

Decree on the Catholic Churches of the Eastern Rite, 211n, 224, 227

Decree on Ecumenism, The, 7, 11, 56-57, 64-228 (*see*

also specific subjects covered by); general principles of, 66-75; text of, 190-228
De Ecclesia. See Constitution on the Church
de Lubac, Henri, 167
de Montalembert, Comte, 37
Denifle, Heinrich, 131, 137-38
De Oecumenismo. See Decree on Ecumenism
Depression, the Great, 123
Determinism, Calvin's, 32-33
Devil, liberalism and, 121
Dialog (periodical), 152
Dialogue, dialogue groups, 84-93; text of Decree on, 197, 203-05, 220
Dialogue on the Way (Schlink), 141
Diamper, Synod of, 212n
Dillenberger, John, 115-16
Diocesan Ecumenical Commissions, 220
Disciples of Christ, 120, 128-29
Diversity. *See* Uniformity and diversity
Divided Christendom (Congar), 48-49
Divine Comedy, The (Dante), 77
Divino Afflante Spiritu (Encyclical), 37-38, 197n
Doctrine and Life (periodical), 43
Doepfner, Julius Cardinal, 38-39
Dominicans, 31-32
Doyle, Bishop James Warren, 42-43
Dumont, Père C. J., 48-49

Eastern Churches Quarterly, 49-50

Eastern Orthodox Churches, 15-22, 43, 46, 96-103, 144, 171, 207-215 (*see also* specific churches); attempts at reconciliation with prior to Vatican II, 43, 46, 48; and collegiality of bishops, 60-61; and concept of Church, 64-65; Decree on Ecumenism and, 67-69, 96-103, 206-15; joint prayer with, 81-82, 93-95; and papal primacy, 147-48; in World Council, 51; and worship in common, 82-84, 93-95, 224-228
Eastern Rite Catholics (Uniates), 97, 102-03, 213n
Ecclesia Catholica (Instruction), 51-53
Ecumenical Councils, 18-19, 101, 208 (*see also* specific Councils); and papal primacy, 151
Ecumenical Directory, 220-21, 229-49
"Ecumenical movement," defined, 177
Ecumenical Review, The, 74
Ecumenism, defined, 4-5
Edinburgh, Scotland, 8-9, 51
Education. *See* Schools
Elizabeth II, 111
England, Bishop John, 49
Enlightenment, Age of, 34-35
Ephesians, Epistle to the, 60, 68, 78, 192-94, 199, 201, 205
Ephesus, Council and Synod of (431), 206, 208n, 210
Ephrem of Syria, St., 210n
Episcopal Church, 119-20, 127-29; and baptism, 112; and ecumenical movement, 171
Erasmus, 6, 41-42

Eucharist, 8, 30, 82, (*see also* Mass); Decree on Ecumenism and, 126, 71-72, 82-83, 99, 110-11, 198, 209-10, 214, 224-28

Ethiopian Church, 206n, 213n

Europe, Europeans, and language of dialogue, 92; and neo-orthodoxy, 123, Protestantism and World War I in, 122-23; Protestants compared with those in U. S., 119; reasons for rise of ecumenical movement in, 7, 9; Reformation in (*see* Reformers and Reformation)

Evangelical Church, German, 66

Evangelicals. *See* Conservatives

Evanston, Ill., 53, 56

Evolution, theory of, 120-21

Existentialism, 124

Exultate Deo (Decree), 195

Faith, 26-28, 86, 132-34, 195; Calvin on, 31; as Protestant principle, 116-17

Faith and Order movement, 43-45, 47, 51; Montreal Conference, 164-65; Oberlin conference, 52-54

Father, the, 17-18, 28-29, 194, 215-16

Federal aid to education, 89

Fellowship, U.S. Protestantism and, 127-28

Finland, Church of, 208n

First Vatican Council. *See* Vatican I

Flanagan, Bishop Bernard J., 227

Florence, Council of, 18, 195, 206n, 212n, 214

Fosdick, Harry Emerson, 121, 123

France, ecumenism in, 46, 47, 49, 92, 152, 202n; liberalism and anti-clericalism in (19th century), 34-35, 36; priest-workers in, 113-14; Revolution in, 18, 35

Franco-Prussian War, 62-63

Franciscans, 31-32

Free will, Luther and, 26

Fry, Dr. Franklin Clark, 51-52

Fundamentalists. *See* Conservatives

Funerals, 225

Furrow, The (periodical), 43

Galatians, Epistle to the, 192, 194, 208n

Garibaldi, Giuseppe, 36

Gazzada, Italy, 46-47

Geneva, Switzerland, 32, 54, 67

Gennadius, Patriarch, 18

Georgia, Church of, 208n

Germany, Germans, 45-47, Evangelical Church, 66; and Reformation (*see also* Luther), 23, 25, 29, 31, 131-32, 138

Gibbons, James Cardinal, 50-52

Glaubenslehre (Schleiermacher), 120

Gnostics, 98

Goa, Archbishop of, 212n

God (*see also* Father, the; specific doctrines): Luther and, 26ff

Graham, Billy, 128-29

Grant, Dr. Frederick, 147

Graymoor Friars, 47-48

Great Britain (England), 111, 125-26 (*see also* Anglican Church); ecumenical activity in, 44, 48, 50; Irish attempts at religious reconcili-

Index

ation with, 42-43; Lambeth Conference, 44-45; liberalism in, 36; Reformation in, 79-81
Greece, Church of (autocephalous), 208n, 213n
Greek Orthodox Church, 18, 21, 208n (*see also* specific branches); and papal primacy, 148
Gregory XVI, Pope, 35
Gregory of Nazianzus, St., 210n
Gregory of Nyssa, St., 210n
Grisar, Hartmann, 131, 138

Halifax, Lord Edward Wood, 44-47
Hamer, Jerome, 48-49, 124
Harbison, E. Harris, 31
Harnish, J. Lester, 73
Hecker, Isaac T., 49-51
Heenan, Archbishop, 48-50
Hegel, Georg Wilhelm Friedrich, 6
Hell, in Decree on Ecumenism, 77-78, liberals reject, 121
Heresy and heretics, 11-12, 16, 18, 69, 151; Barth on Mariology as, 166; Cardinal Bea's clarification of meaning, 11-12, 70; in Eastern Church, 98; modernism as, 36-38; Pope Stephen on baptism conferred by heretics, 109
Herte, Adolf, 131
Hierarchy of truths, 92-93, 205
"Higher criticism," 108-09. *See also* Biblical criticism
Hinsley, Arthur Cardinal, 49
Hitler, Adolf, 45-46
Holland, ecumenical activity in, 46-47; World Council formed in, 50-52
Holy orders. See Clergy; Orders, religious
Holy Spirit, 11-12, 14, 29, 107; in concept of Church, 61-62; Decree on Ecumenism and, 66-79 *passim,* in East-West controversy, 17-18, 209, 212n; and papal infallibility, 154-60
Horton, W. M., 122, 124
Host, the, 102-03
Humani Generis (encyclical), 37-38
Humbert, Cardinal, 17, 19-20, 206

Iakovos, Archbishop, 21
Iconoclast controversy, 207
Ignatius, St., 61-62, 97
Immaculate Conception, 140, 161
Immigrants, 213n
In Ioannem Homelia, 209
Incarnation, dogma of, 92, 106, 157, 162-64
India, Syrian Church of, 206n, 211-12n
Industrial Revolution, 18, 122
Infallibility, 116. *See also* Pope (Bishop of Rome), papacy Inquisition, 61-62
Institutes of the Christian Religion, The (Calvin), 30, 107
Interior conversion. See Personal renewal
International Congregational Council, 144
Iraq, 206
Ireland, Archbishop John, 50
Ireland, and the Irish, 42-43
Irene, Princess of Holland, 109
Irenicism, false, 90-91, 204
Irenikon (periodical), 46

Isaiah, Book of, 194
Isidore, Patriarch, 18
Istanbul, 20-21, 97
Istina Center, 48-49
Italo-Greeks, 211n
Italy, liberalism in, 36-37
Ius Canonicum (Wernz and Vidal), 151

James, Book of, 108, 198
James the Less, St., 208n
Jerusalem, 206n, 208n
Jesus Christ, 76-78 (*see also* Son, the; Word of God); and bishops as shepherds, 12; Catholic vs. Protestant views on, 105-06, 112-13, 116-17, 144-45; East vs. West liturgy and, compared, 102; ecumenism (reconciliation) as response to command of, 5-6, 8, 12, 228; and language of dialogue, 92; Man of Galilee in Liberal Gospel, 121; Mary and, 162-63, 164-66; modernism denies He founded Church, 37-38; papal infallibility and, 153-60; papal primacy and, 145-50; Reformation and (*see* Reformers and Reformation)
Jews, 171
John, St., 167; Book of, 6, 80, 154, 192ff, 201-02, 221, 228
John XXIII, Pope, 4-8, 11-13, 24, 53, 69, 73; Belfast lowers flags at death of, 43; calling of Council, 57; elected to papacy, beginning of era of open Church, 38-39; establishes Secretariat for Promoting Christian Unity, 53-54; opening address to Vatican II, 38-40, 53, 201n; and Orthodox Churches, 19, 21; Pius XII reforms pave way for, 38; reminder on doctrine and manner of expression, 69, 77, 91-92, 201n
John Chrysostom, St., 207, 209, 210n
John of the Cross, St., 61
Johnson, Luci Baines, 109, 110
Justification, Calvin on, 30; in Decree, 195; Luther and, 26-28, 86-87, 117, 132-34, 136-37

Karl Barth (Hamer), 48-49
King, Martin Luther, Jr., 94-95
Kipling, Rudyard, 96
Knox, W. L., 154
Kulturkampf, Bismarck's, 36-37
Küng, Hans, 79-80; on papal infallibility, 157-60; on papal primacy, 149-51

Laetentur caeli, 195, 214-15
Lambeth Conference, 44
Lamentabili (encyclical), 121
Language, for dialogue, 86, 88, 90-3; in U. S. Orthodox Churches, 20-21
Laros, Matthias, 45
Lateran Council, 195, 200
Latinism, 103
Latin Language, 101, 117
Lebanon, 99, 213n
Lectures on Romans (Luther), 30-31
Leo I, Pope, 16
Leo IX, Pope, 17
Leo X, Pope, 23-26, 42, 135
Leo XIII, Pope, 36, 43-44, 50, 113
Liberalism, 34-37, 113, 121-25

Index

Life and Work Movement, 44, 51
Lindbeck, George, 152
Lippmann, Walter, 92
Literature, Protestant, 84
Liturgy, 195 (*see also* Eucharist; Mass); Catholic and Protestant compared, 111; and *Communicatio in sacris*, 223-28; East and West compared, 98-100, 102, 208-15
Living Room Dialogues, 171
Loisy, Alfred, 121
Lord's Prayer, 52, 81
Lortz, Joseph, 131-34, 187
Louvain, University of, 24
Luke, Book of, 147, 163, 192
Luther, Martin, 23-32, 42, 73, 80, 86, 106, 108, 131-39; on the Bible, 108, 134; a casualty of seminary courses, 89; defamation of as obstacle to unity, 130-39; on faith, 26-28, 86, 116-17, 132-34, 136; interest in communal life of Church, 10-11; on "invisible Church," 60, 106; and liberalism, 35; on monasticism, 111-12; neo-orthodoxy a return to, 123; and papacy, 106, 135-37, 156; writings of, 134, 137 (*see also* specific works)
Lutheran Laymen's League, 23
Lutherans, Lutheranism, 25, 126-27, 119, 138 (*see also* Luther); early attempts at reconciliation, 42, 46; ecumenism, 171
Lyons, France, 46, 48, 195

Macaulay, Thomas Babington, 40
Malabar Christians, 212n
Malines Conferences, 43-50
Manning, Henry Edward Cardinal, 36
Maritain, Jacques, 124, 127, 138
Maronite Church, 213n
Mark, St., 208n; Book of, 87, 150, 194
Marriage, 113; Luther and, 136-37; of Orthodox priests, 20; sacrament of matrimony, 102, 225-26
Mary, Virgin, 99, 161-69, 206n, 208, 212-13; Immaculate Conception, 140, 161; Mariology as obstacle to unity, 161-69
Mary, Mother of the Lord (Rahner), 164-66
Mass, 82-83, 99, 208n, 224 (*see also* Eucharist; Liturgy); Anglicanism and, 126; Latin Language at, 117
Matthew, Book of, 8, 146-48, 192, 201, 203, 221, 228
Measure for Measure (Shakespeare), 76
Melchite Church, 213n
Meliton, Metropolitan, 20
Mercier, Désiré Joseph Cardinal, 43-46, 48
Mergers, Protestant Churches', 128-29
Methodist Church, 128-29, 171
Metzger, Father Josef, 45
Meyendorff, J., 148
Michael Cerularius, Patriarch, 17, 20, 206
Michael Palaelogos, 195
Michalon, Father, 47
Missions, missionaries, 8-9; training for, 90; U.S. Protestants and, 127

Modernism, 36-38, 120ff (*see also* "Biblical criticism"); condemned in U.S., 50
Moehler Institute, 46
Monasteries, monasticism, 100, 111, 210
Monophysite controversy, 207n
Montini, Cardinal. *See* Paul VI, Pope
Montreal, Canada, 164-65
Mortalium Animos (encyclical), 43-45
Moscow, Patriarchate of, 208n
Murphy, Rev. Francis X., 38
Muslims, 99
Mystici Corporis (Mystical Body of Christ), 58, 157

Nabaa, Metropolitan Philip, 98
National Council of Churches, 47, 50, 128; centralization in, 10, 125; and ecumenical movement, 170-71
Natural law, 92, 114, 127
Nazis, 45
NCWC's Newsletter, 93n
Negroes, 92-94
Neill, Stephen C., 44, 124
Nelson, J. Robert, 10, 153
Neo-orthodoxy, 123-24, 127, 129
Nestorian Church, 206
New Delhi, India, 53, 191
New Delhi Report, The, 191n, 194n
New Testament (Luther), 31
Nicea, Councils of, 208n
Nicholas, Pope, 16
Niebuhr, Reinhold, 53, 123, 162
Nikodim, Archbishop, 20, 83
Nominalism, 30-31
North American Faith and Order Conference, 52-54

Oberlin, Ohio, 52-54
One and Holy, 46-47
One in Christ (periodical), 49-50
"One true Church" concept, 57-63, 139-45
Orders, religious, 64, 119, 217, 225-26. *See also* Clergy
Oriental Churches. *See* Eastern Orthodox Churches
Osservatore Romano, L' 216n
Outler, Albert C., 73-74

Pacem in Terris (encyclical), 114
Pachomius, St., 210n
Paderborn, Germany, 46
Papal States, 36
Paris, France, 48
Parliament of Religions, 50
Pascendi (encyclical), 121
Pastor Aeternus, 192
Pauck, Wilhelm, 30
Paul, Father (Lewis Wattson), 50
Paul, St., 68, 78, 155, 198, 208n (*see also* specific Epistles); Luther and 26, 30, 192, 208n
Paul VI, Pope, 14; act of contrition for Catholic offenses against unity, at Vatican II, 83, 87, 202n; address at second session of Council, 144-45, 148, 202n; and Anglican reunion, 126; Ecumenism, 190-91, 199, 200n, 211, 212n, 219; on hearing Pope John at Vatican II, 40; and joint prayer, 81, 93-95; on main purpose of the Council, 58; and Mary, 166; as Car-

Index 259

dinal Montini, 46; and Orthodox Churches, 19, 21; warning on false irenicism, 91
Paulist Fathers, 49-50
Peace of Augsburg, 25
Penance, 77-78
Persia, 206
Personal contact, 84-86. *See also under* Protestants, Protestantism
Personal renewal (interior conversion), 73-75, 78-82, 197n
Peter, St., 12, 208n; Book of, 192-94, 204; in Decree on Ecumenism, 68, 192, 195; and papal primacy, 146-51; sets up Church in Rome, 15
Philip, Landgrave of Hesse, 135
Philippians, Epistle to the, 199
Photius, Patriarch, 16-17
Pike, Bishop James A., 110, 126-27; Blake-Pike merger plan, 128-29
Pius IX, Pope, 35-36, 156-57, 161
Pius X, Pope, 121
Pius XI, Pope, 43-46, 109, 113
Pius XII, Pope, 37-39, 103, 113; Assumption defined by, 161-62, 167; *Divino Afflante Spiritu,* 37, 197n; on the nature of the Church (*Mystici Corporis* encyclical), 57-58, 157
Poissy, Colloquy of, 41
Poland, Church of, 208n
Pope (Bishop of Rome), papacy, 60, 97-99, 102; Anglicanism on, 125; and bishops, collegiality doctrine, 18-20, 62-65, 148-49, 152-62; Luther and, 106, 135-36, 156; primacy of, 18-20, 62, 98, 145-52
Portal, Abbé, 45, 47
Prayer in common, 77, 81-84, 201-02; interim guidelines for, 220-28
Praeclara Gratulationis (encyclical), 43
Predestination, Calvin's, 32
Presbyterians and Presbyterianism, 43, 88, 118, 129, 171; Westminster Confession, 107, 152-55
Prophetic criticism, 116
Protestantism (Van de Pol), 46
Protestants, Protestantism, 13-14, 57-64, 73-75, 115-17; and centralization, 9-11; and ecumenism in the Constitution on the Church, 56-65; and ecumenism in the past, 41-54; as heretics, 11; history, teachings of, need to study, 84, 86; and missions, missionaries, 8-9; 19th-century, liberalism and, 35, 37; obstacles to unity, 130-69; personal contact, dialogue meetings with, 84-93, 197, 203-05, 220; and Prayer in common (*see* Prayer in common); variety in unity among Churches, 119-29; and worship of Mary, 99
Prussia, 36-37
Pryzwara, Erich, 124
Psalms, Book of, 138
Puritans, American, 31-33

Quadragesimo Anno (encyclical), 113
Quanbeck, Warren, 161

Index

Rahner, Karl, 164-66
Ramsey, Dr., Archbishop of Canterbury, 126
Rauschenbusch, Walter, 121-22
Real Presence, 31
Redemption, dogma of, 93, 105, 165
Reflections on America (Maritain), 127
"Reform," as used in Decree, 197n
Reformed Churches, 119
Reformers and Reformation, 10, 23-33, 106-07, 116, 125, 156; and concept of the Church, 60-63; Decree on Ecumenism and, 67-68, 79-81, 86, 207; and papal primacy, 149
Regensburg Colloquy, 41
"Renewal," in the text of Decree, 197n
Report from Rome (Congar), 12
Rerum Novarum (encyclical), 113
Riverside Church (New York City), 123
Rochester, N. Y., 67
Roman Empire, 15ff
Romans, Epistle to the, 26, 123, 132, 198, 215, 217, 219
Rome, 15ff, 23, 36
Rome and Reunion (Grant), 147
Rossi, Count Pellegrino, 36
Rousseau, Jean-Jacques, 34-35
Rumania, Church of, 18, 208, 213n
Rupp, Gordon, 134-38 22
Russian Orthodox Church, 18, 21, 83, 213n; in World Council, 51

Ruthenians, 213n
Sacraments, 20, 65, 210, 223-28; giving to the dying, 83
St. Irenaeus Center, 48
St. John, Henry, 49
St. John Lateran, Church of, 166
St. Paul's Outside the Walls, 81, 93
St. Peter's (Rome), 19-21, 23
Saints, Eastern Church and, 99
Santa Sophia, 17
Sartory, Thomas, 45
Scandinavian countries, 138
Schleiermacher, F. D., 120
Schlink, Edmund, 66-67, 141-43
Schmemann, Alexander, 97-99, 148
Scholasticism, Luther and, 30-31, 133
Schomer, Harold, 143-44
Schwarzenberg, Friedrich Cardinal, 148-49
Science, 120, 122
Scotland, 44. *See also* Edinburgh
Secretariat for Promoting Christian Unity, 53, 77, 145; and *Ecumenical Directory,* 220-21
Secularism, 127-29
Seminaries, 89-90, 120, 204
Serbia, Patriarchate of, 208n
Servetus, Michael, 33
Slavic Churches, 208n
Social affairs, 92-94; Protestants and, 10, 111-14, 121-24
Social Gospel, 112-14, 122ff
Southern Baptists, 113-14
Sovereignty of God, 116
Stephen, Pope, 109
Stransky, Rev. Thomas F., 110

Stritch, Samuel Cardinal, 52, 56
Strossmayr, Bishop, 37
Structure of the Church (Küng), 150-51
Suenens, Leon-Joseph Cardinal, 14
Sword of the Spirit movement, 49
Syllabus of Errors, The (Pius IX), 36
Syrian Church, 206n, 211-12n, 213n

Table Talk (Luther), 134
Tavard, George H., 42-43, 45, 48, 50, 150; on visibility of Lutheran Church, 106-07
Tetzel, John, 23
Theodore Studite, St., 207n
Theology: East-West differences, 101, 108
Thessalonica, 208n
Thirty-Nine Articles, 125-26
Thomas Aquinas, 30-32, 109, 133
Three Reformers (Maritain), 137
Tillich, Paul, 124, 162
Todd, John, 50
Tomkins, Bishop Oliver, 5
Transubstantiation, 126
Trent, Council of, 30, 141
Trinity, the, 28, 163; Decree on Ecumenism and, 68, 194, 205, 208, 212n, 227-28
Turks and Turkish Empire, 18

Ukrainians, 211n, 213n
Una Sancta Confraternity, 45-47
Uniates, 97, 102-03, 213n

Uniformity and diversity, 72-74, 98-99, 100-03, 199
United Church of Christ, 128-29
United Nations, 113
United States, 4, 7-8, 11, 22, 47, 49-54, 89-94; and collegiality, 63; Constitution, 9; dialogue in, 89-94; federal aid to education, 89-90; history of Protestants, need to study, 84; image of Pope in, 152; interim guidelines for prayer in common, 220-28; joint prayers, 81, 220; and Mariology, 162; and Orthodox Churches, 20-21, 96, 99; Protestantism, 11, 31-33, 49-54, 112-14, 118-29, 220-28
U.S. Bishops' Commission for Ecumenical Affairs, 21-22, 47-48, 54, 76-77, 171, 220-21
Usury, 112
"Utility," Calvin's, 31-33
Utrecht, Holland, 51

Van de Pol, Dr. W. H., 46
Vatican I, 12, 62, 148-49, 192; anti-Protestantism in, 37; and papal primacy, infallibility, 18-19, 156-60
Vatican II, 4, 6, 12-14, 21; British hierarchy approves Schema, 48-50; collegiality approved, 18, 62-65; Congar at, 48; and Mary, 165-68; and "one true Church" concept, 57-63, 139-45; opening prayers at, 80-81; Pope John's opening address, 39-40, 53, 57; situation in U.S. on eve of, 53
Vesture, priests', 221-22, 225

Veuillot, Louis, 37
Vidal, P., 151
Vigilius, Pope, 208n
Vischer, Lukas, 143
Visser 't Hooft, Dr. W. G., 51, 67-68
von Balthasar, Hans, 124
von Bismarck, Otto, 37
von Hügel, Baron Friedrich, 48
von Leibnitz, Baron Gottfried, 6, 42
von Staupitz, John, 24

Waldensians, 214-15
Wattson, Lewis (Father Paul), 50
Week of Prayer for Christian Unity, 46-48, 51, 228
Weigel, Gustave, 52-54
Welch, Claude, 115-16
Welfare State, 113
Wernz, F. X., 151
Wesley, John, 138-39
Westminster Confession, 88, 107, 152, 154-55
Willebrands, J. G., 46
William of Occam, 31
Winslow, Dom Bede, 49
Wittenberg, Germany, 23-24, 132
Woodlock, Father, 49
Word of God (*see also* Bible; Jesus Christ), Calvin and, 31; Decree on Ecumenism and, 69, 75, 90, 106-09, 111, 116-17, 215-16; Luther and, 28-30, 133; and Mary, 162-64; and papal infallibility, 153-60
Works, salvation and, 86
World Council of Churches, 43-45, 47-49, 50-56, 67, 125-26; and centralization, 10; concern for personal contact, 85; and ecumenical ties, 53-56, 141-43, 171; formation of, 50-52; and Social Gospel, 112-14
World War I, 122-23
World War II, 45, 49, 51, 129, 138
Worms, Diet of, 25, 42, 137
Writers, Protestant, 84

Zamosch, Synod of, 211n